Classic Case Studies in Psychology

The human mind is both extraordinary and compelling. But this is more than a collection of case studies; it is a selection of stories that illustrate some of the most extreme forms of human behaviour. From the leader who convinced his followers to kill themselves to the man who lost his memory; from the boy who was brought up as a girl to the woman with several personalities, Geoff Rolls illustrates some of the most fundamental tenets of psychology. Each case study has provided invaluable insights for scholars and researchers, and amazed the public at large. Several have been the inspiration for works of fiction, for example the story of Kim Peek, the real Rain Man.

This new edition features three new case studies, including the story of Charles Decker who was tried for the attempted murder of two people but acquitted on the basis of a neurological condition, and Dorothy Martin, whose persisting belief in an impending alien invasion is an illuminating example of cognitive dissonance. In addition, each case study is contextualized with more typical behaviour, while the latest thinking in each sub-field is also discussed.

Classic Case Studies in Psychology is accessibly written and requires no prior knowledge of psychology, but simply an interest in the human condition. It is a book that will amaze, sometimes disturb, but above all enlighten its readers.

Geoff Rolls is Head of Psychology at Peter Symonds College in Winchester and formerly a Research Fellow at Southampton University, UK.

D0322441

Classic Case Studies in Psychology

Third edition

Geoff Rolls

Routledge
Taylor & Francis Group

LONDON AND NEW YORK

Third edition published 2015
by Routledge
27 Church Road, Hove, East Sussex BN3 2FA

and by Routledge
711 Third Avenue, New York, NY 10017

First edition published 2005
by Hodder Education

Routledge is an imprint of the Taylor & Francis Group,
an informa business

British Library Cataloguing in Publication Data
A catalogue record for this book is available from the British Library

Library of Congress Cataloging in Publication Data
  Rolls, G. W. P.
  Classic case studies in psychology / Geoff Rolls. – Third edition.
  pages cm
  1. Psychology, Pathological–Case studies. 2. Psychotherapy–Case
  studies. 3. Human behaviour–Case studies. I. Title.
  RC435.2.R65 2015
  616.89–dc23
  2014019987

ISBN: 978–1–84872–269–9 (hbk)
ISBN: 978–1–84872–270–5 (pbk)
ISBN: 978–1–31584–935–5 (ebk)

Typeset in Bembo and Calibri
by Florence Production Ltd, Stoodleigh, Devon

MIX
Paper from
responsible sources
FSC
www.fsc.org   FSC® C013056

Printed and bound in Great Britain by
TJ International Ltd, Padstow, Cornwall

This book is dedicated to my father, Peter Rolls.
I realise how much you taught me and how much
you knew, and wish I'd learned even more.

Contents

Foreword to the third edition

Psychology is commonly defined as 'the scientific study of mind and behaviour' and has, traditionally, modelled itself on the natural sciences (especially physics and chemistry). But not everyone agrees about what 'science' entails, let alone about the validity of trying to study 'mind and behaviour' using methods 'borrowed' from physics and chemistry.

The method that is often taken as distinguishing science from, say, philosophy, is the laboratory experiment; for many 'hard-nosed' scientists, this is the 'method of choice'. Why? Because it allows another researcher to repeat or replicate the study in order to test the reliability and validity of the original findings. In turn, this helps determine general laws or principles, the so-called *nomothetic* approach.

By contrast, case studies, by definition, cannot be replicated. This is because they involve the in-depth investigation of an individual, a pair of individuals (such as twins) or an entire family – rather than groups of 'interchangeable' participants. They illustrate the *idiographic* approach; the study of *unique* individuals: it's their uniqueness that is the focus of study.

Traditionally, the nomothetic and idiographic approaches have been regarded as polar opposites in terms of their scientific value: because only experiments can be replicated and contribute to the formulation of general laws/principles, case studies have been dismissed as 'interesting' but of little importance. This view has been reinforced by the fact that case studies are often derived from the work of *clinicians* (psychologists, psychiatrists, or others who work with people experiencing mental disorders or who display highly unusual cognitive abilities or behaviour). In all of these cases, the case study is a spin-off, a usually unexpected outcome of their work, whereas experiments are designed to test specific hypotheses (another feature that makes them 'scientific').

However, not only is the nomothetic/idiographic distinction a false dichotomy, but it is precisely the uniqueness and novelty of the individuals who become the subject matter of case studies that makes them invaluable in our attempt to understand the human mind – and, hence, ourselves. Conversely, however 'unique' such individuals may be, they're always recognisably human – not some fascinating alien species but, ultimately, not so different from the rest of us that we cannot see aspects of our 'normal' selves in its abnormal – sometimes bizarre – behaviour.

This is perhaps the crucial point. The fact that some other psychologist cannot repeat the case study doesn't invalidate it. On the contrary, the behaviour is likely to be merely an exaggeration or distortion of more common place ('normal') behaviour – it's drawn from the same 'pool'.

As much like novels as reports of scientific investigations, case studies focus on the details that make human beings so fascinating and complex. They tell a 'story' that isn't just inherently interesting, puzzling, and sometimes amusing, but which is also informative about all of us. What makes a case study 'science' rather than literature is that the psychologist or psychiatrist explicitly links the story to some scientific theory or body of research findings, which represent formal, objective attempts to understand and explain the behaviour. Just like experiments, case studies are intended to contribute to our scientific understanding.

Geoff Rolls, as a psychology teacher and author, reflects these various aspects of the case study in this unique and extremely well-written book. He has selected a number of studies that many non-psychologists will probably have some knowledge of. Between them, the studies sample an enormously wide range of human behaviours, both 'abnormal' and merely unusual or exceptional.

One welcome addition to this edition is the Jonestown massacre (the 1978 mass suicide in Guyana), which, while infamous and disturbing in its own right, Geoff links it to, arguably, the most infamous and controversial study in the whole of psychology, namely, Stanley Milgram's obedience experiments conducted in the 1960s. Another is the case of Dorothy Marin/Marian Keech and The Seekers (who predicted the end of the world, in 1954), which is often cited in relation to one of the most influential theories in Social Psychology, namely Leon Festinger's (1957) cognitive dissonance theory. Their inclusion gives the book as a whole a better balance in terms of the traditional areas of psychology that are covered (cognitive, social developmental, individual differences, physiological and comparative).

The other new chapter is the case of Charles Decker – the 'crocodile man'. While less well-known than many of the other case studies, Geoff uses it to highlight several research areas and theoretical issues/debates, namely, the brain's control over behaviour, the causes of mental disorder, biological determinism, and free will.

Each chapter is a summary of the original case study (as reported in a book or academic journal or newspaper), and Geoff's ability to condense huge amounts of information into a single chapter and still tell a good 'story' is an achievement in itself. But, as indicated above, he also weaves into the story the theory and related research that makes these case studies 'science'.

He has done this, I believe, in such a way that both the general reader and the psychology student will learn something about human behaviour they didn't know before – regardless of any prior familiarity with the case study. Both will, I'm sure, also be intrigued and entertained by the 'stories' Geoff has to tell.

Richard Gross, April 2014

Acknowledgements

Although writing may appear a solitary exercise it is only possible with a lot of help. I would like to thank all those people who have worked or contributed to this third edition of *Classic Case Studies in Psychology*.

Russell George has been a most enthusiastic and skilled editor giving me just the right amount of time to complete all the tasks for such a book. Libby Volke came on board to complete the final essential tasks to make it a complete product.

Earlier editions would not have seen the light of day without Liz Wilson, Tamsin Smith, Bianca Knights, Jasmin Naim and, most particularly, Emma Woolf who supported the first edition. I hope the fact that it has now been translated into Italian, Russian and even Korean suggests we were right about the idea. My original psychology writing partner Richard Gross continues to amaze me with his endeavours and I value the many things I learned about writing from him.

Eve Murphy remains the 'rock' by my side. Always contributing useful ideas and thoughts and ever willing to re-read and edit yet another chapter. My children Billy and Ella accept the hours spent on 'their' computer and I thank them for their patience.

Finally and most importantly, having read about these case studies I am filled with a sense of awe for what humans can achieve, often in the face of extreme adversity. I hope that these chapters are an inspiration for all of us. I would like to acknowledge and salute the lives of every one of the individuals documented in this book. Writing about their lives made me feel very humble and their unique lives provide lessons for us all.

List of abbreviations

ASL   American Sign Language
CBT   cognitive behaviour therapy
CSF   cerebrospinal fluid
DID   dissociative identity disorder
EEG   electroencephalogram
EWT   eye witness testimony
GSR   galvanic skin response
LAD   language aquisition device
LTM   long-term memory
MPD   multiple personality disorder
OCD   obsessive-compulsive disorder
PET   Positron Emission Tomography
PTSD   post-traumatic stress disorder
REM   rapid eye movement
STM   short-term memory
SWS   slow wave sleep

Introduction

This is a strange book full of even stranger stories. Psychology is a fascinating subject with many fascinating stories to tell. But the most fascinating stories are told by case studies. They range from stories of people with no memory to stories of people who can't forget. Stories of wild, abandoned children to stories of child prodigies. Without doubt, these are the most interesting aspects of psychology.

They can also be the most revealing in terms of furthering our understanding of human behaviour. The problem is, we all want to know more than is available in the textbooks. Scientific journals concentrate on the scientific aspects when we also want to know what happened on an everyday, human level. What was it like to do that? What was it like for the individuals concerned? How did they feel? How did they cope? What happened next? This book tries to bridge that gap.

Important findings in psychology have often been discovered first through one-off case studies. Such case studies always fascinate both the psychology student and the lay reader alike. The use of the case study method helps bring psychology to life – it puts a human angle to psychological ideas.

Psychologists continue to argue about the scientific status of psychology. There is little doubt that scientific findings tend to be given greater credence than hearsay or subjective experiences. However, when it comes to the human mind and behaviour, it can be difficult to conduct scientifically controlled experiments that don't break ethical and moral boundaries. This is where the use of case studies can be particularly useful. They enable the scientist to investigate avenues of the mind and behaviour that are not ordinarily available. By exploring the extraordinary we can learn much about the ordinary.

The use of the case study method in psychology has a long tradition. Indeed, it is one of the very earliest methods and Itard's first report on the 'Enfant Sauvage' dates back to 1801 (see Chapter 9). In recent years, there have been numerous books giving unique insights into people's unusual deficits or excesses. However, these books tend to be written by neurologists and the case studies relate to patients they have met during their medical careers. This book is different in that it provides more detail on the most famous case studies in psychology – the studies that are in many of the psychology textbooks. Of course, entire books and numerous papers have been written about some of the more famous ones, but here, each chapter is condensed into a more easily digestible 'chunk' dealing with the most interesting and revealing aspects of each case. In addition to the scientific importance of each case study, the human aspect of each person's experience is included. The hope is that we will begin to understand the people presented in the case studies as humans with a unique ability or difficulty rather than merely as 'scientific case studies'.

Professor Luria who worked at the Moscow State University outlined two contrasting approaches to the study of human behaviour. These he called 'classical' and 'romantic' science. Classical science has the aim of formulating 'abstract general laws', which can result in the 'reduction of living reality with all its richness of detail to abstract schema'. He noted that this has become more and more pronounced with the advent of computers in that observations can now be reduced to complex mathematical analysis. This book seeks to adopt the so-called 'romantic' or literary science view. The stories have a scientific point and help to illustrate areas of psychology but are written from a human viewpoint. They are *human* stories.

Case studies are used extensively in law, business and medicine, but their use is less common in psychology. This is a shame since we often seem to remember the case studies most vividly because they help to humanise science as well as illustrating psychological findings.

A case study involves gathering detailed information about an individual or group. It will usually include biographical details as well as details of the behaviour or experiences of interest. Case studies allow a researcher to examine a particular individual in far greater depth than experimental methods of investigation. Case studies lend themselves to so-called qualitative research methods and thus findings are not easily reported in a numerical fashion. Written, descriptive reports are often used. These outline what the person feels or believes about a particular issue.[1] These methods tend to be criticised as being less 'scientific' and less worthy than more rigorous experimental methods using statistical analysis.

An additional criticism levelled at case studies is that sometimes the researcher conducting the study may be biased in their interpretations or reporting method. This 'subjectivity' means that it could be difficult to determine factual information from researcher inference. An awareness of this does not detract from the stories that emerge. Indeed, much of the rich detail from the first-hand accounts would not have been possible, had the researcher(s) not formed warm and friendly relationships with their participants. This might be viewed as a strength of the approach not a weakness.

Case studies can help shed light on both specific and general psychological issues. Case studies allow psychologists to study behaviours or experiences that are so unique that they could not have been studied in any other way. Examples in this book illustrate this. These case studies allow the researcher to explore possibilities in human behaviour that may not have been previously considered or thought possible. Often a case study can span several different areas of psychology. With this in mind, readers may argue about the grouping of the case studies into specific approaches. Does the David Reimer case cross from developmental psychology into both social and physiological psychology and perhaps even further? I will leave the reader to be the judge of this. Thus, these headings may be a little artificial but at least they illustrate how case studies are drawn from many different areas of psychology.

Bromley (1986) has argued that case studies are 'the bedrock of scientific investigation' and that psychologists' preoccupation with experimental procedures has led to a neglect of this area. Case studies have the advantage of providing greater depth and understanding about an individual and acknowledge and celebrate human diversity. Because case studies are about 'real, genuine people' they have a special feeling of truth about them. This helps to make them memorable. However, case studies are also criticised for being unreliable (no two case studies are alike) and therefore results cannot be easily generalised to other people. The question arises as to whether we always have to find out universal truths of behaviour. Sometimes surely, it's enough to explore the lives of a unique individual.

Students of psychology will recognise many of the stories but will want to know more. Those new to psychology will find it a useful and interesting introduction to the greatest mystery of all: understanding the human mind and human behaviour in all its facets.

Note

1   There are more quantitative methods for single case studies – these tend to be rather different to the 'naturally occurring originals' we are dealing with here.

Reference

Bromley, D.B. (1986). *The Case Study Method in Psychology and Related Disciplines.* Chichester: John Wiley and Sons.

Part 1

Cognitive psychology

Chapter 1

The man who couldn't forget

The story of Solomon Shereshevsky ('S')[1]

One day in 1905, a 19-year-old Moscow newspaper reporter, called Solomon Shereshevsky, turned up for work as usual and waited for the daily meeting with the editor of the paper during which assignments for the day would be given out. Unlike any of his colleagues, but as was his usual practice, Solomon did not take any notes about the meeting. The editor had noticed this before with surprise and this time decided to reproach Solomon. After all, often there were numerous names and addresses given out and Solomon ought to record the details. The editor decided to test Solomon by asking for details of what he had said. Solomon proceeded to repeat all that he had been told word for word. This incident changed Solomon's life forever and was the starting point of his new career as the world's greatest mnemonist or 'memory man'.

Solomon's memory

The editor was amazed by Solomon's memory whereas Solomon was amazed that anyone should think his memory was remarkable. Didn't others have equally good memories? The answer he would discover over the coming months and years. Sensing an interesting story, the editor sent Solomon to the local university for some further tests of his memory ability and this is where he met Alexander Romanovich Luria, a Russian professor who was to spend the next 30 years systematically studying the most remarkable memory ever examined.

Luria started the examination by collecting biographical details. Solomon, a Latvian by birth, was in his late 20s, his father owned a bookstore and therefore, not surprisingly, his mother was well read. His father could apparently recall the location of every book in the store and his mother, a devout Jew, could quote long paragraphs from the Torah. His brothers and sisters were well-balanced individuals and there was evidence of some musical talent within the family. Indeed, Solomon trained as a violinist until an ear infection put paid to that choice of profession and he turned to journalism instead. Given the suggested link between exceptional ability and mental illness, Luria noted no history of mental illness in the family.

Luria began by giving Solomon a series of tests to ascertain his memory capacity. Words and numbers were presented to him in spoken or written form and he had to replicate them in their original form. Luria started with 10 or 20 items but increased this gradually to 70 items. Solomon recalled all the items perfectly. Solomon occasionally hesitated with his answers, and stared into space, paused but then continued with the word-perfect recall.

Solomon could also report the letters or numbers in reverse order or determine which letter or number followed another in a sequence. This is known as a serial probe technique whereby a list of letters or numbers is read out and then one item is repeated and the item that follows has to be recalled. This can be conducted as a test of short-term memory (recall duration of up to about 30 seconds). Most people find this task extremely difficult especially with a long sequence of items but Solomon had no difficulty providing that the initial presentation of the list was at a pace that he dictated. This pace tended to be fairly slow, which is the exact opposite of so-called 'normal' participants who tend to perform slightly better on a serial probe task if the items are presented quickly. This is because with normal participants the quicker the presentation the less time the items have to decay in their short-term memory. However, with Solomon it was discovered that he was using a different system for remembering the items – not one based on normal acoustic or sound processing – but one that involved images or pictures. This also meant that once learned, Solomon would remember the sequence of items indefinitely, whereas most normal participants would have little recall for the items beyond the minutes that the experiment would take.

Luria began to present Solomon with different memory tasks. Most people find meaningful words far easier to recall than nonsense syllables or trigrams (three consonants with no meaning) but Solomon had no problem with any of them. The same findings occurred with sounds and numbers, all Solomon required was a 3- or 4-second delay between each item to be recalled. In order to test the capacity of memory, researchers have devised a technique developed originally by Jacobs in 1887 called the serial digit span technique. This involves gradually increasing the items to be remembered until the

Figure 1.1 Professor Alexander Luria who studied Solomon Shereshevsky ('S') for decades

Source: © RIA Novosti/Alamy

participant becomes confused and can no longer recall the items in the correct order. If you try this, you'll find that the typical digit span is seven plus or minus two items. However, with Solomon it was Luria who became confused since Solomon appeared to have no limit to his digit span! Indeed, Luria had to give up in the end since there appeared to be no limit to his memory capacity.

Luria arranged for Solomon to return to the university for further tests of his memory. At these sessions, Solomon could recall perfectly all the previous items he had learned. These results confused Luria even more, since Solomon seemed to have no limit either to the capacity of his memory or to the durability of the traces he retained. As Luria writes: 'I soon found myself in a state verging on utter confusion. An increase in the length of a series led to no noticeable increase in difficulty for S., and I simply had to admit that the capacity of his memory had no distinct limits' (p. 11).

Luria couldn't measure either the capacity or duration of Solomon's memory, both of which can usually be tested fairly easily in a laboratory. Indeed, even more amazingly, Luria found out 16 years later that Solomon could recall the items learned at his original sessions. Luria reports Solomon saying: 'Yes, yes . . . This was a series you once gave me when we were in your apartment . . . You were sitting at the table and I in the rocking chair . . . You were wearing a gray [sic] suit and you looked at me like this . . . Now then I can see you saying . . .' (p. 12). This gives a clue as to how Solomon's memory worked – images were the key to his remarkable memory.

Luria had a problem. He realised that there was no way to measure Solomon's memory since it seemed to have no capacity limit. A quantitative analysis of his memory was impossible. For the next 30 years, he decided to concentrate on *describing* Solomon's memory: to provide a qualitative account of its structure.

Solomon used one particular mechanism to aid his memory. Regardless of the type of information or its form (words, numbers, sounds, tastes and so on) Solomon always converted these items into visual images. Providing Solomon was given the time to convert the items into images there was no limit to the capacity or duration of his memories. A table of 50 random numbers would typically take him about 3 minutes to commit to memory. How was this done? Solomon stated that if numbers were written on paper, when asked to recall them later, he would recall the image he had of the paper and recall them as though he was still staring at it. If you were to stop reading now and try to report all that you could see if you glanced up from the page you would probably recall only a fraction of what you actually saw. For Solomon, his recall was as though he was still looking at the page! Solomon could still picture the page in his mind's eye in perfect detail.

Many memory tasks work on the basis of errors made during recall. Such memory experiments are called 'substitution error' studies. Mistakes that are made during recall often provide a clue as to how the memory works. It would be wrong to give the impression that Solomon never made any mistakes – they did not occur that often and they were usually of a similar type – they give us a further clue as to how his memory worked. For example, Solomon occasionally misread one number for another, especially if the numbers appeared similar i.e. 3 and 8 or 2 and 7. Such errors again suggested that his memory was almost exclusively dependent on visual or so-called orthographic processing.

When given a list of words or numbers to recall, 'normal' people often recall the first and last items on the list. Recall of the first items is called the 'primacy' effect and the last is called the 'recency' effect. This pattern of recall is known as the 'serial position effect'. It is suggested that the first words have been transferred to long-term memory through rehearsal and the last items on the list are still held in short-term memory. Once again, as with Solomon's duration and capacity of memory, Luria did not record this phenomenon, since Solomon could recall all the items wherever they appeared on a list!

Solomon had the most amazing memory. Indeed, he had memories dating back to childhood that few of us possess. It is suggested that our memories of our first few years aren't recalled because we haven't learned to encode the material due to a lack of development in terms of memory and/or speech. However, Solomon encoded his memories in a different way and since this ability was innate he possessed it at a very early age. Solomon reported memories from lying in his cot as an infant when his mother picked him up: 'I was very young then . . . not even a year old perhaps . . . What comes to mind most clearly is the furniture in the room . . . I remember that the wallpaper in the room was brown and the bed white . . . I can see my mother taking me in her arms' (p. 77). He even recalls his smallpox vaccination: 'I remember a mass of fog, then of colours. I know this means there was noise, most likely conversation . . . But I don't feel any pain' (p. 78). Of course, it's impossible to discover the accuracy of these memories but their vividness certainly suggests an element of truth.

With such an amazing memory, Solomon was brilliant at spotting contradictions in stories, often pointing out things that the writers had failed to notice. He reports a character in the Checkhov story entitled 'Fat and thin' who takes off his cap where earlier he is mentioned as having not worn a cap.

Given his precise ability, one might have imagined Solomon becoming a detective or lawyer. Solomon could 'see' every detail and could not fail to spot any contradictions.

Synaesthesia

Luria reports that Solomon often had difficulty with encoding or processing information if there was a distraction during the encoding process. This included the experimenter merely saying 'Yes' or 'No' to indicate whether Solomon had heard an item correctly. Solomon reported that these words 'blurred' the image in his head and created 'puffs of steam' or 'splashes', which made it more difficult for him to see the items. Later, during his stage shows, coughs in the audience would have a similar distracting effect. It seemed that all information created an image in Solomon's head regardless of whether or not he wanted it to.

Psychologists have consistently shown that the use of imagery is a particularly effective technique for improving long-term memory. Solomon seemed to have a particular visual ability related to synaesthesia. Synaesthesia comes from the Greek words *syn* meaning 'together' and *aesthesis* meaning 'perception'. Synaesthesia is therefore a form of combined perception where two (or more) senses become intertwined. This means that when one of the senses is stimulated, it automatically triggers another sense that acts involuntarily. For example, days of the week may be associated with particular colours. A student of mine states that 'Tuesday' is definitely a 'blue' day. When asked why, most synaesthetes just say that it just is! There's no explanation for why the senses intertwine. Other synaesthetes might 'taste shapes' or 'see sounds'. These experiences are always the same; the same stimuli consistently evoke the same reactions. This is because they are not learned, they just occur naturally. Synaesthesia tends to be one-directional, meaning one sense may spark off another sense but it doesn't tend to work the other way round. Since synaesthesia is the crossing of two or more senses, there are 31 different possible combinations of sight, smell, touch, taste and hearing. The most common combination tends to be colour and hearing (chromasthesia). Most synaesthetes experience the fusion of only two senses, but Solomon appeared to have four senses joined! Only his sense of smell did not intertwine with his other senses.

The ability Solomon possessed to form visual images for words was the key to his remarkable memory recall. Whenever he heard a word, whether it made sense or not, an immediate visual image was created. He reported that if he heard the word 'green', he would see a green flowerpot, with the word 'red' he would see a man in a red shirt waving towards him, 'blue' conjured up an image of someone waving a blue flag from a window. Even nonsense words conjured up immediate visual impressions that he could continue to 'see' clearly years later.

When Solomon was asked to listen to tones or voices he saw images. An example of this is the report he gave when asked to listen to a tone of 30 cycles per sec at 100 decibels: 'I saw a strip 12–15cm. in width the colour of tarnished silver. Gradually this strip narrowed and seemed to recede: then it was converted into an object that glistened like steel' (p. 22). Such examples clearly show how his synaesthesia worked. Repetition of the tones months later led to exactly the same images being recalled. Every sound he heard summoned up a memorable visual image with its own distinct form, colour and taste.

Solomon's recall of numbers worked in a similar way. He reported the shape of the number 1 as being 'pointed, firm and complete'; the number 2 as being 'flatter, rectangular, whitish in colour, sometimes almost a grey'. Numbers also produced more concrete images: the number 1 was a 'proud, well-built man'; the number 2 was a 'high spirited woman', and so on. For Solomon, vision, taste, touch and hearing all merged together. Later on in his career, as a professional mnemonist, audiences tested him with nonsense words or foreign languages and even these unfamiliar words produced sensations of taste, touch or vision. These additional bits of extra information helped to cue his recall. Solomon even reported an association with the 'weight' of a word. For Solomon, these sensations were so vivid that he reported 'I don't have to make an effort to remember it – the word seems to recall itself' (p. 28).

The method of loci

The method of loci is a mnemonic (memory enhancement) technique that Solomon used in order to remember items in a particular sequence. The method of loci refers to 'objects to be remembered that are imagined in known locations' and dates back to Ancient Greece where orators would use it to remember long speeches.

A story that is associated with this technique relates to the orator Simonides of Ceos who was due to give a speech at a banquet in the 5th century BC. In order to receive a message, he left the building whereupon the hall collapsed. All the guests were killed and their bodies were unidentifiable. Using the method of loci, Simonides was able to locate the bodies of the guests based on where he had last seen them in the building. The relatives were thus able to identify their relative's remains. This shows not only how useful the method can be but how important it is to pay attention to messages!

In order to use the method of loci, you need to imagine a familiar route or location. Solomon often used a street or road in his hometown in Latvia or a well-known route in Moscow such as Gorky Street. Once imagined, the images to be remembered need to be placed at points on the walk. Items are thus distributed at various locations such as in houses, by gates, trees or shop windows ('the loci'). In order to recall the list, you need to retrace your steps and 'see' the items placed there.

Solomon's amazing visual memory meant that he had no difficulty retracing these 'walks'. For him, it was as though he was actually walking along the route. On the few occasions when he failed to recall an item, he explained that he had placed the item in a location, which made it difficult to see on retracing the route. Sometimes, he placed the items in a dimly lit spot, say, in the shadow of a tree, and therefore he would not notice the item in question. For Solomon, these mistakes were defects of perception (not seeing them on the route) rather than defects of memory. One example of this involved the word 'egg', which he placed against a white wall and then failed to spot on retracing his steps. When Solomon later became a mnemonist he became more careful at placing objects in appropriate places and mistakes such as these became rarer.

Memory performance

When it became clear to Solomon that people might be interested in his memory ability, he quit his newspaper job and became a professional mnemonist performing his memory feats on stage.

Audiences often tried to catch him out by giving him nonsense or made-up words to recall. Although Solomon found he could do this, all the visualisations that he had to make to recall these 'words' meant that he took quite a long time to process the information. He recalls one of his most difficult performances when he was asked to recall a long series of repetitive syllables (over 50) such as MA VA NA SA NA SA VA MA and so on. Solomon stated:

> no sooner had I heard the first word than I found myself on a road in the
> forest near the little village of Malta, where my family had a summer

cottage when I was a child . . . The third word. Damn it! The same consonants again . . . I knew I was in trouble . . . I was going to have to change paths in the woods for each word . . . but it would take more time. And when you're on stage, each second counts. I could see someone smiling in the audience, and this, too, immediately was converted into an image of a sharp spire, so that I felt as if I'd been stabbed in the heart.

(pp. 52–3)

Despite these reservations, Solomon still managed to reproduce the sequence correctly. Eight years later and without prior warning, Luria asked Solomon to repeat this monotonous list of syllables and he had no difficulty whatsoever!

As a mnemonist, Solomon tried to simplify his recall techniques in order to speed up his memory performance. As mentioned, he ensured that mental images were clearly 'seen' and he also developed a shorthand system of his images. He tried to create images that were more simple and less detailed. Solomon found that he could still recall the words and that the less-detailed images took less time to encode. With nonsense syllables that audiences gave him to recall, he linked image associations with lots of different syllables. He worked on this for hours each day and became a master at forming images of nonsense syllables. Using such techniques, he could recall words in a foreign language, meaningless mathematical formulae and nonsense syllables.

Luria was adamant that Solomon's memory was an innate characteristic, that he had been born with. The use of mnemonic techniques during his stage performances were simply devices to enhance and speed up his natural ability to satisfy a demanding audience.

Other associated abilities

Solomon's incredible visual memory ensured that he could perform bodily feats due to the power of thought. As he put it: 'If I want something to happen, I simply picture it in my mind' (p. 139). This was no idle boast and he could regulate his heartbeat and even alter his perception of pain through imagery.

To alter his heartbeat, he merely had to imagine that he was running for a train or imagine he was lying perfectly still and relaxing in bed. These images were so real for him that his body altered its physiological responses. In addition, he was able to alter the temperature of his hands by imagining placing one of them in a hot stove while holding ice in the other hand. Recordings of the temperature of the skin on each hand showed that they had changed by a couple of degrees.

In addition, Solomon could alter his perception of pain. While at the dentist, he would imagine watching someone else having their teeth drilled. This meant that the 'other person' experienced the pain, not Solomon! He could also adapt his eyes to the dark by imagining himself in a darkened room and could produce a cochlear-pupil reflex using his imagination of 'hearing' a piercing sound. Despite being studied at a specialist neurology clinic, few explanations for these abilities were forthcoming.

Memory problems

It is clear by now that Solomon possessed a unique memory. However, there were downsides to his abilities. Due to the abundance of images that were associated with each word he heard he had to have information read to him fairly slowly in order for him to process the word as an image.

Apparently, on meeting Solomon for the first time many people reported him as appearing rather disorganised, dull or slow-witted. This was certainly true if he was read a story at a fast pace. Solomon found that the array of images each word created meant that they collided with the images of the reading voice and those of any extraneous sounds. The result would be a complete chaos of images. A simple passage of writing sometimes became a herculean effort of processing. Skim-reading a passage or taking just the gist of a passage seemed beyond him since each word summoned up such a rich array of images. Solomon found it impossible to single out the most important or key points from a text. Each detail in any text produced further images that often took him further and further away from the central point of any passage.

Solomon was also very poor at processing abstract ideas. To Solomon, everything was processed visually. He said 'other people *think* as they read, but I *see* it all' (p. 112). He often found that one word in a passage sparked off an image and then from that image he would move to a related one not associated with the original text. His own thinking would guide his linked images rather than the text itself! Abstract words were a real problem as well since they could not easily be visualised. For example, he said that it was impossible to see the word 'infinity'. He saw the word 'something' as a dense cloud of steam and 'nothing' as a thinner, completely transparent cloud. In effect, he could not grasp an idea or word unless he could see it and some ideas and words cannot be easily visualised! Solomon's torment was to spend many hours of his life trying to grapple with these things that the rest of us cope with quite easily.

Solomon was spectacularly poor at coping with synonyms or metaphors due to the images that crowded in on him. To him, a 'child', 'youngster', 'infant', 'toddler' and so on meant many different things whereas a writer might use them interchangeably without a great deal of thought. To Solomon they were processed in completely different ways. Furthermore, words with many alternative meanings such as 'wear' as in 'to wear away' or 'to wear a coat' would cause serious problems since the image would always be the same despite the different meanings. Often, Solomon would get so bogged down in the detail that he couldn't see the overall picture. Poetry was almost impossible for him to read. Every word would form an image whether or not it was the one that the poet intended, and the image Solomon saw, would, more often than not, disguise the associated meaning.

Another skill that Solomon was also particularly poor at was spotting any form of logical organisation of material. Solomon did not readily spot patterns that might have aided recall, indeed, he never used any logical means of recall at all. Solomon's over-reliance on imagery techniques meant that he often didn't take notice of the meaning of many words. Once he was given a list of bird names to recall – he recalled the list perfectly but failed to note that the list was a list of different birds! His imagery technique meant that each word conjured up one or more separate images and these were disconnected from the next word in the list. The same thing happened when he was given numbers that followed a particular sequence. Solomon usually failed to spot any logical sequence. Indeed, he commented: 'if I had been given the letters of the alphabet arranged in a similar order, I wouldn't have noticed their arrangement . . . I simply would have gone on and memorized them' (p. 60).

Perhaps surprisingly, Solomon had a fairly poor memory for faces, or voices heard on the telephone. He complained that faces and voices were so changeable and depended on the mood or expression they had at the time. Solomon saw faces as constantly changing. The recognition of faces was compared to watching a wave changing its shape. Solomon claimed that a person's voice could change as much as 30 times a day. Each voice change produced a different set of images for Solomon and hence recognition of one voice was difficult. Indeed, he was known to become so preoccupied by the sound of a person's voice that he didn't register what they were actually saying. Of course, this might be seen as an advantage with some people!

Solomon's synaesthesia enabled him to have a phenomenal memory but the lack of a dividing line between his senses did result in rather strange occurrences. For example, he reported that in order to eat in a restaurant there had to be the right kind of background music playing. Otherwise, the sound of the music would interfere with the taste of the food. Solomon stated that: 'if you select the right kind of music, everything tastes good. Surely people who work in restaurants know this' (p. 82). One occasion is reported when he fancied eating an ice cream and went to buy one from a nearby stall. However, when asking what flavours were available the ice cream seller replied 'fruit ice cream' in such a tone of voice that: 'a whole pile of coals, of black cinders, came bursting out of her mouth, and I couldn't bring myself to buy any ice cream after she'd answered that way' (p. 82). Another example of this concerns the Russian word *svinia*, which stands for 'pig'. For Solomon, this word evoked fine and delicate images quite at odds with the qualities usually associated with pigs. For Solomon both the sound of a word, the voice of the speaker and the meaning of the word would be encoded together. For Solomon, all of these things had to fit together.

Trying to forget

Unlike most people, who spend time trying to devise strategies for remembering, Solomon spent time trying to devise strategies to forget! It became increasingly clear to him that he needed to forget information. After becoming a professional mnemonist, when he would give several performances a day in the same venue, Solomon found that he was having difficulty organising all the material he had to remember. Solomon developed a number of strategies to try to overcome this.

First, he deliberately tried to restrict the images that he used to aid recall. He tried to focus his attention and limit the images to the essential details that he would need to recall the item to be remembered. In effect, he began to make shorthand versions of his images. He still remembered the material perfectly but did not need to encode all the rich details that each item would normally evoke. Although this helped, he still needed a way to completely forget material rather than just code things in a simpler form.

One way he tried to forget was to mentally rearrange material on paper that he had remembered on previous performances. He then imagined screwing up the paper and throwing it away. However, he still reported difficulties of forgetting. Solomon found interference occurred if material in a subsequent performance was similar to that presented during an earlier performance. This is an example of proactive interference where older memories affect newer memories. Furthermore, the more similarities between the material, the greater the interference. For once, Solomon's memory seemed to work like everyone else's since interference is one of the suggested explanations for forgetting. Although it must still be recorded that Solomon did not actually forget any of the material, he merely found it more confusing to learn and recall.

So Solomon still needed to develop a technique for forgetting. He realised that many people wrote things down in order to try to aid recall, which, to him, seemed ridiculous. Nevertheless, he wondered if he might write things down in order to forget. He reasoned that if something was written down, there would be no reason to continue to remember it! He tried this technique and then discarded the pieces of paper, even burning them on occasion. Unfortunately, he found he could still see the numbers on the charred embers!

It seemed to Solomon that he would be forever affected by the inability to forget and this became an increasing worry to him. Then, out of the blue, Solomon found a method for forgetting that neither he nor the psychologists studying him fully understood. He explains that after giving three performances in one evening, he was worried about interference effects during his fourth performance. He thought:

> I'll just take a look and see if the first chart of numbers is still there. I was afraid somehow that it wouldn't be. I both did and didn't want it to appear . . . and then I thought: the chart of numbers isn't turning up now and it's clear why – it's because I don't want it to! Aha! That means if I don't want the chart to show up it won't. And all it took was for me to realise this! . . . At that moment I felt I was free . . . I knew that if I didn't want an image to appear, it wouldn't.
>
> (pp. 71–2)

Strangely, this technique of deliberately trying to forget seemed to work although, to this day, no-one knows how it worked.

The paradox of Solomon Shereshevsky

So what can we make of Solomon Shereshevsky? Solomon's life was a paradox. His greatest ability was also his greatest handicap. His amazing memory meant that he found it difficult to forget, but despite this he did appear slow and forgetful to others. His memory created practical difficulties for him on a day-to-day basis and he continued to have difficulty distinguishing reality from the images created in his head. He spent hours each day daydreaming on a journey through his remarkable memory. Although successful as a stage mnemonist for a time, he had many other jobs and never really found a satisfying career that exploited his astounding abilities. It is particularly difficult to draw parallels from his memory to 'everyday' memory ability since his capacity and processing techniques differed so markedly from the norm. Solomon ended up working as a taxi driver in Moscow and never had any excuse for going the wrong way! There are mixed reports about what happened to Solomon, and to some extent he disappeared off the radar. *The New York Times* reported that he married and had one child and that he died in 1967 aged 72. Solomon was always striving to do something great in his life but probably felt he didn't succeed. However, his legacy to psychology may mean that in the end he actually achieved his goal. Professor Luria continued with his successful academic career until his death in 1977, and in 1972 he wrote about another famous case of a man called Zasetsky who had suffered a major brain injury.

Note

1   Solomon Shereshevsky is his actual name, although his surname is sometimes spelt slightly differently. Often, participants' real names are kept confidential and individuals are referred to by their initials only. In many articles and books, Solomon Shereshevsky is referred to simply as 'S'. However, since his name is now well known, it seems reasonable to refer to him by his actual name. Material in this chapter has been drawn from Luria (1968).

Reference

Luria, A.R. (1968). *The Mind of a Mnemonist*. Cambridge, MA: Harvard University Press.

Chapter 2

The man who lived for the present

The story of H.M. (Henry Gustav Molaison)

One summer day in 1953, brain surgeon Bill Scoville tried an experimental technique to cure one of his patient's debilitating epilepsy. With his patient still awake, he cut a hole in his head and sucked up a part of his brain through a silver straw. As he later joked, instead of removing his epilepsy, he removed his memory. H.M. as the patient was referred to, was destined to become one of the most famous neurological cases in the world.

H.M.'s past

Henry Molaison (H.M.) had a fairly uneventful childhood. He was born on 26 February 1926 in a working class area of Hartford, Connecticut, the product of small town America. He was a quiet, reserved and shy boy who did the typical things of his age. He'd spend time with his friends at the local soda shop and swim in the local reservoir. He had a particular interest in shooting and would spend many happy hours exploring the woods near to his home hunting for birds and pheasants for the pot. One incident that was later seized upon by doctors occurred when he was knocked unconscious by a boy on a speeding bike. Seventeen stitches were needed to mend the wounds to his face and head. It has been suggested that some of his subsequent neurological problems may have had their origins in this incident.

On his sixteenth birthday he was driving with his parents to town in order to celebrate his birthday. Suddenly, his body stiffened and he had the first of many full-blown 'grand mal' epileptic seizures. H.M. lost consciousness and his body stiffened and yet he also began jerking uncontrollably. He bit his tongue so severely that it bled and he lost bladder control. His breathing became shallow until the jerking stopped after a minute or so. These are the classic symptoms of a 'grand mal' seizure. These seizures are the symptoms of epilepsy. Prior to this, H.M. had noticed moments when his mind went blank but these effects were only temporary. H.M.'s three first cousins on his father's side also had epilepsy, suggesting a family trait.

Epilepsy is a neurological condition that makes people susceptible to seizures (the old name for a 'seizure' was a 'fit'). A seizure is caused by a temporary change in the way the brain cells work. In the enormous network of neurons that make up the brain, billions of electrical messages are fired to and fro. These determine virtually all our thoughts, feelings and behaviours. Occasionally, without warning an upset in brain chemistry causes these messages to become scrambled. The neurons 'fire' faster than normal and in bursts. It is this disturbance that causes a seizure. A seizure usually only lasts a few seconds or minutes and then the brain cells return to normal functioning. Epilepsy can be inherited but often no cause is readily found.

Unfortunately, H.M. was not treated very sympathetically by either his family or peers. He was teased at school and ended up leaving and having to graduate at a different school. On graduation day, his teachers refused to let him collect his diploma on stage in case he had a seizure. His father, Gustav, was horrified

Figure 2.1 Photo of Henry Molaison by Suzanne Corkin

Source: © Suzanne Corkin, used by permission of The Wylie Agency (UK) Limited to have 'a mental' in the family. Gustav sought solace in alcohol and left his son's future in the hands of his wife. H.M.'s plans to follow in his father's footsteps and become an electrician were abandoned and by the age of 26, he seemed destined to a life of dead-end jobs. H.M. lived in constant fear of epilepsy and by the summer of 1953 was having as many as 10 minor blackouts and one 'grand mal' (major) seizure every week.

His doctor made a decision to seek 'expert' help from the local neurological hospital. There were two doctors who could have taken his case. One was Bill Scoville who specialised in lobotomies and the other specialised in epilepsy. Scoville took the case.

The caring profession?

When physicians first became interested in insanity or madness in the 1800s, they believed that the mentally ill had lost their reason, the thing that makes humans uniquely human. The mentally ill were often treated in barbaric ways with little or no understanding of their humanity. They were often confined with physical restraints for weeks on end. Doctors were developing more and more therapies that now seem little more than innovative forms of torture. One doctor developed a gyrating chair, another shook his patients for hours on end and collapsing bridges were made that unexpectedly plunged patients into ice-cold water. The hope was that such treatments would restore sanity by shocking their disturbed minds. Surprisingly, many of these treatments were reported as being effective in improving manic behaviour. It seems certain that the patients were merely frightened into submission. Doctors were increasingly desperately searching for the cure to mental illness.

In the 1930s the incidence of serious mental illness was increasing, but an understanding of its cause or how to treat it was not. A Portuguese doctor called Egas Moniz was impressed when he was shown at a conference how placid a previously temperamental chimpanzee was after having had its frontal lobes removed. Moniz wondered whether a similar process would work for the mentally ill? Moniz suggested that mental illness might be caused by malfunctioning nerve cells. If these were destroyed, might not the patient show some improvement? Although Moniz had no real scientific evidence for his hypothesis, he started performing psychosurgery on human patients. Using his own subjective, biased criteria, Moniz declared the operations successful.

An American professor, Walter Freeman, enthusiastically welcomed these new 'invasive' techniques and began extolling their virtues on that side of the

Atlantic. Moniz and Freeman published an influential book promoting the use of lobotomies to treat the mentally ill (Freeman, 1949a, 1949b; Moniz, 1994). The number of lobotomies performed in the USA increased from 100 in 1946 to 5,000 in 1949. The technique seemed to offer hope where none lay before. Freeman seems to have been a rebellious, controversial character. He developed a technique that involved lifting a patient's eyelid and inserting a leucotome (an instrument similar to an ice-pick) through a tear duct. He would push the leucotome about an inch and a half into the frontal lobe and move the sharp tip to and fro. He would repeat this with the other eye socket. He liked to show off his skill by performing two-handed lobotomies on both eye sockets simultaneously. Being the showman he was, he ordered his own handmade leucotome to be made out of pure gold. Unbelievably, he once killed a patient when he stepped back to take a photo and accidentally allowed his leucotome to sink deep into the person's brain. Around this time, Moniz received the Nobel Prize for his discovery of the frontal lobotomy (this was later described as the most disgraceful award in the history of the prize). During this time, Scoville was studying medicine at university and could not help but be influenced by this new found 'miracle' procedure.

Bill Scoville was also a rather wild character known to the local police for his reckless driving in his red Jaguar and for his high risk pranks, such as climbing the cable tower of the George Washington bridge at night. In his professional life, he also appeared willing to take risks in the hope of gaining high rewards. Local mental hospitals used to 'volunteer' suitable patients for pioneering operations and Scoville used to take them on. He used to believe in the motto of Walter Freeman, 'Lobotomy gets them home.' However, by 1953, concerns about the effectiveness of lobotomy were being raised. Scoville saw a chance. Could he find a new site in the brain that might be the seat of mental illness? Quite openly, he reported in the papers that he was cutting new and different areas in the brains of patients (mainly schizophrenics) and investigating the effects. In none of the papers is there any mention of ethics. Scoville reported that there had been no adverse effects, except in one case (Scoville et al., 1953). This is the first reference to H.M. in any medical journal.

Although Scoville had previously been warned of the dangers of his operations, H.M sat in his operating chair on 25 August 1953. With no pain receptors in the brain, H.M. was awake with a local anaesthetic administered when Scoville started to cut across the skin on his forehead. Using a hand drill, Scoville bored two holes into his skull to access his brain. He inserted a metal spatula in order to lever up his frontal lobes to access the deeper structures within the brain. Years later brain scans would show that his frontal lobes remained slightly pushed up and squashed. Next, he inserted a silver straw and sucked up an orange sized mass of grey matter from both hemispheres. Specifically, Scoville removed most of the hippocampus (a small seahorse shaped organ), the amygdala and the entorhinal and perihinal cortexes. Many of the functions of these areas are still not fully understood. The amygdala, for example, appears to play a part in organising sensory and cognitive information in order to interpret the emotional significance of an event or thought. Due in no small part to the case of H.M. it is now clear that the hippocampus plays a part in organising memory storage. In a moment, H.M. had lost the ability to encode new memories. He was stuck in the past and the present but with no future to look forward to.

Bill Scoville had not finished his operation. He decided to place metal clips inside H.M.'s brain in order to mark the edge of the cuts. If the operation was a success, this would enable researchers using x-rays to locate precisely where his cuts had been. However, on the first day after his operation, H.M. suffered another 'grand mal' seizure. There were immediate fears that the operation had been of no benefit. However, this was not true. H.M.'s seizures did become less frequent and were reduced to about one major seizure every few months. Somewhat fortuitously, Scoville had been partially correct about his hypothesis regarding the spreading nature of the epileptic seizure within the brain. (It is also now clear that the hippocampus is involved in mental illness. In both schizophrenia and some types of depression, the hippocampus appears to shrink.) Unfortunately, Scoville did not foresee the intractable side effect that would afflict his patient. H.M. was, and remained for the rest of his life, incapable of updating his memory. Despite this, Scoville wrote on H.M.'s discharge notes 'Condition improved.'

H.M.'s memory loss was immediately apparent. His mother regretted agreeing to the operation and was angry with her husband for leaving the decision to her and with Scoville for persuading her that there was a chance it would be a success. Scoville went home and joked to his wife: 'Guess what? I tried to cut out the epilepsy of a patient, but took his memory instead! What a trade!' He showed no guilt about the operation and, indeed, published papers reporting it but at least he did warn other scientists of the dangers of precisely this sort of operation. He telephoned one of the most famous neurologists at the time, Wilder Penfield in Canada, to tell him of his patient. Penfield was angry with him and could not believe that he had conducted such a procedure but, after calming down, decided that H.M. provided an opportunity to find out more about the workings of the brain.

'Waking from the dream'

One of Penfield's colleagues, Brenda Milner, visited H.M. and started a systematic investigation. Largely because of her work with H.M., Milner is now regarded as one of the world's leading memory researchers (Milner et al., 1968). H.M. had one of the clearest memory deficits ever documented. He found it virtually impossible to acquire any new memories at all. Although Milner worked with him for the next 20 odd years, each time he met her she appeared as a stranger to him. From the day of the operation, H.M. was destined to live his life in the past. H.M. would often repeat the same material over and over again. He was unaware that he was repeating himself. Milner became fond of H.M. but in much the same way you might develop affection for a pet. She claims he lost some uniquely human quality during the operation since it was impossible to build a genuine friendship with a person who could not remember you from one moment to the next.

So what exactly could H.M. remember? He still had a normal short-term memory. He could repeat lists of numbers or letters just heard. His digit span (the number of items you can recall immediately in short-term memory) was normal (that is, he could recall approximately seven items). He was certainly aware of what had happened a minute or so before. But beyond this, or if he was distracted, he could recall nothing. He was suffering from the most severe form of anterograde amnesia. Anterograde amnesia refers to the loss of memory for any events after the trauma or, in this case, the operation. In other words, he was almost totally incapable of forming any new memories. At first, H.M. also seemed to be suffering from retrograde amnesia (loss of memory from before the trauma) but gradually he did begin to retrieve memories from before the operation. He remembered incidents from his childhood. He recognised pictures of famous people from the 1940s. Eventually, most of his memories up to the age of 16 were retrieved, but along with his almost total inability to form any new memories he suffered from an 11-year retrograde amnesia. That is, he could not recall events from 11 years prior to the operation. It has been suggested that this provides evidence that memories take a long time to be permanently consolidated in memory.

After his operation, H.M. continued to live with his parents, and his mother in particular encouraged him to work to regain both his memory and his independence. For example, he would be asked to go and mow the lawn. He remembered the procedure of lawn cutting and could work out where he'd cut by judging the height of the grass. However, if his attention was diverted halfway through, he would be unaware that he was cutting the lawn. It became clear that he would be unable to lead a 'normal' independent life.

H.M. occasionally surprised researchers by reporting a few memories that had been encoded after the operation. He had a vague recollection about the assassination of President Kennedy, although he often confused this with the 1933 attempt on Franklin D. Roosevelt. He learned what contact lenses were and reported that 'Magnum' was the name of his favourite television detective. It seemed that after hundreds of repetitions he was capable of encoding some new (but often confused) memories. This may be because later advanced brain scans showed that minute pieces of his hippocampus remained from the original surgery.

Despite the devastating situation he found himself in, H.M. remained an intelligent, amusing and polite man. His intellectual powers were not affected by the surgery, indeed his IQ test scores rose after his operation from 104 to 117. The average IQ of the general population is 100. Once, a researcher accidentally locked his keys in the experimental room. H.M. smiled and pointed out that at least he'd know where to find them, something that H.M. realised would have been impossible for himself! H.M. continued to do crossword puzzles. He would spend hours and hours completing them, perhaps because all the clues were there on the page. He could return to them at any time and immediately see where he had got to. He continuously told visitors that he did crosswords unaware that he was repeating himself. In a reference to his amnesic state and his love of crosswords he once declared himself 'the king of puzzles'. He could still read and write but read the same rifle magazine over and over again. Each time he forgot that he had previously read it.

As with many amnesiacs, H.M. developed strategies to try to hide his memory loss. For a number of years after the operation, H.M. worked in a machine tool shop doing menial, repetitive jobs. He could do these so long as he didn't stop or was distracted. If he went to the toilet he would never find his way back. His surperviser used to ask him to collect tools. He would give him the picture of the tool that he required and then H.M. would usually succeed in locating it. H.M. also learned to notice subtle non-verbal cues that familiar acquaintances exhibited. These helped him to realise that these were people he should have known. However, this was not always the case. When he returned home to live with his mother soon after the operation, he would

Figure 2.2 H.M. could collect tools if his supervisor gave him a picture
Source: © Shutterstock

invite all callers to the house in for a cup of tea. He assumed that all callers must be friends and, not wishing to appear rude, invited everyone in!

Eventually the research on H.M. switched to the Massachussetts Institute of Technology (MIT) and a former student of Milner's called Suzanne Corkin took charge in 1966 and continued to test H.M. three times per year until his death in 2009. At this time, H.M.'s anonymity ceased and we found out his real name was Henry Molaison.

After the operation, Henry had no idea of his own age or the date. He believed he was about 33 years of age and often guessed the year to be about 1930. He was often shocked when he saw his reflection in the mirror. Indeed, he had been known not to recognise current pictures of himself. When he was shown a picture of Muhammad Ali, he said that it was Joe Louis. He didn't remember the operation but was aware that he had a problem with memory loss. He was often worried that he may have said something that may have been upsetting to others and that he couldn't remember it. He constantly worried about this and asked people if that was the case. He did seem to realise that his situation could help others. He once said: 'I keep thinking that possibly I had an operation . . . somehow the memory is gone . . . I'm trying to figure it out. It isn't worrisome in a way, to me . . . they'd learn from it. It would help others.' Although cheerful for the most part, Henry did occasionally show hurt at being referred to as 'a case'. He described his life as like 'waking from a dream . . . every day is alone in itself'. He found it difficult to hold conversations and ask questions because he was aware that he couldn't remember 'what went just before'. He often reverted to telling a dozen or so anecdotes that he repeated over and over again for the last 50 years of his life.

Psychological tests showed that Henry was extremely poor at estimating time. Beyond 20 seconds, he seemed incapable of accurately estimating it. His estimations were so poor that researchers believed that to him a few days passed like minutes, weeks like hours and years like weeks. This may have been a godsend for someone in Henry's position since it would mean that his last 50 years of memory loss may have seemed no longer than a few months.

Henry's gift to science

One of Henry's gifts to science was the discovery that there are many different forms of memory and that they are located in different areas of the brain. His memory loss involved 'the processing of memory', that is, the forming, sorting and storing of new memories. This seems to be a major role of the hippocampus. Not only does it file away new memories but it connects them with related memories and thus helps to give the new memories meaning.

It is possible to determine whether amnesiacs can learn new things without them being consciously aware of it. Henry managed to learn a number of procedural memories. Procedural memories (sometimes called 'muscle memory or implicit knowledge') involve the storage of skills and procedures. This includes memories of skilled tasks such as playing tennis, swimming or riding a bike. Memories such as this are most easily demonstrated by performing the actual skill. People have great difficulties describing procedural memories. For example, try describing the front crawl swimming stroke to someone.

Specifically, procedural memory is now thought to comprise three types: (1) conditioned reflexes; (2) emotional associations; and (3) skills and habits. Each of these memories are related to different areas of the brain. The learning of conditioned reflexes is thought to be related to the brain structure called the cerebellum. The most famous example of this was reported by Claparede in 1911 (Claparede, 1911). One of his amnesic patients never remembered him from one meeting to the next. One day Claparede held a pin in his hand and pricked her when shaking hands. Next time they met, the patient again did not recognise him but refused to shake his hand. She could not explain why but was very reluctant to do so. This is an example of simple conditioning (learning). Henry's cerebellum was unaffected by his operation and so we would expect that he should have been able to acquire and learn things in this way even though he would not have been aware of having learned it. However, conditioning tests on Henry had to be abandoned when it was found that he had an abnormally high tolerance to electric shocks. He seemed able to tolerate shocks that any normal person would find painful. The exact reasons for this remain unclear but it is suggested that this must be another symptom of his widespread neurological damage. Emotional associations such as knowing when to feel afraid or angry are related to the amygdala. Much of this brain structure was removed in Henry and although he did appear to feel fear and anger he was unaware of *why* he felt such emotions. For example, since the operation, Henry occasionally showed extreme outbursts of anger. He once broke a finger when he banged his fists repeatedly against his bedroom door shouting: 'I can't remember, I can't remember', and he threatened to kill himself on at least one occasion. There were fears that he was beginning to realise how empty his life had become due to his memory loss. However, most often, he could not remember why he was angry nor indeed his actual display of anger. It seemed that the feelings of anger arose but he could not remember why he felt angry. This, in itself, must have been a frustrating and confusing situation.

It is still unclear which brain structures are associated with the skills and habits of procedural memory. Both the cerebellum and hippocampus are thought to be implicated. Henry could demonstrate the acquisition and retention of new skills. For example, Corkin taught him the technique of mirror drawing. This involves tracing a drawing onto paper while only viewing the image of it in a mirror. At first, this is extremely difficult but with sufficient practice, people soon improve on the task. Henry showed normal learning ability for the task but on subsequent occasions when he was asked to perform the task he was totally unaware that he had learned the particular skill. Later on, he also learned the techniques of mirror writing and mirror reading. These examples echo the case of an amnesic patient who learned to play table tennis to a good standard but was unaware of his ability or, indeed, the rules of the game or how to keep score. Another amnesic pianist was taught a new piece of music. Later, he could not recall it but after being given the first few notes he could play the tune perfectly.

What was missing from Henry was the ability to encode new memories for episodes that occurred in his life (for example, his birthday). This type of memory is called 'episodic' memory. Henry could not store the events in his life but had also lost the ability to learn new factual information (for example, who the president of the United States was). This type of memory is called 'semantic' memory. It is clear that the brain structures that Henry lost were not involved in procedural memory but are essential for retaining episodic and semantic memories.

Henry's legacy

So how can we summarise what we learned from the 50-year study of Henry? Researchers found that short-term memory is not located in the hippocampus, that there are different forms of long-term memory, that the hippocampus is not involved in the encoding or retaining of procedural memories, that the hippocampus *is* involved in the formation of new (episodic and semantic) long-term memories and that personality is not greatly affected by the loss of the hippocampus.

Henry outlived his family, but he never had any recollection of their deaths. When he was told about his mother's death, he grieved afresh each time. However, he did sometimes report that he had a feeling that she may have left him somehow. With his intellect intact, by estimating what his age might be from looking in a mirror, he could deduce that it was most likely that his mother was dead.

In a striking contrast to many of the researchers that dealt with other cases such as Genie (see Chapter 9), Suzanne Corkin who spent much of her academic career studying Henry became a 'guardian' of him, looking after his interests and helping to organise various aspects of his life. She helped him in the nursing home in which he resided up to his death and arranged his research visits to MIT. She became a valuable adviser to Henry despite the fact that he never remembered her.

Henry always stated that he wanted to help others in a similar predicament and he and his court-appointed guardian gave consent for his brain to be donated to science on his death. As Corkin (2002) put it: 'His wish to help other people will have been fulfilled. Sadly, however, he will remain unaware of his fame and of the impact that his participation in research has had on scientific and medical communities internationally.'

People have often pondered what life would be like without memory. Without memory where would the human race be? There would be no language, no science, no art, no history, no family, no meaningful existence.

Our existence would be from moment to moment. We would only have our innate reflexes to cope with the world. A world that would be completely different from the one we know today. Because of Henry we can answer some of those questions.

It may be possible to view Henry's memory loss as a blessing in some respects. Henry's memory loss also served to protect him from fully realising what a meaningless life he led after his operation. The case of Henry is tragically ironic. The man without a memory has taught us so much about the nature of memory and will continue to do so to this day. When told of his massive contribution to brain science he would quickly forget it but it would also make him very happy if only for a few seconds.

Henry Molaison died of respiratory failure aged 82 on 2 December 2009 at his Connecticut nursing home. As previously agreed, Suzanne Corkin arranged for his brain to be taken to the Brain Observatory at the University of California San Diego. His brain was dissected and sliced into specimen segments during a 53-hour live web broadcast in order to allow researchers to access his brain in the future (www.brainobservatory.usd.edu/hm). Corkin has revealed plans to write a memoir of her time working with Henry and the film rights to Henry's life story have recently been sold to Columbia Pictures. It seems that the man with no memory will never be forgotten.

References

Claparede, E. (1951) [1911]. 'Recognition and "me-ness"'. Trans. D. Rapaport. In D. Rapaport (ed.), *Organization and Pathology of Thought: Selected Sources*. New York: Columbia University Press.

Corkin, S. (2002). 'What's new with the amnesic patient H.M.? Nature reviews'. *Neuroscience*, 3: 153–60.

Freeman, Walter (1949a). 'Mass action versus mosaic function of the frontal lobe'. *Journal of Nervous and Mental Disease*, 110: 413–18.

Freeman, Walter, (1949b). 'Transorbital lobotomy'. *American Journal of Psychiatry*, 105: 734–40.

Milner, B., Corkin, S. and Teuber, H-L. (1968). 'Further analysis of the hippocampal amnesic sundrome: 14-year follow-up study of H.M.'. *Neuropsychologia*, 6: 215–34.

Moniz, E. (1994). 'Prefrontal leucotomy in the treatment of mental disorders'. *American Journal of Psychiatry* (Sesquicentennial Supplement), 151: 236–39 (original work published in 1937).

Scoville, W.B., Dunsmore, R.H., Liberson, W.T., Henry, C.E. and Pepe, A. (1953). 'Observations on medial temporal lobotomy and uncotomy in the treatment of psychotic states'. *Association for Research in Nervous and Mental Disease*, 31: 347–69.

Chapter 3

The man who was disappointed with what he saw

The story of S.B.[1]

S.B. lost his sight aged 10 months. His particular eyesight problem was declared inoperable. However, many years later, science had progressed to the point where his sight was restored. At the age of 52, S.B. could see again. He would see his wife for the first time and everything else besides. He would surely be delighted with his newly restored gift of sight. However, he quickly became dispirited, depressed and within 2 years died a broken man. He was disappointed with what he saw.

The life of a blind child

S.B. was born in 1906. He was one of seven children born into a relatively poor home in Birmingham, UK. He became blind at the age of 10 months due to an infection following a smallpox vaccination. His elder sister used to take S.B. to his weekly eye clinic sessions in order to have his bandages removed and for his eyes to be cleaned. She reports that his eyes were continually bandaged since his eyes wept so much with an unpleasant discharge. As a game, the family used to test S.B.'s vision and she recalls his ability to distinguish light and to be able to point to some 'large white objects'. He could also distinguish hand movements at a distance of about 8 inches with his right eye. However, for the most part during his childhood, S.B.'s head was covered in a bandage. He himself reported that he had only three visual memories, these being the colours red, white and black. To all intents and purposes, he led the life of a blind child. He attended the Birmingham Blind School from the age of nine and left with a good education and the skills necessary to be a cobbler in 1923.

During these school years he was described as a good, nice mannered and smart boy, only occasionally disobedient. He started work as a boot repairer in a garden shed at his home in Burton-on-Trent. All his tools and equipment were provided for him. The quality of his work was reported as good and he led a largely independent existence and yet he earned only a meagre wage compared to his sighted colleagues. He set up home, married and is reported as being a jovial and active person. He was confident enough to cross any road unaided and generally would not carry a white cane when going out. It was not unknown for him to injure himself by walking into parked cars or other unexpected obstructions on his familiar routes to the pub or shops. He was a keen cyclist and would go for long rides holding on to a friend's shoulder for guidance. He enjoyed gardening and was described as a positive and enthusiastic person who embraced life.

Such was his life – relatively uneventful, but full – until a routine eye examination in 1957 opened the door for him to regain his sight. The ophthalmic surgeon, Mr Hirtenstein, tested S.B. and suggested that since he was not actually blind (technically, this means *totally* insensitive to light), that there might be an operation that could improve his corneal functioning and thus restore his sight. The cornea is the window at the front of the eye. It should be transparent and allow light to enter the eye. When this cannot occur, the path of light to the retina is distorted and/or blocked with a corresponding loss of vision. A corneal graft involves removing a part of the cornea and replacement with a similar piece from a donor eye. Advancement in surgical techniques meant that such operations were now possible and on 9 December 1958 he received a corneal graft on his left eye to be followed a month later with a similar operation on the right.

A national newspaper, *The Daily Express*, got to hear about this and reported the case. A psychology professor called Richard Gregory read the story and immediately wrote to the surgeon requesting access to his patient (Gregory, 1986). To this day, Gregory remains one of the world's leading experts in visual perception. Gregory and his assistant Jean Wallace were given the necessary consent and visited S.B. 48 days after the operation on his left eye.

Restored sight

S.B.'s first visual experience after the operation was the sight of the surgeon's face as his bandages were removed. *The Daily Express* story reports that he saw a dark shape with a bump sticking out and heard a voice, feeling his own nose, he realised that the 'bump' in front of him must also be a nose and therefore the dark shape must be a face. He therefore concluded that this must

Figure 3.1 Richard Gregory who examined the case of S.B.
Source: Heini Schneebeli/Science Photo Library

be the surgeon's face. Later reports by S.B. himself suggest that he recognised 'the confusion of colours' as the surgeon's face purely because he remembered the surgeon's voice. He admitted that he wouldn't have known this was a face without the vocal accompaniment and his pre-existing knowledge that voices came from faces. Initially, S.B. did not find faces very easy objects to identify. He described his wife as 'just as bonny as I thought she would be'.

A well-controlled study would have enabled the researchers to examine and test S.B. both pre- and post-operatively and have given the researchers more time to prepare various perceptual tests. Nevertheless, by the time Gregory and Wallace met S.B. they were armed with an array of various tests of his visual abilities. They first saw him strolling confidently down a hospital corridor. He walked through a door without the need of the use of touch and they reported him as appearing confident, extrovert and cheerful. He seemed to have normal sight. However, they soon realised this was certainly not the case. His gaze was focussed ahead and he did not scan round the room. Only if asked to look at something in the room, did he give it any attention and then he would peer at it with inordinate concentration and deliberation.

S.B. could name all the objects in the room and could even tell the time from the wall clock. Given that many people with 'restored sight' struggle with such object recognition, Gregory and Wallace asked him to explain why he was so good at identifying objects. S.B. explained that most of the items he could guess from his touch experiences as a blind man. He showed them his watch that had had the glass removed and demonstrated how he had learned to tell the time by touch. Furthermore, he said that he could identify letters in capitals because he had been taught at the blind school to identify capital letters from touch. It was noticeable that he couldn't recognise letters in lowercase (he hadn't been taught to recognise these by touch) but that he could often use intelligent guesses to cover up any such perceptual abnormalities. This 'filling in the gaps' of his knowledge has echoes with the case of H.M. who also used 'educated guesses' to try to overcome his lack of memory.

S.B. was not so certain about colour recognition. Previous reports suggested that yellow is often seen as an unpleasant colour by restored sight patients. S.B. complained of the many different types of yellow. He showed a marked preference for greens and blue and liked bright colours in general. He was disappointed with 'dingy' colours. He found the world rather drab and became upset at flaking paint and the imperfections on things.

S.B.'s perception of depth was extremely poor. He would look outside his hospital window, which was 40 feet up and believe he could reach out and touch the ground. His estimation of size also suffered from inaccuracies. He estimated that buses were the right length but believed that buses were too high. It was assumed that this was because he would have been familiar with touching the length of buses when blind but that he wouldn't have had any experience of the correct height. In essence, his size estimations were reasonably accurate if he had previously known the objects by touch.

There were two objects that particularly fascinated him. Three days after the operation, he asked the matron what the object was in the sky. He showed great surprise to be told that it was the moon. He thought that a quarter moon would be like a quarter piece of cake rather than a crescent shape! Again, the moon was an object that he could not have previously experienced by touch. He also showed a fascination with mirrors that continued for the rest of his life. A 'regular' at his local pub, he would sit for hours in his favourite seat opposite the mirror enjoying the reflections he could see.

Psychological testing

Gregory and Wallace asked S.B. to complete a number of different perceptual tests. These included well-known visual illusions that tested depth and length perception, perspective changes and colour vision tests. In marked contrast to 'normal' people, S.B. did not seem to be confused by the illusions. In essence, they did not work as illusions. For example, after careful consideration, he declared the verticals in the Zollner Illusion to be parallel (see Figure 3.2). People usually perceive the verticals as angled towards one another (i.e. non-parallel). Similarly, with the Necker Cube (see Figure 3.3), S.B. did not see the figure as representing a three-dimensional object nor did he find that the faces of the cube reverse. That is, after staring at it for a period of time many people find the front side 'reverses' to the back and vice versa.

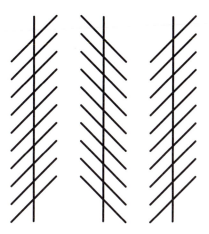

Figure 3.2 The Zollner Illusion

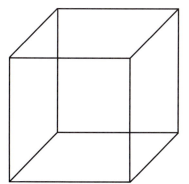

Figure 3.3 The Necker Cube

S.B. was also shown a number of pictures of objects and landscape scenes. He was shown one of a bridge over a river in Cambridge. S.B. made nothing of this. He did not recognise that there was a river or a bridge. He occasionally recognised colours but could not make out what they represented.

He was not aware of the concept of overlapping (sometimes called overlay or interposition). This gives us information that an object blocking part of another object from view must be nearer than the partially covered object. S.B. also appeared to have limited knowledge of the concept of relative size or size distance perception. This refers to the fact that objects of the same size but of varying distances cast different retinal image sizes. Hence, objects that appear smaller may merely be further away and vice versa.

S.B. was given a colour blindness test called The Ishihara Colour Vision Test. This involves numbers or letters marked out in coloured dots against a contrasting coloured background. S.B. read every single number correctly without hesitation. He had normal colour vision.

S.B. was also asked to draw a number of objects including a bus, a farmhouse, a hammer, and so on. It was found that his drawings were typical of those of the blind. Features that he would previously have recognised by touch were present and recognisable whereas many features that he could not have previously experienced through touch were missing. For example, his drawing of the bus had exaggerated windows (very familiar objects) but missed out the bonnet and radiator since he had little experience of them. The wheels had spokes since he was more familiar with the wheels on bikes and carts. The drawings always presented the bus in profile facing to the left since this is how he would have always perceived them through touch at bus stops (admittedly most people would draw them this way). The drawings showed that although S.B. could now see the world, he still saw the world through the eyes of a blind man heavily dependent on touch.

The case of S.B. provides very good evidence for cross-modal transfer from one sense to another (in this case, touch to sight). S.B. certainly had the ability to see and make sense of objects with which he had been previously familiar through his sense of touch. For example, he visually recognised uppercase letters that he had learned by touch, but not lowercase letters.

'Tired of London and tired of life itself'

Soon after his operation, S.B. was invited to London to see the sights. On the drive down, he appeared down and unresponsive. He took no interest in the journey despite the unfamiliar scenery. He complained that the world seemed 'dull' and was disappointed when the sun set. He appeared to have changed markedly from the cheerful extrovert he had been immediately after the operation, or, indeed, before it. He took little interest in the sights. Trafalgar Square was boring, the buildings were dull and he found the traffic frightening. He lacked the confidence to cross even the quietest road whereas when blind he would cross the busiest thoroughfare.

On a visit to the Science Museum, he showed little interest in any of the tools or machinery until an attendant allowed him to feel one of the lathes. He immediately became animated and said: 'Now that I've felt it I can see.' At London Zoo, he could correctly identify some of the animals (giraffe, elephant, monkey, lion) but could not identify others (bears, seals, crocodiles). The only occasion Gregory and Wallace ever saw S.B. laugh was when two giraffe heads looked at him over the top of a cage. The trip to London was not a success. S.B. seemed disinterested in seeing the sights and generally disappointed in life itself.

Allied to his disappointment in colours and the imperfections so noticeable on objects, he admitted to being disappointed with faces. He stated that 'I always felt in my own way that women were lovely, but now I see them as ugly.' S.B. never learned to interpret people's facial expressions, he could not determine what people were feeling from a smile, grimaces and so on. However, he could work this out from the sound of their voice.

'Seeing' not to let us down

Gregory and Wallace visited S.B. at home six months after the operation. They watched him using his tools for cobbling and woodwork with amazing dexterity. He used machine tools to cut up firewood with frightening speed and proficiency. He confided in them that he found sight a grave disappointment. Whereas previously as a blind man, he had been admired for his self-reliance and had gained enormous self-respect for his achievements despite his handicap, he now seemed to realise that the gift of sight did not enable him to live the life that he desired. Sight afforded him fewer opportunities than he imagined it might. Indeed, in some respects he continued to live the life of a blind man. In the evenings, he would often sit in the dark and not bother to put on the lights.

Neighbours and workmates no longer admired him for his achievements but regarded him as 'odd'. Some teased or tricked him about his deficits, in particular, his inability to read. He could see now, so why couldn't he recognise objects and read? S.B. himself realised that his achievements as a blind man had been admirable but his achievements in the world of the sighted were less so. Perhaps, he realised what a handicap his lack of sight had been. As an intelligent man, perhaps he could have achieved much more in his life if he had not been blind for 50 years. Although reluctant to talk about the subject, S.B. admitted that he had shown initial enthusiasm after the operation due to his gratitude to the surgeons and those people who had taken such an interest in the case. He was obviously suffering from depression and stated that he had lost more than he had gained from the operation. His initial enthusiasm for the operation was attributed to his desire 'not to let anyone down'. Many people had invested a great deal of time, knowledge and expertise in his case and he didn't want to appear ungrateful. However, as time went by, he could not hide his disappointment.

The relevance of the case of S.B. to perception

As is true with all the case studies in this book, it is difficult to draw conclusions from a single case study. In S.B.'s case, it remains unclear whether what applies after the recovery of sight can be applied to the development of sight in infancy. Psychologists such as Donald Hebb have suggested that the 'crisis of motivation' that S.B. experienced and noted in other cases of sight recovery is due to the difficulty in acquiring the perceptual skill of vision (personal communication reported in Gregory and Wallace, 1961). However, Gregory and Wallace argue that it is an *overall* sense of inadequacy that affects patients adversely rather than the slow pace by which they can learn to acquire perceptual skills. Patients such as S.B. respond as a result of realising that they will remain handicapped in the world of the seeing rather than as a result of their slowness in perceptual learning. Hebb draws close comparisons between child perceptual learning and restored sight learning. Gregory and Wallace question this view. For example, they ask why a child does not seem to suffer a crisis at the slowness of perceptual learning and they add that people of restored sight have spent years making sense of the world through touch. This is very different to the child who starts from scratch. Gregory and Wallace conclude that the development of visual perception in the child and the restored-sight adult are very different and few meaningful comparisons can be made. They conclude that the main difficulty with S.B. was not learning per se but changing his learning from a reliance on touching to one of seeing. He had to unlearn his perceptual habits in order to learn new ones. This is always more difficult than learning something afresh. For example, if you have learned to touch type incorrectly it is much more difficult to change this than learn correctly in the first place.

With regard to the tests of visual illusions, the evidence suggests that S.B.'s spatial organisation was not normal. He did not perceive the illusions as illusions. This suggests that these cues to perception are learned and not innate. S.B. had not learned them yet. It is interesting to speculate as to whether he would have started to see them as illusions over time.

Looking to the future

S.B.'s health continued to decline. His nerves became worse, his hands developed a marked tremble, he was signed off from work, collapsed on a couple of occasions and was referred to a psychiatrist. With his 'handicap' gone, he had lost his self-respect. S.B. died on 2 August 1960, less than 2 years after his operation. It may not be an exaggeration to say that he died disappointed with what he saw.

Richard Gregory continued with a brilliant career as a psychology lecturer at Bristol University, reaching the position of Emeritus Professor of Neuropsychology and gaining an MBE in the Queen's honours list. He was instrumental in setting up the Exploratory Applied Science centre in Bristol, UK, which has undoubtedly enthused thousands of people with a love of all things scientific. He suffered a stroke and died on 17 May 2010.

Note

1   S.B.'s real name was Sidney Bradford, as reported by Gregory (1986).

References

Gregory, R. (1986). *Odd Perceptions*. London: Routledge.
Gregory, R. and Wallace, J. (1961). *Recovery from Early Blindness. A Case Study*. Reproduced in March 2001 from Experimental Psychology Society Monograph No. 2.

Chapter 4

Kim Peek
The *real* Rain Man[1]

In the Academy Award winning film *Rain Man*, Tom Cruise plays Charlie Babbitt, a young man who finds that he has been written out of his recently deceased father's 3 million dollar estate. The beneficiary is his previously unknown older brother called Raymond (played by Dustin Hoffman). Raymond lives in a world of his own and is institutionalised. The film revolves around a road trip the brothers make to the West Coast of America – a voyage of discovery for both the brothers but particularly for Charlie who begins to recognise the very special gifts his older brother possesses. Although the film is a work of fiction, the inspiration for the film was a real-life megasavant called Kim Peek. In many ways, Kim Peek is even more remarkable than the character Dustin Hoffman played in the film; he has been called a 'living google' and is the world's most famous savant. Sadly, Kim Peek suffered a major heart attack and was pronounced dead at a hospital in his home town of Salt Lake City, Utah on 19 December 2009.

Childhood

Kim Peek was born on 11 November 1951. It would be highly unusual for most of us to know which day of the week this was, but Kim would have known in an instant not simply because it was his birthday but because he had the mental ability to know which day of the week any date in history was. Although his parents, Fran and Jeanne Peek, noticed nothing unusual about the pregnancy, it became obvious at birth that Kim was somewhat different. His head was about 30 per cent larger than normal; indeed it was so big that his neck muscles could not support its weight. As time progressed Kim did not show the usual stages of development – his eyes moved independently of one another, he didn't play and didn't respond to stimuli that children would normally be expected to respond to. A blister-like growth (called an encephalocele) started to grow on the back of Kim's head, which doctors did not remove for fear that it may have actually contained part of his brain.[1] During an examination at the age of 9 months, Kim was pronounced 'mentally retarded' and it was recommended that he should be placed in an institution in order to 'free' his parents from the inordinate amount of care that they would be forced to devote to Kim over the coming years. At this stage, Kim was spending most of his time propped up on the sofa at home and when crawling he had to push his head along much like a snowplough because he still could not support its weight. Fran and Jeanne ignored the medical advice about institutionalisation – they took Kim home and lavished their attention on him. They spent hour after hour reading to him and tracing the words on the pages with his fingers. When Kim turned three, the blister retracted into his head but it is believed that about half of his cerebellum had either been destroyed or had failed to develop.

About this time, an extraordinary incident occurred that provided the first clue to Fran that he had a very special son. Fran Peek recalls that Kim asked him what the word 'confidential' meant. As a joke, he told his son to look it up in the dictionary. Kim did exactly that, located it and read it out to his amazed father. Kim loved reading from an early age and devoured anything he could read. His parents found that he would remember any information he had read and be able to recall it verbatim simply when they mentioned the page number of the book! By the age of six, Kim had read and memorised the entire set of encyclopedia in the family home.

Kim's school career was over almost before it started. Kim had to leave his first class after only 7 minutes because he was considered a disruptive influence due to hyperactivity. It was suggested that Kim might benefit from a lobotomy – a procedure thought to be an appropriate therapy at that time. Luckily given the chequered history of the lobotomy his parents rejected this out of hand and instead they decided to home educate him. Although Kim's factual knowledge was gaining at a terrific rate, other areas of his life were less successful. Kim was very shy, withdrawn and introverted and couldn't dress or wash himself. The first indication that Kim might be capable of interacting with people other than his close family came one Christmas when he was 12 years old. It was a tradition in the Peek family to gather at his grandmother's house and recite stories and sing carols. This particular year, Kim successfully volunteered to recite the entire Christmas story in front of all his relatives.

Mainly home educated with the additional help of a few hours of formal teaching each week, Kim had completed all his high school requirements by the age of 14.

'Kimputer'

Kim continued to be a voracious consumer of factual knowledge – usually hidden away in his room, hour after hour, adding to his phenomenal memory, never forgetting any detail that he learned.

One of Kim's favourite activities and one that he did on a weekly basis involved visits to his local library. Kim spent a lot of his time there in his favourite place – the Salt Lake City public library reference section in Utah. He usually took down several reference books or phone directories and spread them on the desk. He carried a notebook where he made a note about where he had got to last time and then he began to read at an amazing speed. In fact he flicked through the pages so quickly that the innocent observer would conclude that he was not actually reading the information contained in the pages. He could read the left-hand page with his left eye and the right-hand page with his right eye although he did not usually do this. Typically he read two pages in about 15 seconds and once read the Tom Clancy novel *The Hunt for Red October* in 85 minutes.

In a typical library visit he might read eight or nine books. When tested he recalled 98 per cent of what he had read – far better than most people. Indeed, 4 months after reading the Tom Clancy novel he could recall the name of the Russian radio operator in the book. Once a book had been read, Kim turned it upside down on the shelf to indicate that it was now on his 'hard drive'. His friends affectionately nicknamed him 'Kimputer' due to his prodigious memory capacity – the main difference being that Kim seemed to have no limit to his memory capacity and no delete button. At the end of any library session with a phone directory he was able to recall the names, address, city, ZIP (post) code and phone number of any entry. Indeed, Kim was able to recall all the area codes and ZIP (postal) codes in the United States.

Kim loved learning for its own sake and enjoyed storing information in his computer-like memory. Fran Peek described his son's mental storage system as a 'self-contained internet'. However, Kim was not very good at conceptual thought. He tended to accept words at face value and thus had difficulty with metaphors and proverbs. He was also poor at performing tasks that required new thinking nor was he very good at reasoning out maths problems. One

Figure 4.1 On a typical library visit Kim might read eight or nine books
Source: © Shutterstock

incident illustrates how literally he took things. One day a professor asked Kim about Abraham Lincoln's Gettysberg address. Kim replied without realising the humour of his answer: 'Will's House, 227 North West Front Street, but he only stayed their one night before delivering his speech the next day.' His forte was his prodigious memory. However, it would be wrong to categorise Kim as simply a recorder of factual information. Kim did understand and comprehend most of the material he memorised – an ability that isn't always evident with other savants. Indeed, in more recent years, Kim started to enjoy reading fiction after realising how much people enjoy talking about certain novels.

Kim had other remarkable abilities. For example, he could read a page of a book turned upside down or turned sideways. He could also read mirror images with little difficulty. Kim seemed to make links or associations between seemingly unconnected items. It was suggested that one idea could spark off countless other facts that Kim could recall and link to one another. Unfortunately it was not always easy for others to understand these connections and thus sometimes his thought processes could seem confusing and incomprehensible. However, when this did occur it was sometimes possible to trace back the thinking process and see how Kim had linked one thought to another. It seemed that his ideas swirled around his brain too quickly for the words or, indeed, for other people to keep up.

Kim had always had an interest in classical music and could recall every piece of classical music he had ever heard and when and where each was composed and performed. He would know the name of the composer and details about their life. Kim had perfect pitch and could hum or sing any piece of music after having heard it only once. Another area of his savant skills began in 2002 when he met April Geenan, a professor of Music at the University of Utah. Under her tuition, Kim learned to play the piano. With perfect pitch and his encyclopedic knowledge of music, Kim gradually improved his manual dexterity to the point where Prof. Geenan made comparisons between Kim and Mozart!

Although Kim had extraordinary abilities in some areas of his life, he found it hard to cope with more mundane day-to-day activities. Every day he needed his father's help to shave, brush his teeth and dress because of his relatively poor motor co-ordination (probably due to the damage in his cerebellum). Kim's father showed extraordinary resilience and patience over the years and Kim always said that his father and he 'share the same shadow'. Kim also had moments when he seemed to lose focus and concentration and he called these moments 'pop offs' where he got very angry and agitated. An inclement change in the weather (hence the 'Rain Man' title of the film) or upsetting news were topics that could make him agitated – when this happened he was known to make car- like engine noises and pace up and down. However these emotional outbursts lessened after the release of the film *Rain Man*, which appeared to have a very positive effect on Kim.

Rain Man and the call of Hollywood

In 1984, a Hollywood scriptwriter called Barry Morrow accepted an invitation to assist on the Committee of the National Association for Retarded Citizens. Fran Peek was the chair of the committee and this is how Morrow came to meet with Kim. After chatting to Kim for a few hours and finding out about his amazing memory, Morrow suggested that he write a screenplay loosely based on Kim's abilities. Two years later the Peeks got the phone call from Morrow to say that the script had been sold to United Artists – the film was going to be called *Rain Man*.

Hollywood films are not made overnight but eventually Kim and Fran heard that Dustin Hoffman would play the lead role and that, as part of his research for the role, Hoffman wanted to meet the real-life 'Rain Man'. This involved a challenging but exciting trip to Hollywood where Fran and Kim spent some time with Barry Morrow and enjoyed the hospitality of the Century Plaza Hotel in Beverley Hills. On entering the foyer, Kim declared to the concierge 'Rain Man is here!' They spent a little time meeting up with the people working on the film and had a meeting with Dustin Hoffman. On first meeting Hoffman, Kim leaned forward, touched noses with Hoffman, and said 'Dustin Hoffman,

Figure 4.2 Kim Peek, the real 'Rain Man'
Source: Dmadeo, from wikimedia.org

from now on we shall be as one!' Hoffman obviously found Kim to be an engaging and charismatic person and enjoyed their meeting. Kim gave him a T-shirt with his face emblazoned on the front, which Dustin immediately put on. For about an hour Kim showed Hoffman some of his mannerisms, which Hoffman tried to imitate as best as he could. When watching Hoffman in the film it is clear that he used many of these in his portrayal in the film. At one point Dustin introduced Kim to Denis Hopper who was working down the corridor. Immediately Kim started singing the theme to *Easy Rider* 'Get your motor running, head out on the highway . . .'. Hopper and Hoffman joined in with the chorus 'Born to be wild'! When it was time to depart, Hoffman embraced Kim and said to him 'I may be the star, but you are the heavens.' Hoffman spoke to Fran Peek and suggested that Kim was such a special person that he 'should be shared with the world'.

Of course the film was a resounding success and won plaudits from the critics and public alike. Hoffman won a Best Actor Oscar for his portrayal and the other awards included Best Picture, Best Director and Best Screenplay. On accepting his Oscar, Hoffman started his speech by saying: 'I would like to thank Kim Peek for his help in making *Rain Man* a reality.' Kim and his father were in the audience that night and the shy introverted boy was no longer, seemingly enjoying the attention in the full glare of the media spotlight.

The film *Rain Man* had some surprisingly beneficial effects on Kim. Prior to the film, Kim was a very introverted and shy person. Kim himself declared that *Rain Man* changed his life and partly as a reaction to the public's response, Kim and his father began to contemplate the possibility of Kim making public appearances in an attempt to educate the public and to promote a positive image of disability. Although most of his family were against the idea for fear of turning Kim into some kind of freak show, after careful consideration, Kim and his father decided that it would be a good idea to meet the public and become an ambassador for people with special needs. Gradually Kim started to make appearances and speeches at conferences, seminars and workshops. These became very successful and popular and Kim seemed to gain much from these outings. Usually the public were all too keen to test Kim's memory capacity and see how many facts he had managed to absorb. His father always accompanied him at these events to help guide him and ensure that no problems arose. The once introverted Kim met well over 2 million people in his public appearances. Kim showed clearly that people with developmental disabilities are capable of making considerable progress. Through this interaction, Kim became more adept at meeting new people and he gained many more social skills.

Brain scans

Kim was given a brain scan at the age of 32 years and it was shown that his brain was one solid brain hemisphere, with tissue areas that seemed to be fused together. Typically, humans have two separate hemispheres connected by a bundle of tissues called the corpus callosum. In Kim's case his corpus callosum was non-existent and hence his two hemispheres had fused into one solid mass of brain tissue. Later scans confirmed these initial findings and also showed that the right-hand side of his cerebellum had split into eight or so pieces. This damage had probably been caused when the swelling on the back of his head had retracted back into his head. The cerebellum is usually associated with motor activity and thus this was probably the cause of many of Kim's movement difficulties. There are known cases of other people who do not have a corpus callosum and sometimes there appears to be no accompanying abnormalities. Similarly, some people who have their corpus callosum cut in an attempt to reduce epilepsy (this operation restricts the seizures to only one hemisphere) manage to function well with two independently functioning hemispheres. However, those people like Kim who are born without a corpus callosum seem to operate one giant hemisphere. It remains unclear what the exact purpose of the corpus callosum is. Indeed some neurologists suggest that the only two functions of the corpus callosum that we can be sure of is (1) to spread seizures and (2) to hold the brain together! (Treffert and Christensen, 2005).

There were also some structural abnormalities to Kim's left hemisphere. One theory that was put forward that may account for this involved the fact that males are more prone to savantism, autism and dyslexia than females. Male foetuses have more circulating testosterone and this is toxic to brain tissue development. The left hemisphere develops slower than the right hemisphere and thus is more likely to be affected over a longer period of time. With Kim's brain you might have expected that he would have something extra, something that might have explained his talents over and above the deficit, but his brain was clearly damaged. With the damage to the left hemisphere it seems his right hemisphere was freed from the tyranny of the usually dominant left and thus a kind of dis-inhibition occurred with his right hemisphere abilities allowed full rein. The damaged left hemisphere might also have encouraged his right to compensate for the damage and this may have led to his special abilities. After all, it is often claimed that some blind people develop better hearing as a compensation for their lack of sight. It is also interesting to ponder, therefore, whether Kim's abilities might be present in all of us but are suppressed by our fully functioning left hemispheres. The phenomenon of Kim was not that he could store so much information (given our enormous brain capacity this is entirely feasible) but that he had such ready access to it all.

Savants

So-called 'savant syndrome' is defined as a rare condition in which individuals have one or more deep areas of expertise, ability or brilliance, and these are usually in marked contrast with their overall limitations. Although the disorder is often associated with autism this is certainly not always the case – it is generally estimated that only 10 per cent of autistic individuals possess some savant-like skills and half of all savants are autistic or have some other disability. However a more recent study by Howlin et al. (2009) found 28 per cent of autistic individuals displayed some savant-like skills and they recognised that even this figure might be a slight underestimation. Darold Treffert (2009) suggests that one feature shared by almost all savants is a prodigious memory. Strictly speaking Kim was not merely a savant but a megasavant since he had special abilities in as many as 15 different areas – these included history, Shakespeare, classical music, geography, sports, movies, actors, literature, the Bible and church history. It is estimated that by the time of his death, Kim had read as many as 12,000 books. Kim was also classified as a prodigious savant, that is, someone whose ability level in one domain qualified him as a prodigy or exceptional talent. The most common ability of savants is that of a prodigious memory but there are other abilities, such as artistic ability, embodied in British born artist Stephen Wiltshire[2] and musical ability, seen in the phenomenon of American musician Tony de Blois.[3]

The term 'idiot savant' was first coined in 1887 by John Langdon Down (who is more famous for the eponymous Down's Syndrome classification). The term 'idiot' was adopted in the early 1900s by scientists and medics to describe a person with an IQ score below 25 (the mean average in any population is 100). The use of 'idiot' as a scientific term has now been abandoned due to its derogatory use in everyday language. In either case the term was inappropriate for savantism. That is because (even accepting all the possible criticisms associated with IQ tests) savants tested in recent years have always been found to have IQ scores of above 40 and, indeed, some savants have been known to have well above average IQs. Thus mental retardation is not a prerequisite of savant syndrome. The term 'savant' or 'knowledgeable person' was chosen because it is derived from the French word 'savoir' meaning 'to know'.

Much remains to be discovered about savant syndrome. There is no single well accepted theory, which explains the so-called 'skills and ills' displayed by many savants. One theory suggests that savants focus their cognitive abilities on details and this helps with their savant-like memory abilities. Another suggests that they possess heightened perception or that these individuals can access poorly processed information in the brain that normal people are not aware of. Another suggests that some kind of left hemisphere brain injury has lead to over-compensation in the right. The skills demonstrated by most savants tend to be associated with the right hemisphere and those skills typically missing are associated with the left hemisphere. Brain scans tend to support the idea of left hemisphere damage in savants. Further support for this hypothesis comes from people who have developed savant-like skills in adulthood (called 'acquired savant syndrome') as a result of damage to their left hemisphere or more specifically the left anterior temporal lobe. There have also been cases where elderly people with fronto-temporal dementia have displayed savant-like skills. There have even been isolated examples of people who have shown exceptional memory ability when their brains have been stimulated during neurosurgery. Examples such as these suggest to some that savant-like abilities may lie dormant in all of us. It is not clear why we cannot or do not use such abilities but one suggestion is that procedural or rote memories (typified by savant memories) are overlaid by a broader more all-encompassing semantic knowledge circuit that proves more successful with day-to-day living. Future research opens up the exciting possibility of using magnetic circuits to temporarily inhibit specific brain area function to see if other brain areas can compensate and produce and display differing cognitive abilities. Savant skills tend to be restricted to five general areas such as music, art, mathematical calculations and mechanical (e.g. repairing machines) and spatial skills (e.g. map reading and route memorising).[4] Calendar calculating, which is so rare in the general population, seems almost commonplace in savants (as demonstrated by Kim). The exact reasons for this remain elusive and Kim himself had no idea how he did it! Musical ability, including possessing perfect musical pitch is also relatively common and is a gift possessed by both Kim Peek and Stephen Wiltshire. Other savants have been shown to have special language ability skills or extraordinary sensitivity to smells or touch and some are able to precisely estimate the passing of time. Indeed, work with savants has prompted psychologists to wonder whether brain damage might lead to compensatory development, or does it allow latent abilities to emerge? Do these special abilities actually lay dormant in us all?

The future?

On a typical day, Kim would rise at 5 a.m. and read the paper for an hour, check his mail and in the early afternoon potter downtown to visit the reference section of the Salt Lake City library and take on board more and more facts. He continued with his ambassadorial role for people with special needs. He remains an inspiration to all who have met him. Throughout Kim's life, his father showed remarkable love and devotion to his son. A love that all fathers would hope to be capable of, although there must inevitably have been difficult times to endure. Kim himself rightly declared that his father had the patience of a saint and that they remained inseparable. With Fran Peek's advancing age, however, there were worries about Kim's future. Somewhat unexpectedly, on 19 December 19 2009, Kim suffered a heart attack and died aged 58. Kim Peek was, and indeed remains, an inspiration to us all – an extraordinary mix of disability and brilliance that neurologists and psychologists are still trying to understand. Described as the 'Mount Everest of memory', both Kim, and indeed his father Fran, have touched the lives of every person who has read or heard about their unique and uplifting story. It may also be the case that one day savants will provide the key to unlock the true potential that may reside in the brains of all of us.

Kim ended many of his public appearances with this: 'Learn to recognise and respect differences in others – treat them as you would like to be treated so we can have a better world to live in – you don't have to be handicapped to be different – everybody is different'.[5]

Notes

1   Much of the material in this chapter comes from the brilliant and fascinating book written by Fran Peek (1996) called *The Real Rain Man: Kim Peek* published by Harkness Publishing Consultants.
2   More information on Stephen Wiltshire is available at: http://stephenwiltshire. co.uk/art_prints.aspx?page=9
3   More information on Tony de Blois is available at: http://tonydeblois.com/

4   More information available from: http://wisconsinmedical society.org/savant_syndrome
5   Quoted from a recording by Verklighetens: 'Rain Man: English excerpts from a Swedish documentary', Anders S. Nilsson, with comments by Kim and Fran Peek, Drs Treffert and Christensen, and Barry Morrow. Available at: http://wisconsin medicalsociety.org/savant_syndrome/savant_profiles/kim_peek

References

Howlin, P., Goode, S., Hutton, J. and Rutter, M. (2009). 'Savant skills in autism: Psychometric approaches and parental reports'. *Philosophical Transactions of the Royal Society of Biological Sciences*, 364(1522): 1359–67.

Peek, F. (1996). *The Real Rain Man: Kim Peek*. Salt Lake City, UT: Harkness Publishing Consultants.

Treffert, D.A. (2009). 'The savant syndrome: An extraordinary condition. A synopsis: Past, present, future'. *Philosophical Transactions of the Royal Society of Biological Sciences*, 364(1522): 1351–7.

Treffert, D. and Christensen, D. (2005). 'Inside the mind of a savant'. *Scientific American*, December: 108–13.

Chapter 5

Holly Ramona and the nature of memory

The prosperous Ramona family seemed to be living the American dream in Napa Valley, California. But on 5 September 1989, aged 19, Holly Ramona visited a therapist for treatment for her depression and bulimia. The therapist Marche Isabella told Holly that sometimes bulimia is a consequence of childhood sexual abuse. Gradually during the sessions, Holly reported detailed memories of 12 years of horrific abuse that she had suffered at the hands of her father Gary Ramona. These revelations split the family apart, led to a sensational court case and brought into the public eye the concept of repressed memories. Academics and therapists confronted each other over the evidence – disputes that continue unabated to this day.

This chapter must be the most controversial of all the case studies examined. Protagonists on both sides of the argument about the existence of repressed or dissociated memories have received hate letters and even death threats. Academics who dispute the existence of repressed memories have been accused of protecting paedophiles while those who believe in the existence of repressed memories have been accused of exploiting vulnerable people, splitting families apart and, in extreme cases, helping to put innocent parents in prison. Suffice to say, research has clearly shown that all memories can be fallible and they *can* be altered by past experiences (this is not to say that all memories are affected in this way). Given this position, it has to be recognised that there is every likelihood that this chapter also suffers from this possible distortion.

The 'perfect' family and the American dream

The Ramona family consisted of Gary, his wife Stephanie and their three daughters Holly, Kelli and Shawna. They lived in Napa Valley, California, and with Gary making a six-figure salary from the Mondavi Wine Company they seemed, from the outside at least, to be the stereotypically perfect family. In reality, beneath the surface there were tensions within the family between Gary and his wife and obsessions with cleanliness and jealousy resulting in an uncomfortable marriage. Holly was a quiet, shy girl and she had started gaining weight. By 1988, Holly weighed over 11 stone (70 kilograms or 155 pounds) and yet was only five foot four inches tall. When she started college, Holly started binge eating and it was a short step to start purging. Holly had developed bulimia. In August 1989 she made her first visit to Marche Isabella, a therapist who was reported to be a specialist in the psychological treatment of eating disorders. In an early interview with Stephanie, Marche claimed that about 70 per cent of bulimics had been sexually molested. These statistics are controversial and remain difficult to substantiate and Marche was laying herself open to later charges of professional malpractice.

Soon after Holly started the therapy, she had some flashbacks or 'memories' of her father abusing her. Holly went to group therapy sessions with other sufferers and when she was asked by Marche to test whether these flashbacks might be actual memories, Marche suggested using sodium amytal (known as the 'truth drug'). Her mother, Stephanie became aware of the accusations against her husband and was unsure what to do. She had never seen Gary touch the children in this way and she knew that if she confronted him it would mean the end of their dream – the 'happy' family, the luxury house, the $400,000 salary that Gary was now earning and the end of their marriage. The problem was that despite no corroborating evidence Stephanie did believe in Holly. Stephanie took advice and was told that she must deal with the allegations immediately or it might appear that she had colluded with Gary. So Stephanie collected her children, told them about Holly's allegations and immediately started divorce proceedings. The younger children were asked whether Gary had ever made any improper advances towards them and they categorically denied it. Both Holly and Stephanie wanted to see if they could find any corroborating evidence of the abuse and so they arranged an internal examination of Holly. There was no conclusive evidence that her hymen had been broken by penetration – the examination showed a minor tear but this could have been caused by any number of other factors such as menstruation, cycling or horse riding.

Holly wanted to talk to her father Gary about her abuse, although at that time Gary wasn't aware that he was being accused of being the abuser. Indeed, Gary questioned whether Holly had been molested by anyone and initially it seems he thought that any such allegations might have been directed at a teenage neighbour from Holly's childhood. The sodium amytal interview took place the day before Holly had arranged a confrontation with her father. The sodium amytal interview seemed to confirm to Holly and Marche that Gary Ramona had indeed raped his daughter Holly. Holly remained worried that she may have lied under the influence of the drug but Marche reassured her that this was highly unlikely. The next day Gary attended the hospital and Holly confronted him and told him that he had raped her. Gary responded to the accusation with disbelief and was equally dumbfounded that everyone in the room appeared to believe Holly's version of events and not his own. His wife Stephanie never even asked him if it was true; she completely believed her daughter Holly and from that moment on Gary Ramona's life fell apart. Stephanie and the younger daughters took Holly's side and they tried to instigate charges of child molestation against Gary. However, without enough evidence for a criminal trial Gary could not be charged.

Gary's life was in complete turmoil. He suspected that Holly's memories might have been implanted by Isabella Marche to fit her theory of the cause of Holly's bulimia and depression. Despite trying to keep a lid on the events as they unfolded, friends began to suspect the truth behind the break-up of the family and inevitably each family member had confided in a few trusted close friends.

The court case

The family were split apart and Gary lived separately from his wife and daughters. A divorce was granted and Gary soon found himself out of work when the Mondavi Wine Company decided that they no longer needed his services. He lost his standing in the community as friends and associates took sides with either Stephanie and his daughters or Gary. The fortune that he and his family had worked to build was soon lost. Gary decided that he would sue Holly's therapist for professional malpractice and damages and as a consequence of this also clear his name. The court case proved a sensation, with Holly and her therapist Marche Isabella being allowed to give their evidence against Gary (something which had earlier been denied due to a lack of evidence). Other academics came to provide expert witness including a professor of psychology called Elizabeth Loftus from the University of Washington who spoke about the reconstructive nature of memory, as well as the psychiatrist and child abuse expert Lenore Terr who spoke on Holly's side.

During the trial, Holly recounted her evidence of sexual abuse. She reported dreams of snakes inside her, refused gynaecological examinations, said that she hated Tom Cruise who had 'pointy canine teeth' (like her father), told the court that she couldn't eat whole bananas (they had to be sliced) and reported that she disliked melted cheese and mayonnaise because they reminded her of oral sex with her father. She also reported detailed memories of her father raping her repeatedly. Her therapist Marche Isabella stated that these were all the classic symptoms of child abuse. Others disagreed with her, questioning her unflinching and uncritical belief in Holly's repressed memories. With no clear corroborating evidence as to the proof of the abuse, the jury had to listen to the witnesses and weigh the 'preponderance of evidence' to come to a judgement about malpractice. Although some of the jurors believed that 'something had happened' between Gary and Holly, the decision was reached that there was not enough evidence of sexual abuse. Jurors later reported that they felt there would have been more physical evidence after 12 years of the most violent and horrific abuse than a partially separated hymen. The jury argued that Gary had been a poor parent but not an abuser. The jury were forced to assign proportionate blame to the damage suffered by Gary. The jury

Figure 5.1 Expert witness, Elizabeth Loftus
Source: © Jodi Hilton/Pool/Reuters/Corbis

argued that 40 per cent was the fault of Isabella Marche the therapist, 5 per cent was Gary's own making and 40 per cent to all other persons (the other smaller percentages were allocated to the hospital and another Doctor who treated Holly). The court case did not mention who these 'other persons' were but it is reported that later the jurors mentioned Stephanie and other women in her circle of friends who gossiped and thus condemned Gary as a child abuser in the absence of proof. The jury awarded Gary $500,000 in damages although his counsel had requested $8 million. The case was a watershed for recovered memory therapy and a warning to such therapists about the controversial techniques that they had pursued. Stephanie was outraged and shouted that Gary should not receive a penny for raping his own daughter. To this day Stephanie and Holly are adamant that the abuse took place.

After the trial, Holly Ramona pursued a civil case against her father in the Los Angeles Superior Court, but later the Court of Appeal ordered the case dismissed. In 1997, Holly Ramona decided against appealing this decision and finally drew a close to her legal battle against her father Gary. Holly argued that if she had lost this final case it might have harmed other lawsuits filed by victims of sexual abuse.

To date, the family remain divided, although in later years there were reports that one of Gary's daughters, Shawna, agreed to meet her father for coffee and a chat so perhaps there is the small possibility of future reconciliation.

The nature of 'repressed' memory

The Ramona case brought into sharp relief the problem and status of repression or recovered memory syndrome. Of course, the idea of repression is not new. Freud (1901) believed that some forgetting is an unconscious but motivated process. He believed that we forget because certain memories are too psychologically painful to allow them to remain conscious. Therefore, we repress or push the memory out of consciousness. These memories aren't 'lost', they just remain inaccessible in our unconscious. Repression is thus a 'defence mechanism' to protect our conscious mind. The term repression can describe memories that have been dissociated from awareness as well as those that have been repressed without dissociation. Repressed memories may sometimes be recovered years after the memory was encoded and may be triggered by any number of environmental stimuli such as a particular smell, taste, similar event or any other cue related to the original memory. As was alleged in the Ramona case, repressed memories may be recalled via suggestion during psychotherapy (this does not presuppose that they must therefore be false).

Experimental studies on repressed memories are almost impossible to conduct. However, one study that provided an experimental test of Freud's repression theory was conducted by Levinger and Clark (1961) in their emotionally charged words study. Participants were given lists of negatively charged words (e.g. 'hate', 'anger', 'fear') and neutral words (e.g. 'window', 'cow', 'tree'). They were then asked to say exactly what came into their mind when they saw each word. This is called a free association task. During this task, the participants' galvanic skin responses (GSRs) were measured. GSR detects minute traces of sweat on the fingers and is a measure of emotional response. Finally, participants were given the cue words again and asked to recall the associations they had just reported. Levinger and Clark found that participants took longer to think of associations to the emotional words and that GSRs were higher for the emotional words. Also, recall of the associations of the emotionally charged words was poorer than the neutral ones.

Levinger and Clark concluded that the emotional words were more anxiety-provoking and therefore the formation of associations or recall of these words was more difficult as a result of repression. This study is accepted as one of the best experimental demonstrations of repression. Laboratory evidence for repression is difficult to conduct, since you would have to get participants to experience an anxiety-provoking event and this would break ethical guidelines. However, it's been claimed that arousal adversely affects short-term memory (STM) but actually helps long-term memory (LTM). Repression cannot explain this enhanced LTM effect (Eysenck and Wilson, 1973). A methodological problem with the experiment is that the emotionally charged words were less easy to visualise and thus more difficult to form associations with. If you accept this then it might be that results had nothing to do with repression!

Dr Bessel van der Kolk also believes in the idea of repressed memories. Dr van der Kolk is an internationally recognised leader in the field of psychological trauma and founder and medical director of the Trauma Center in Brookline, MA, USA. In 1995 he wrote that traumatic emotional memories were more durable and accurate than ordinary memories and that they could be banished by dissociation only to re-emerge much later as reliable conscious memories. He applied this in a study of post traumatic stress disorder (PTSD) and childhood trauma where 46 people with PTSD reported recalling traumatic memories, at least initially, in the form of dissociated mental imprints. Over time, the participants reported the gradual emergence of further details and of the 35 subjects with childhood trauma, 15 (43 per cent) had suffered significant, or total amnesia for their trauma at some time of their lives. Van der Kolk reported that 27 of the 35 subjects with childhood trauma (77 per cent) reported confirmation of their childhood trauma (van der Kolk and Fisler, 1995). Practising therapists supported such studies with clinical evidence. For example, Richard Kluft, director of dissociative disorders at the Institute of Pennsylvania Hospital, USA, claimed that over 60 per cent of patients with repressed memories of child abuse were able to document at least one episode of the abuse they had alleged in therapy.

There have been many anecdotal and experimental accounts of inaccurate memory recall. Jean Piaget one of the most famous developmental psychologists once reported a memory that he had of a time when a man tried to kidnap him when he was only 2 years old. Piaget recalled sitting in his pram while being looked after by a nurse on the Champs Elysees. He recalled the nurse struggling with the man and the scratches she received in the struggle. The kidnapping was unsuccessful and the nurse received an expensive watch from Piaget's parents in gratitude. However 13 years later Piaget was surprised to find that the former nurse had returned the watch with a letter to his parents stating that she had entirely made up the kidnapping event. Piaget realised that he must have heard the story being retold during his childhood so often that he had come to recount it as though it was an accurate memory that he had actually recalled and experienced.

We have all experienced memory distortions or inaccuracies but the key question here is whether entire memories, which never existed in the first place, can be created. There is evidence that some 'memories' must be untrue and created by suggestion or hypnosis. Studies by Spanos et al. (1991) showed in four studies that some participants would report regressing to beyond birth and to a previous life. The credibility that participants assigned to their past-life experiences was influenced by whether the hypnotist defined such experiences as real or merely imagined.

Experimental research

There are other academics who do not believe in the idea of repressed memories. Elizabeth Loftus, now the Distinguished Professor of Social Ecology, Law, and Cognitive Science at University of California, Irvine, has spent much of her professional life investigating the nature of memory. Loftus testified that

Holly's repressed memories were the result of suggestion and not accurate recollected memories.

Loftus cited scientific studies that she had conducted, which, she claimed, had shown how memories are reconstructed based on previous experiences, prior expectations and suggestion. Bartlett (1932) was one of the first researchers to demonstrate that memory doesn't work accurately like a camera, rather it is prone to inaccuracies and interpretations based on prior experiences or schemas. In other words, memories are subject to reconstruction errors. Loftus herself had made her name at the University of Washington investigating the practical application of memory reconstruction, namely the accuracy of eye witness testimony (EWT). Loftus showed that eyewitness memories can be affected by the wording of questions that are asked after someone has witnessed a crime. Loftus identified two types of (mis)leading questions that appear to affect EWT:

- leading questions: a question that makes it likely that a participant's schema will influence them to give a desired answer; and
- 'after-the-fact information' questions: this is where new, misleading information is added in the question after the incident has occurred.

One study that examined the effect of leading questions was conducted by Loftus and Palmer (1974). Here, student participants were shown slides of a two-car accident. Some were asked 'About how fast were the cars going when they smashed into one another?' whereas for others the verbs 'hit', 'bumped', 'contacted' were used instead of 'smashed'. Estimated speed was affected by the verb used. Using 'smashed into' the average speed estimate was 41 mph whereas 'contacted' was 32 mph. This study (and many others) appeared to show that memory recall can be distorted by the language used.

Another study that demonstrated the power of adding 'after-the-fact information' involved two groups of participants who watched a film of a car being driven through the countryside (Loftus, 1975) past a 'Stop' road sign. Group A were asked 'How fast was the white car going when it passed the "Stop" sign while travelling along the country road?'. Group B were asked 'How fast was the white car going when it passed the barn while travelling along the country road?' (there was no barn but the question presupposes that there was one). A week later 17 per cent of Group B reported seeing a barn compared to just 2 per cent of Group A. The 'after-the-event' question had falsely suggested to them that there had actually been a barn. The explanation for this is source misattribution, where witnesses confuse the *actual* event itself with post-event information. The questions are: can these studies apply to real-life memories and are they of any relevance in the case of recovered child abuse memories?

In these studies, participants don't expect to be deliberately misled by university researchers and therefore the reconstructive findings might be expected since they believe the researchers to be telling the truth. Furthermore, the consequences of inaccurate memories are minimal in a research setting compared to real-life crimes and so participants may not be so motivated to recall the events accurately. Foster et al. (1994) showed that eyewitness identification was more accurate for a real-life crime as opposed to a simulation. Indeed, there is evidence that memory for important events isn't easily distorted when the information is obviously misleading and that misleading information only affects minor, relatively unimportant, aspects of the memory (for example, the 'barn' details in the research above).

Can such research really be applied to 12 years of sexual abuse? Can such a traumatic series of events be completely lost to memory rather than just reinterpreted in a fairly minor way? Can memories be so distorted that a person is convinced that something happened when it can be clearly shown that it did not? Loftus agreed that these were important and relevant criticisms so sought to investigate this with her so-called 'Lost in a shopping mall' study.

'Lost in a shopping mall'

Loftus arranged for her students at the University of Washington to recruit 24 participants aged from 18 to 53 to take part in the study (Loftus and Pickrell, 1995). Each participant was provided with a booklet containing brief accounts of three true childhood incidents that had previously been provided by a relative. Each relative also provided 'information about a plausible shopping trip to a mall or large department store' so that a fourth false incident that supposedly occurred when the participant and close family member were together could be included in the booklet. Participants were told that they were participating in a study on childhood memories, and that the researchers were interested in how and why people remembered some things and not others. Participants were asked to complete the booklets by reading what their relative had told the researchers about each event, and then writing what they remembered about each event. If they did not remember the event, they were told to write that they didn't remember it. Seven (29.2 per cent) of the 24 subjects 'remembered' the false event, either fully or partially.

Participants were then interviewed about their memories a week after completing the booklets. At this point, only six (25 per cent) participants still believed that the false memory they recalled was true. Participants also had a second interview another week later and then were told that the researchers had tried to create a false memory. Participants were asked to select the false memory from those in the booklet. Five people (20.8 per cent) incorrectly selected one of the true events as the false one. The percentages were not of paramount importance, but according to Loftus and Pickrell this study showed that false memory syndrome does exist and that some people can be affected by it. However the study is not without criticism. Researchers have questioned the relevance of this study in cases of childhood sexual abuse. There is a notable difference between being told a believable but untrue event by a relative and one involving sexual abuse by a close relative. For example, a study by Pezdek (1995) found that although three (15 per cent) of 20 participants recalled a plausible false memory of getting lost in a shopping mall, none of the participants accepted an implausible false memory that they had received a painful enema as a child from their parent.

Loftus's work remains controversial, both for the ideas it contains, the way it has been represented in court and in the media, and the way that some of the research was conducted. Loftus has provided testimony at the trial of Oliver North, the Rodney King beatings, the Menendez brothers murders, the Michael Jackson abuse case and the Ted Bundy murder trial. There have also been challenges to the work both methodologically and ethically. It is always difficult to judge the relative merits of any work and this is compounded by the controversial nature of the topic. As Loftus herself acknowledges in all areas of science it is important not to accept any work on face value and to adopt a standpoint that seeks to achieve rigorous scientific scrutiny.

Loftus continues to work in the field of memory and helps individuals who have been accused of child abuse as a result of recovered memories. Soon after the turn of the millennium, Loftus reports receiving a letter from a husband and wife whose daughter had accused family members of abuse. Once again, the memories had been recovered during therapy. Loftus asked for the therapist's name and was surprised to hear that the therapist involved was Holly Ramona (reported by Wilson 2002).

It may be the case that some therapists are guilty of seeing smoke when there is no fire. As Gary's defence attorney said in the trial 'As Freud said:

"sometimes a cigar is just a cigar".' The American Psychological Association states that it is not currently possible to distinguish a true repressed memory from a false one without corroborating evidence. The Royal College of Psychiatrists in Britain has officially banned its members from using therapies designed to recover repressed memories of childhood abuse. The British Psychological Society (1995) has not gone this far but has urged therapists to 'avoid drawing premature conclusions about memories recovered during therapy'. However, the same report concluded that there was no evidence that therapists are creating false memories in their patients.

Repressed or implanted memories?

Most psychologists would agree that every memory involves a process of reconstruction, and therefore involves some degree of distortion. People can believe that they hold a genuine memory and yet be entirely mistaken. Sometimes these memory mistakes have extremely damaging effects. There is mixed research on both sides of the divide into the existence of recovered or implanted memories. Those who argue for the existence of recovered memories tend to rely more on clinical case studies whereas those who favour an implanted memory stance emphasise the lack of proof in such cases and the scientific evidence in favour of the malleability of memory.

The research that demonstrates that it is possible to retrieve false memories is compelling and the consequences of these false memories are indeed profound. However, it would be a tragedy if we let this research blind us to genuine cases of abuse. Repressed memories or implanted memories? There remains the possibility that both might exist and, at present, we cannot tell with absolute certainty one from the other.

References

Bartlett, F. (1932). *Remembering: A Study in Experimental and Social Psychology*. Cambridge: Cambridge University Press.

British Psychological Society (1995). 'Recovered memories: Report of the BPS Working Party'. Leicester: The British Psychological Society.

Eysenck, H.J. and Wilson, G.D. (1973). *The Experimental Study of Freudian Theories*. London: Methuen.

Foster, R., Libkuman, T., Schooler, J. and Loftus, F. (1994). 'Consequentiality and eyewitness person identification'. *Applied Cognitive Psychology*, 8(2): 107–21.

Freud, S. (1901). *The Psychopathology of Everyday Life*. Trans. A.A. Brill (1914). London: T. Fisher Unwin.

Johnston, M. (1997). *Spectral Evidence: The Ramona Case: Incest, Memory and Truth on Trial in Napa Valley*. New York: Houghton Mifflin.

Kolk, B.A. van der and Fisler, R. (1995). 'Dissociation and the fragmentary nature of traumatic memories. Overview and exploratory study'. *Journal of Traumatic Stress*, 8: 505–25.

Levinger, A. and Clark, J. (1961). 'Emotional factors in the forgetting of word associations'. *Journal of Abnormal and Social Psychology*, 62: 99–105.

Loftus, E. (1975). 'The myth of repressed memory: False memories and allegations of sexual abuse'. *Psychology*, 7(4): 560–78.

Loftus, E. and Palmer, J. (1974). 'Reconstruction of automobile destruction: An example of the interaction between language and memory'. *Journal of Verbal Learning and Verbal Behaviour*, 13: 585–9.

Loftus, E.F. and Pickrell, J.E. (1995). 'The formation of false memories'. *Psychiatric Annals*, 25: 720–5.

Pezdek, K., Finger, K. and Hodge, D. (1997). 'Planting false childhood memories: The role of event plausibility'. *Psychological Science*, 8: 437–41.

Spanos, N., Menary, E., Gabora, N., DuBreuil, S. and Dewhirst, B. (1991). 'Secondary identity enactments during hypnotic past-life regression: A sociocognitive perspective'. *Journal of Personality and Social Psychology*, 61(2): 308–20.

Wilson, A. (2002). 'War and remembrance'. *Orange County Register*, 3 November.

Part 2

Social psychology

Chapter 6

The girl who cried murder

The story of Catherine 'Kitty' Genovese

On 13 March 1964, 28-year-old Catherine Genovese began the walk back to her apartment after work. There was nothing unusual in that except that it was to be her last walk. She was stabbed and murdered by an unknown assailant after being sexually assaulted. In New York City, such crimes are not unknown but this particular crime was to send shockwaves around the world. The horrific crime had lasted half an hour, been witnessed by 38 neighbours and during this time no-one had called the police. The case of 'Kitty' Genovese (as she was known in the media) is regarded as the catalyst for research into the phenomenon of bystander behaviour. Indeed, psychologists still debate the causes of what is sometimes known as the 'Genovese syndrome'.

As New York psychology professor Stanley Milgram said, 'The case touched on a fundamental issue of the human condition . . . If we need help, will those around us stand around and let us be destroyed or will they come to our aid?'

The murder

Leaving her job as a bar manager in the early hours, Catherine parked her red Fiat in the car park near to her apartment. She lived in Kew Gardens, a relatively crime-free, middle-class area in the Queens' district of New York. On the short walk to her front door, she noticed a figure walking towards her. The assailant later testified that she immediately started running away from him. She must have spotted the knife in his hand and tried to reach a nearby police phone box that linked directly to the 112th Precinct. The assailant ran and jumped on her and stabbed her in the back several times. Catherine screamed out: 'Oh my God! He stabbed me! Please help me! Please help me!' At this point, many neighbours turned on their lights. Irene Frost heard the screams clearly and could see the tussle. Irene reported: 'There was another shriek and she was lying down crying out.' On the seventh floor, Robert Mozer opened his window, saw the struggle and yelled out 'Hey, let that girl alone!' The attacker heard his shouts and hurried away. On the sixth floor, Marjorie and Samuel Koshkin reported that they saw the assailant run to his car, but noticed that he was still prowling around 10 minutes later. Unfortunately, that was not the end of the ordeal.

Catherine, although bleeding badly, managed to stagger to the side of her apartment block and collapsed into the lobby area. She looked up to see her assailant had returned. He stabbed her again and once more Catherine shouted out 'I'm dying! I'm dying!'. Again, many of her neighbours heard her screams. As the murderer said later 'I came back because I knew I'd not finished what I set out to do'. He proceeded to sexually assault her and leave her for dead. In all, the attack had lasted 32 minutes. During this time, it was reported that none of the witnesses had telephoned the police.

The assailant rushed back to his car and fled the scene. A few blocks away, while waiting at a red light he noticed that the driver in the car next to him was asleep. He got out and woke the driver and warned him about the dangers of falling asleep at the wheel. A surprisingly altruistic act from someone who still had blood on their hands.

Catherine Genovese, as it turned out, had been his third victim.

The assailant: Winston Moseley

One week later, Winston Moseley, 29, a manual worker was arrested for murder. He had no previous convictions and lived with his wife and two children nearby. Under police interrogation, he soon confessed to the murder saying that he'd had an uncontrollable urge to kill. He went on trial for murder 3 months later. Despite pleading guilty on the grounds of insanity, on 11 June 1964, Winston Moseley was sentenced to death by electric chair. However, the judge had made a mistake by not allowing evidence regarding Moseley's mental health to be presented at a pre-trial hearing. His sentence was commuted to life imprisonment.

A year later, Moseley attempted a prison breakout. He assaulted a prison guard, stole his gun and held five civilians hostage. He raped one of the women and eventually gave himself up after a half-hour stand-off with armed FBI agents. Moseley remains in Great Meadow State Prison, N.Y. to this day. So far, all his applications for parole have been refused. At a recent hearing in

April 2008, Moseley claimed that some of the blame for his behaviour lay with his upbringing and that his father was a vicious wife-beater who had contemplated killing his mother.

The details of this crime were horrific and caused a sensation in their day. However, the sensational story reported in the newspapers did not surround the actual murder details but the fact that it was reported that as many as 38 people in the neighbourhood witnessed Catherine's murder but that no-one had called the police during the assault. One person did ring the police but by that time Catherine was already dead. It is reported that they arrived within 2 minutes of receiving the call. The man who did finally ring the police only did so after ringing a friend in Nassau County for advice. His friend told him to ring the police. Even then, he popped next door to a female neighbour and asked her to make the call. Later he explained that he hadn't wanted to become involved. If any of the witnesses had rung the police as soon as they were aware of the incident then there seems little doubt that Catherine Genovese would still be alive today. The question everyone was asking was: Why had no-one called the police when what they had clearly seen was an innocent woman being attacked?

Too many witnesses to help?

Soon after this crime, many experts tried to explain the apathy of the bystanders. There were numerous suggestions put forward. These included the alienation of the individual ('deindividuation') due to a lack of community feeling inherent in city living. Indeed, in subsequent years there would be reports of crowds 'baiting' suicide victims to 'jump'. On one occasion, when police talked down a potential suicide victim, they were booed by the onlookers. Ironically, a theologian asked to remain unidentified when he stated depersonalisation in the city had gone further than ever imagined! Most of the explanations remained mere conjecture and so two New York-based psychology professors decided to research the area of bystander behaviour. They started this area of research as a direct result of the Catherine Genovese murder. Their names were Bibb Latané and John Darley.

Latané and Darley wondered whether it was precisely because there were so many witnesses to the murder that no-one helped. The first explanation they proposed was 'pluralistic ignorance' (Latané and Darley, 1969). It is suggested that in ambiguous situations people look to others for help as to what to do (social reality). In an emergency situation, if all the other bystanders are also uncertain and looking for guidance, then looking to others can produce the wrong guidance, sometimes resulting in no action at all. Perhaps, the other witnesses looked for signs of action in the other apartments, saw none and simply didn't interpret it as an emergency situation. Put simply, if no-one else is helping, then perhaps it really isn't an emergency. Alternative explanations are sought, such as 'a lover's tiff' or 'just a couple larking around' to write off what's been seen. A French witness, Madeleine Hartmann, later admitted that she might have misinterpreted the incident and not thought of it as an emergency. She reported that 'so many, many times in the night, I heard screaming. I'm not the police and my English speaking is not perfect'.

The second explanation they proposed again relates to the number of witnesses present. It is suggested that the presence of other people can influence the decision-making process. If there are lots of people present, then a so-called 'diffusion of responsibility' occurs whereby each person feels less responsible for dealing with the emergency. In essence, someone else can help. Given the large number of witnesses in the Genovese case and the fact that people knew there were many others watching the events unfold (they could see lights on and people at their windows) it might be the case that people

Figure 6.1 Catherine 'Kitty' Genovese
Source: *NY Daily News* via Getty Images

believed others would take responsibility. In any case, if no-one helped it wouldn't be entirely your fault. You could always say 'Well, don't blame me. No-one else did anything either!' Each bystander assumes that another witness will call the police.

This diffusion of responsibility explanation was supported by the testimonies of the witnesses. Remember Mr and Mrs Koshkin on the sixth floor? Mr Koshkin wanted to call the police, but Mrs Koshkin thought otherwise. 'I didn't let him,' she later said to the press. 'I told him there must have been 30 calls already.'

Rather surprisingly, Moseley appeared to be aware of the likelihood of bystander apathy. He later reported that he was relatively unconcerned by the shouts from the apartment building. He stated 'I had a feeling this man would close his window and go back to sleep and sure enough, he did.'

Psychological research

Latané and Darley carried out a series of elegant experiments where they tested the so-called bystander effect.

In the first, students were invited to discuss 'the personal problems faced by college students'. To avoid embarrassment, the students sat in separate cubicles and communicated via intercom. Taking turns, each student was allowed to talk for 2 minutes. During the first turn, one participant mentioned that he had seizures when stressed. On the second turn, it became obvious that this person was, indeed, having a seizure. He cried out: 'Give me a little help here . . . I think I'm having a seizure . . . I think I'm gonna die here . . . er . . . help.' Eighty-five per cent of those persons who thought that they were alone with the seizure victim offered help within 2 minutes. Of those who thought they were in a three-person group (participant, victim and bystander), 62 per cent reported the seizure. Only 31 per cent of those people who thought they were in groups of six (participant, victim and four bystanders) went to help the victim within 2 minutes. This is a clear example of diffusion of responsibility: the presence of others meant that each person felt less responsible for helping.

In the second study, students were asked to sit on their own but in the same room as other participants and complete a questionnaire on the pressures of urban life. While they were completing this, smoke (actually steam) began pouring into the room through a small wall vent. Within 4 minutes, 50 per cent had taken action, and 75 per cent acted within 6 minutes. However, in the groups of three participants, only 4 per cent of people reported the 'smoke' within 4 minutes and only 38 per cent reported it within 6 minutes. When two confederates joined the naïve participant and answered 'dunno' to all the questions they were asked (such as 'Do you think we ought to do something?'), only 10 per cent of participants reported the smoke within 6 minutes. This demonstrates the phenomenon of pluralistic ignorance: people didn't want to over-react and lose their cool. In the presence of others, we look to others for guidance. If they appear calm, then there can't be a problem.

A combination of diffusion of responsibility and pluralistic ignorance probably explains why the Genovese bystanders behaved as they did. Presumably they believed that since nobody else was reacting as if there were an emergency, it probably was not an emergency. Furthermore, even if some of them suspected it might be an emergency, the diffusion of the responsibility effect made them less compelled to take action. In a group situation, it is much easier for an individual to assume that s/he does not have to do anything and hope someone else will take care of it by calling the police or yelling out of the window.

The Genovese case still poses the question 'Why don't we want to appear to have over-reacted in an emergency situation?' Surely it's better to have over-reacted than not to have acted at all? Many people have explained this in terms of fear of ridicule or embarrassment. But why is it embarrassing to be doing what you thought was right? Perhaps people carry out a cost–benefit analysis and realise that the potential costs to themselves (time, effort, danger) outweigh the likely benefit to themselves. Would these behaviours be the same in other cultures?

Predictable apathy?

The controversy surrounding the Catherine Genovese case continues to this day. How could all those bystanders have ignored Catherine's cries for help? Why didn't they do something? Why were so many of them indifferent to their inactivity when interviewed afterwards? Armed with the insights provided by Latané and Darley it seems that the bystanders acted in an entirely predictable way. Entirely predictable and entirely in line with what we now know about social behaviour in group situations. Remember, the fact that the witnesses were aware of each others' presence suggests it was a group situation. Writing in 1985, Shotland concluded that: 'After close to 20 years of research, the evidence indicates that "the bystander effect," as it has come to be called, holds for all types of emergencies, medical or criminal.'

Manning, Levine and Collins (2007) question whether individual witnesses standing at windows can be seen as an unresponsive group, let alone a crowd and yet the case is most often viewed in this light. Whatever the truth about these doubts, there is no doubt that the Catherine Geneovese murder prompted research into the bystander effect. Prior to this case, psychology tended to concentrate on the danger of the crowd as a cause of action or mob rule – after this case the issue was redressed in terms of the danger of crowd inaction and passivity.

Lessons to be learned

So did Catherine's cries go in vain or have any lessons been learned that might benefit others when they need help? What would you do in Catherine's situation that might increase your chance of survival?

Given the increased knowledge of the 'Genovese syndrome' there are some simple rules to remember if help is ever required. The first imperative is to try to overcome the possibility of bystanders being in any doubt as to whether they are witnessing an emergency situation requiring their help. For example, you need to make it clear that you have been assaulted and are not merely drunk. You need to be explicit. You need to overcome the 'diffusion of responsibility' effect by singling out one individual for help. It's far easier to ignore a general cry of 'help' rather than 'Hey, you with the grey jacket, come here, this is an emergency. I need YOUR help. Ring the police immediately.' You need to take charge and assign responsibility. Once one person helps, the social norm in the situation changes from non-helping to helping. It's likely that others will now perceive it as an emergency and all act to help. You have overcome the 'pluralistic ignorance' effect. As Darley et al. (1973) state, communication between bystanders helps to inoculate against the bystander effect. You will be inundated with offers of help! Make the psychology work for you, not against you.

There is another way that this case can have a beneficial effect. A few years ago, there was a drunk staggering all over the road outside my house. I lived on a busy road. He must have walked all the way down the road and there was a serious chance of an accident. I thought of calling the police but figured that they must have already received lots of calls. Yet quoting the Genovese syndrome to my wife, I changed my mind and called the police. They arrived in 5 minutes and took him away. Next day, the police returned to thank me.

Mine had been the first call that night. They said that they never minded however many calls they get. The drunk was released unharmed next morning.

A clearer understanding of the psychological explanations behind the Genovese case allows people to be better equipped to cope with life's emergencies. Such an understanding could save your life or that of another person.

Unfortunately the Catherine Genovese story does not end here. Every year, there are regrettable incidents that echo her case. In 2003, the Swedish minister for foreign affairs, Anna Lindh, was stabbed in a crowded department store after being pursued by her assailant up an escalator. There were dozens of bystanders but none intervened to help. The 'Genovese syndrome' had occurred again.

Recent doubts

In recent years there has been further research into the Catherine Genovese case. A resident of Kew Gardens for the last 35 years called Joseph de May began re-investigating the exact details of the case (de May, online). De May argues that there is evidence that some people did indeed call the police during the attack. For example, Michael Hoffman who was 15-years-old at the time swore that he told his father that he saw Winston Moseley running away and that he witnessed his father call the police. The police had no record of the call but Hoffman later became a New York policeman and appears to be a reliable source. Furthermore, de May estimates that there were only three witnesses who may have had a good view of the initial attack and the fact that the assailant left the scene and Catherine continued on to the side of her apartment might have suggested to witnesses that she was relatively unharmed. Only three witnesses were called to give evidence at the trial (Irene Frost, Andre Picq and Robert Mozer) (People vs Mozer, 1964), although Charles Skoller, the assistant district attorney at the time argued that there may have been more witnesses but that they were not called because their apparent inaction and callousness might have proved a distraction for the jurors. Given the speed of the first attack any other witnesses would not have got to their windows in time to witness anything. The second violent and sexual assault took place in the apartment building where no-one could have seen anything. Any witnesses who heard screams or shouts would most likely have concluded that it was late night revellers from a notoriously noisy local bar. Thus it is questionable how much the supposed inaction of witnesses was due to apathy or due to a misinterpretation of the evidence.

Figure 6.2 Scene of Catherine Genovese's murder, Kew Gardens, NY, 1964
Source: *NY Daily News* via Getty Images

Another enlightening interview occurred in 2004 when the person that shared Catherine's apartment at the time of the murder came forward to talk about the incident. Mary Ann Zielonko was Catherine's long-term partner and revealed that they were lovers. Some people have questioned whether some of the neighbours may have suspected this and a kind of 'homophobia' prevented people from wanting to become involved. Despite the different views and attitudes that may have been prevalent in 1964 towards gay people it seems extraordinarily unlikely that people would consider this as affecting their decision about whether to call the police or not. In any case, Zielonko says that they didn't openly advertise the fact that they were gay and most neighbours were probably unaware of it. Most of the witnesses spoke of Catherine in the highest possible terms as a polite and likeable young woman.

An apology?

What can we say about the Catherine Genovese case? Perhaps it can be summed up as follows: 'The crime was tragic, but it did serve society, urging it as it did to come to the aid of its members in distress or danger.' This is an extract from a letter published in *The New York Times* in 1977. It was written by Winston Moseley. Moseley finally apologised for his crimes and even gained a sociology degree while in prison. He continues to apply for parole but has been refused 13 times so far and has shown little remorse for his horrendous crimes. Catherine's brothers and sister have vowed to continue to contest any such release. They bear no grudge against the apathetic witnesses, only the murderer.

References

Darley, J.M., Teger, A.L. and Lewis, L.D. (1973). 'Do groups always inhibit individuals responses to potential emergencies'. *Journal of Personality and Social Psychology*, 26: 395–9.

Latané, B. and Darley, J. (1969). 'Bystander "apathy"'. *American Scientist*, 57: 244–68.

Manning, R., Levine, M. and Collins, A. (2007). 'The Kitty Genovese murder and the social psychology of helping: The parable of the 38 witnesses'. *American Psychologist*, 62(6): 555–62.

May, Joseph de (online). 'Kitty Genovese: A picture history of Kew Gardens', available at: http://web.archive.org/web/20070416121525/http://www.oldkewgardens.com/index.html (accessed July 2014).

People vs Moseley (1964). 43 Misc. 505.

Shotland, R.L. (1985). 'When bystanders just stand by'. *Psychology Today*, June: 52.

Chapter 7

Jonestown and the dangers of obedience

On 18 November 1978 in Georgetown, Guyana, 907 people committed suicide by poisoning because they were told to do so. Inhabitants of the place known as 'Jonestown' were influenced into taking their own lives through blind obedience to their charismatic 'religious' leader, the Reverend Jim Jones. Such was the influence that Jones had on his followers that many commentators (and the few survivors) now refer to the events as mass murder. This incident involved the largest loss of civilian American lives in a non-natural disaster prior to September 11th, 2001. Psychologists became fascinated by the Jonestown case, appearing as it did to show the dangers of blind obedience, compliance, propaganda and persuasion in affecting people's behaviour in a catastrophic way.

The Rev. Jim Jones and The People's Temple

James (Jim) Warren Jones was born on 3 May 1931 in Crete, Indiana, USA. He was the only child of a disaffected couple who were somewhat untraditional in their beliefs towards religion. His mother had managed to acquire such a scandalous reputation around the town that the young Jim felt quite alienated and outcast from his community. Jim came from a dysfunctional family and did not have a secure father figure. He was a lost soul who felt disengaged and without purpose in life. This all changed one day when a neighbour took the young Jim to a pentecostal church service where he became mesmerised by the charismatic preacher. Jim had found his calling and at the age of 10 he practised his sermons in the barn behind his house. School friends at the time considered the young Jimmy Jones somewhat odd – he was already obsessed with religion and death and they later reported that he killed small animals including cats in order to hold funerals for them. By the age of 16, he took to preaching on street corners in the black areas of Richmond. A white boy preaching Christian inclusion to discriminated blacks ensured that he soon cultivated a close following and after some training in the methodist church he founded his own movement, which, by 1956, he had called the 'People's Temple Full Gospel Church'. No-one could have guessed at that point the calamitous events that would ensue.

In the following years, Jones developed his oratory style, becoming an engaging speaker – using all the tricks of the trade. Dramatic pauses, changes in tone, shouting and even dramatic healings or miracles to convince all-comers of his religious power and brilliance. On the surface, the message he told was appealing. At a time when many felt very marginalised by traditional churches, Jones, the white preacher, was promoting rights for women, blacks and the poor. He adopted several non-white children and it can be easily imagined why people fell under his spell. Jones made people seem special, that they were on earth for a purpose and he offered them whatever they wanted. His popularity exploded and church membership soared. He became an influential political figure and politicians were keen to be seen with him by their side. Jones appeared to be at the forefront of the civil rights movement, although with the benefit of hindsight (which is always 20:20), people now claim that his words and actions were simply devices to attract and deceive his followers. As Jones himself preached 'some people see Christ in me' but by the end of his ministry people could see only evil.

In 1965, Jones managed to convince some of his followers, scared by him about the prospect of an imminent nuclear war with the Soviet Union, that they would be safer if they moved to California. The large commitment that his congregation made to move to California ensured that Jones had his most committed followers on board and once the move was completed they set about gaining new followers.

During his sermons, Jones often appeared to demonstrate remarkable clairvoyant powers or be capable of performing so-called miracles. In truth, these were set up by Jones who had arranged for members of his own staff to pretend to be disabled in order to suddenly walk from their wheelchairs after the Jim Jones 'miracle cure'. Close followers were instructed to merge with the congregation and report back snippets of overheard conversation, which he then used to convince members of the audience that he was clairvoyant.

Jones boasted of his amazing powers of concentration and energy but it seems clear that he was actually using the drug dextroamphetamine or 'speed' during this time to maintain his boundless energy. One of the side effects of

Figure 7.1 Jim and Marceline Jones seated in front of their adopted children, with Jones's sister-in-law (right) and her three children, California, 1976

Source: Photo by Don Hogan Charles/New York Times Co./Getty Images

the drug is paranoia and Jones was becoming increasingly paranoid in his behaviour. Jones staged many apparent 'attacks' on his church in order to help close ranks with his most trusted members. The siege mentality – suggesting that 'others are out to get us' – helped to bind people to the cause. Jones would exploit this aspect to the hilt over the coming years as he was preparing the ground to move his entire congregation to the 'promised land' in Guyana.

Jones was always worried about people who abandoned his movement. He used every technique to prevent followers from leaving his People's Temple. He got followers to sign blank sheets of paper, which he called 'attendance sheets', but anything could be typed above the signatures turning them into 'signed' confessions. He exhorted his congregation to kill anyone who harmed the movement and gradually introduced verbal and physical abuse into meetings. Ritual beatings became more and more commonplace and escalated into parents whipping their children on stage so violently that the children had to be carried off the stage. After punishment, people had to say 'Thank you, Father'.

Jones had always been impressed by people who were so immersed in their revolutionary goals that they were prepared to commit suicide for their cause. Jones wondered whether his followers felt so strongly about his movement. He realised that members who committed suicide in the name of the movement would generate a lot of publicity so he asked whether any members would be willing to throw themselves off the Golden Gate Bridge. Although members refused, Jones kept the idea in mind and at a meeting on New Year's Day 1976 he gave a glass of wine to the 30 odd members present. After drinking the 'wine', Jones informed them all that it was poison and that they would all be dead within the hour. While some did not believe him, others tried to rush out to seek help. Three-quarters of an hour later, Jones informed them it had merely been a test of their loyalty to see if they would accept their fate and die for their true beliefs.

At this point, Jones decided on a much bigger and more elaborate plan. He wondered how devoted his followers really were. How far could he push them? He would form a new society in the middle of the jungle in Guyana and this 'promised land' or 'freedom land' would be called Jonestown.

Jonestown

British Guyana was liberated from the British in 1965 with a socialist government and an English speaking, black population. Unlike other Caribbean countries, Guyana did not have a thriving tourist industry (the beaches were mud not sand) and, in addition, could not grow enough food to feed its inhabitants. Nevertheless, Jones felt it was a suitable place to start a new community. The Guyanese government offered 3,800 acres to the Temple at 25 cents per acre on a 25-year lease. The prime minister, Forbes Burnham, was keen to show the locals that co-operatives could be sustainable and so Jonestown was born, in February 1976. A promised land that would end as a land of torture, misery and death.

In the early days, a few dozen settlers arrived to try to put up some buildings, plant and prepare the land for crops. An air of expectancy and enthusiasm prevailed before the arrival of Jones, and members seemed reasonably happy despite their difficult physical daily work regimes. However, the soil was poor and as more and more members arrived it became clear that the project could not be self-sustainable. Jones visited Guyana and kept the recruitment process going by falsely producing films that showed a utopian lifestyle. Members were generally disappointed on arrival but had no recourse left open to them – they had sold all their possessions and this was their only option. They had no money, no possessions and they were 4,000 miles from home. No-one could hear their voices even if they had been brave enough to use them.

Jones was a brilliant negotiator and strategist. He organised a group of women called the PR Crew to 'work' with the men who held the political power in Guyana. Jones's main 'political prostitute' (as she called herself) was Paula Adams who began dating the Guyanese ambassador to the United States, giving Jones unprecedented access to the workings of the Guyanese government. Some members of the Temple did manage to leave and reported that the Temple was nothing more than a slave colony but in contrast there were always people ready to support and argue that Jonestown was actually a paradise. Jones managed to organise fake assaults by 'hostile' external agencies and pretend that the movement was under attack.

Gradually, Jones's behaviour became ever more controlling. Beatings continued, people were drugged and marriages and family relations were deliberately wrecked by Jones. People who wished to leave were not allowed to do so. They had no physical means of escape nor the finances to facilitate it. People who had questioned Jones's thinking were informed on and sent to join the 'Learning Crew' where, under armed guard, they were forced to perform hard physical labour for 16 hours a day. Punishments in Jonestown became increasingly harsh, public humiliations where people were ridiculed or paraded naked were the prelude to physical beating and even solitary confinement for days on end in a shipping crate used as a deprivation and isolation chamber. It was reported that people took weeks to regain some semblance of normality after their experiences in 'the box'. All the residents of Jonestown apart from Jones himself and his trusted lieutenants were left isolated, tired and perpetually hungry. Their disorientated state made them all the more easily manipulated.

Jones continued to maintain a siege mentality in the community arguing that the Guyanese government, the CIA and other capitalist forces were preparing to attack them. He kept planting the idea of revolutionary suicide into people's heads – he argued that it was better to commit suicide and die freely by their own hands than be killed by fascists and capitalists. People realised that Jones had complete control over every aspect of their lives and soon accepted that it was futile to argue with him.

One day Jones set up a test of loyalty involving a suicide drill. He made everyone line up and drink a 'potion'. Guards forced people to drink and any who refused were branded as anarchists or traitors who would be shot if they attempted to flee. Some people were so dispirited that they felt suicide was a better option than another day in the hell that had become Jonestown. Others believed that the potion was not poison and just another test, although some did refuse to drink it only to serve days or weeks of harassment. These 'fake' poisonings were nicknamed 'white nights' by the people. Of course, this time it had been a hoax by Jones and the potion had not been a poison but merely another test of obedience. However, in the coming months things would get worse: the next time the drink would be cyanide. Residents were becoming ill, food production was inadequate and most realised that Jonestown was doomed.

The Concerned Relatives

Needless to say many of the people in Jonestown had left close relatives behind in the USA. Some of these relatives were concerned by a lack of information or questioned the veracity of the stories they did receive. Eventually, 25 relatives of Jonestown residents filed lawsuits against the Temple requesting information about their relatives. The group called themselves The Concerned Relatives. Jones was furious – the story hit the newspapers and Jones knew that his attempts at manipulating all media sources was starting to unravel. Questions would continue to be asked in America and eventually the US government would take more than a passing interest in the welfare of almost 1,000 of their citizens. Jones did not have a clean record and there were numerous stories circulating about conditions in Jonestown involving physical and mental abuse and imprisonment. Jones forced family members of The Concerned Relatives to make scripted tapes detailing how happy they were in Jonestown and stating how they would torture their relatives if they were ever given the chance.

As Jones predicted, the US government did start to take notice of the US residents in Jonestown and the US consul Richard McCoy visited Jonestown to interview residents in order to see whether they wanted to leave. None did so and McCoy concluded that it was highly unlikely that the residents were being held against their will. It looked as though Jones was going to successfully sit out the storm until Debbie Blakey, a trusted Jones aide and a member of the PR team and a Temple member for 7 years, defected and told McCoy about the reality of Jonestown. Back in the safety of San Francisco, Blakey foretold of the possibility of mass suicide and urged the US government to safeguard Americans living in Jonestown. McCoy found it hard to believe that almost 1,000 people could be controlled in this way. Furthermore, the US had a problem in that the First Amendment prohibited interference in the privacy and religious freedom of its citizens. Jones, worried by this turn of events ordered a 'lock down' of the community and sealed the area from the outside world. With little concrete evidence against Jonestown both the US and Guyanese authorities were unsure exactly what to do. During this stand-off, Jones ordered his trusted Doctor Schacht to order quantities of sodium cyanide and potassium cyanide – more than enough to kill 1,000 people.

At this time, Democrat congressman Leo Ryan from San Mateo California decided, at the request of some of his constituents, to try to visit Jonestown to discover the truth about the situation there. Jones was beside himself and worried that at least one resident would inform Ryan about the real situation at Jonestown and then others would choose to leave. Jones was never going to allow that.

The end game

Jones had a trusted Temple member who had infiltrated The Concerned Relatives group and kept Jones informed about Ryan's visit. He also had paid allies in the Guyanese government who did everything in their power to delay or obstruct the visit. Jones informed the Ryan party that their visit was not welcome, that Jonestown was private property and that if they attempted to enter it they would be arrested for trespassing. Nevertheless, the party flew to Guyana. Once there, Jones changed his mind and decided to let the visit proceed. The numerous reporters that had accompanied Congressman Ryan were left at the airfield but eventually Ryan and three others were escorted in. Jones had briefed the residents as to what to say and on the day of the visit they were given a proper meal of barbecued pork and coffee. This put them in good spirits for the visit and the carefully orchestrated events such as a talent show seemed to be portraying Jonestown in a good light. Ryan was even shown on NBC film talking to an audience and saying 'there are some people here who believe this is the best thing that ever happened to them in their whole life'. The inspection appeared to be going well although two people had smuggled notes to the visitors asking them to help them to leave. By the next day, 20 defectors had identified themselves to Ryan and were sent to collect their belongings from their huts. There were disputes between families as to whether children would be allowed to go with one parent if another wished to stay behind. The crowd were baying at the defectors and the whole situation was becoming unmanageable. Some of the defectors were worried that Jones would kill them all there and then, and indeed one Temple member did attack Ryan with a knife trying to slit his throat before being wrestled to the ground. Ryan had seen enough – it was time to leave with as many defectors as possible. One of Jones's most trusted aides, Larry Layton, decided at the last minute to defect and chose to accompany Ryan to the airbase. Other defectors didn't believe that he wanted to leave but Ryan had promised to take anyone so he was forced to accept Layton's word.

After a frantic drive to the airport, the defectors and newspapermen were all keen to get on the planes and out of the area as quickly as possible. The first small plane had been delayed and there was a nervous wait while people boarded the planes after their arrival. Before either plane took off a pick-up truck drove towards them stopping 10 metres or so away. From the truck's trailer six men got out and started shooting at selected members of the congressional party. Congressman Ryan was shot dead, Bob Brown, the NBC film reporter, was also gunned down. Larry Layton started firing at people with a gun that he had concealed on his person. Jones's assassins escaped back to Jonestown to report on events at the airport. When Jones heard what had happened he realised that his social experiment was at an end – bar one final act. Jones called members to the pavilion for one last 'white night' meeting.

18 November 1978: The final 'white night'

Jones called his group together and explained the events that had taken place at the airport and said that these actions would undoubtedly prompt an invasion by Guyanese or US forces. Jones said that they had no other option than to commit revolutionary suicide rather than be captured, 'tortured and killed'. Jones's egotistical approach ensured that he tape recorded many of his speeches and this particular 45-minute tirade was no different; it would be known in the future as the 'death tape'. Jones had been training his residents for years for this night and he made sure they were going to follow him to the end.

As the group returned to the compound to relay the news of Congressman Ryan's demise, Jones's aides carried drums of poison from the kitchens. The drum contained flavoured grape juice (Kool Aid) and the lethal dose of cyanide. One member who survived the massacre reported looking around to see 25 armed guards outside the pavilion. Although these guards were supposed to be protecting the Temple members the witness noticed that their guns were turned on the residents, not at any threat from the jungle. On the final recorded death tape, there were isolated voices questioning the wisdom of revolutionary suicide, but by now Jones had manipulated the people into largely doing as he willed. Mothers were requested to bring their children forward first to administer the poison, some using needle-less syringes to squirt the liquid into the children's mouths before taking their own dose and going to sit in the jungle clearing outside. All the time, residents were encouraged by Jones and his aides that they were doing the right thing. Some Temple members talked about the ecstasy of reincarnation. The children died first as they began to convulse and froth at the mouth. Their parents destined to die moments later would have seen this in their last few living minutes. Most of the people dying were doing so out of sight of those still in the pavilion so the full horror of the events may not have been known to those yet to take the poison, until a 15-year-old lad burst into the pavilion convulsing in front of the waiting members. It was clear that this was not another rehearsal. Jones had made true his threat of revolutionary suicide. Those people who didn't volunteer for the poison were forced to take it at gunpoint. With almost 1,000 dead bodies in front of him Jones must have felt that his goal had been achieved – he had become famous, he had left his mark on history. Perhaps he felt strangely satisfied with his life's endeavours as he pulled the trigger of the revolver he had aimed at his head.

Before the final killings, Jones had sent a radio message to Temple members elsewhere to kill themselves and other members as part of the pact. The Jonestown basketball team who were in Georgetown for a game were ordered to try to kill The Concerned Relatives who were still there as part of Ryan's visit (they had been refused entry to Jonestown itself). The team did not carry out this order.

The final death toll was 909. The number that committed suicide willingly and gave up their lives for what they believed was a worthy cause will never be truly known. Even those who did die 'willingly' were undoubtedly tricked by Jones throughout their membership of the People's Temple. The United States requested that the bodies be buried where they lay but the Guyanese government refused. It took four days to repatriate them, by which time in the heat of the jungle they had decayed to such an extent that they could only identify 631 of the 909 dead. In total, 304 children were murdered including 131 under the age of 10. Many of the identified dead were not even buried by relatives. They either had no known relatives or their relatives were too ashamed to retrieve their bodies. The People's Temple members were all portrayed as child murderers and there was little attempt to see the victims as 'innocents' who had been manipulated by Jones. The general public could not comprehend how anyone could commit such acts without everyone present being truly evil. A total of 408 victims were returned to the US and buried in the Evergreen Cemetery in Oakland. Jim Jones was cremated and his ashes dropped into the Atlantic Ocean.

The aftermath

Very few people survived the Jonestown massacre. Some escaped to the jungle fearing that they would be tracked down and some feigned dead and managed to avoid taking the poison. Some fortunate members had been on visits and not been at Jonestown on that fateful day. Afterwards most of the survivors shunned publicity although a few conducted lecture tours and wrote accounts of the People's Temple, earning money from selling their stories. Michael Prokes a prominent member of the movement had been given the task of taking funds from the jungle for safekeeping and thus had avoided the suicides. He called a press conference a few weeks later in a Californian hotel and shot himself in the head leaving behind a message stating that Jones had been misunderstood. Larry Layton served 18 years in a US prison for his role in the murder of Congressman Ryan. There were reports that a small number of Temple members who had previously abandoned the movement were murdered by unknown assailants, but whether these killings were directly related to Jonestown remains unclear.

Jonestown itself was looted and ransacked by the locals and a fire consumed many of the buildings including the pavilion. The site is now overgrown and a solitary tree marks the location of the pavilion. Occasionally there are plans for the pavilion to be rebuilt for tourists to visit although nothing has actually come of this. Some of the members managed to resume their lives but for others life fell apart.

The lessons to be learned

There is no doubt that the personality of Jim Jones managed to attract a remarkable number of people to the People's Temple. It is always easiest to regard such appalling events as 'unique' cases in which one evil man managed to turn many people's minds towards committing atrocious acts. However,

there are various social and psychological processes that can also help to explain the members' blind obedience to Jones's destructive orders and should help us to predict and prevent future atrocities of this nature. Why did people join the movement in the first place? Why didn't they leave once they realised that Jones couldn't deliver what he had promised? What led them to murder innocent children and then kill themselves? Such aspects can be explained in terms of persuasion, propaganda, compliance, conformity and obedience.

If you have absolute power over someone then it is certainly possible to give them no other option but to do what you want them to do. There is little doubt that Jones gradually and insidiously gained more and more control over his followers. Dissent and disagreement was punished as severely as possible and soon members learned that resistance and argument was futile. Recall that Jones organised public humiliations, physically threatened defectors and many members believed the stories that circulated about ex-members who had suffered from surprising and inexplicable deaths. However, there have been a number of psychological studies that have shown that people will destructively obey an authority figure even without a great threat of violence or intimidation. The best known studies of this kind were conducted by Stanley Milgram in the early 1960s.

Stanley Milgram

Obedience can be defined as a type of social influence in which somebody acts in response to direct instructions from an authority figure. Obedience or its sister, conformity (behaviour that follows the majority view), are often viewed in negative ways but of course society would function far less successfully if people did not follow the laws that the majority have agreed upon or the unwritten social rules in society. Indeed Milgram (1974) wrote 'Obedience is as basic an element in the structure of social life as one can point to; some system of authority is a requirement of all communal living'.

Usually in terms of obedience it is assumed that the person acts in such a way that they would not have done so without the authoritative order. Stanley Milgram was fascinated by how the Nazis managed to get so many ordinary people to actively participate in the Holocaust atrocities. The common view at the time was that 'evil' people behave in an evil way (the dispositional hypothesis) but Milgram wondered whether the power of the situation may play a part in making ordinary, even 'good' people behave in an evil way if

asked to do so (the situational hypothesis). He tested these hypotheses in a series of brilliant experiments.

The aim of Milgram's (1963) experiment was to measure the level of obedience of participants who were told by an authority figure to administer electric shocks to another person.

The participants consisted of 40 males aged between 20 and 50 years of age who were recruited by a newspaper and direct mail advertisement asking for volunteers to participate in a study of memory and learning at Yale University. Milgram deliberately chose people from all walks of life who appeared to be average or normal members of the public. For obvious reasons, participants had to be deceived about the true aim of the study.

When each participant turned up for the experiment, they were introduced to another participant (called Mr Wallace). Mr Wallace was actually a confederate of Milgram's; he was not a participant but already knew exactly what would happen and was simply playing the role of a friendly, middle-aged man. Both the participant and Mr Wallace then drew a slip of paper from a hat to determine which of them would be the 'learner' and which would be the 'teacher'. The draw was fixed so that the participant always played the role of teacher and Mr Wallace that of the learner. This ensured that participants felt that simply by chance they could well have been the learner rather than the teacher in the study.

Mr Wallace was then taken to another room and, in full view of the teacher (participant), was strapped into a chair and electrodes attached to his wrist. It was explained to the teacher that the 'learner' could not escape any subsequent electric shocks. The naive participant was informed that although 'the shocks can be extremely painful, they cause no permanent tissue damage'. Milgram had manufactured a realistic looking shock generator with 30 switches on it starting from 15 volts and going up in 15-volt increments all the way to 450 volts.

In order for the teacher to understand what 15 volts felt like, they were given a 15v electric shock (this was the only real electric shock given during the entire study). The teacher was then seated in front of the shock generator and asked to read a series of word pairs to the learner. The learner (Mr Wallace) was asked to memorise the words. He was subsequently 'tested' for his learning ability of the words, and when Mr Wallace gave a wrong answer the teacher was instructed by the experimenter to administer an electric shock. Hence the participant thought they were testing the effects of punishment on learning. In reality the test was a study of destructive obedience. If Mr Wallace gave a

correct answer they moved on to the next word pair. If Mr Wallace gave an incorrect answer the teacher had to inform him of the correct answer and tell him the level of shock punishment he was going to receive. For each subsequent wrong answer the teacher was required to move one switch up the scale of shocks (15 volts higher than the voltage of the last shock delivered).

If at any time the teacher showed any disobedience or reluctance to administer the shocks, the experimenter gave him encouragement that this was the correct course of action using pre-arranged 'prods' (prompts) such as 'Please continue' or 'The experiment requires that you continue'. So did any of the participants give electric shocks to the innocent and mild mannered, friendly Mr Wallace? Of course they did! Although all participants showed marked signs of stress and nervousness, all obeyed the experimenter to a greater or lesser extent. Of the 40 participants, 14 exhibited nervous laughing fits and three of the participants had uncontrollable seizures as a result of the stress. The power of the situation was such that all 40 of the participants obeyed the experimenter and delivered shocks up to 300 volts. As many as 65 per cent (26 out of 40 participants) delivered shocks up to the maximum 450 volts (Milgram, 1963, 1974). After the maximum level had been reached and the experiment ended most of the participants showed immense relief or shook their heads in regret. Some participants even asked if they had seriously harmed Mr Wallace (the learner).

Milgram put forward a number of possible explanations for this high level of obedience, including the fact that the experiment took place at the prestigious Yale University, that the participant believed that the experiment was for a worthy purpose and that the participant believed the victim had volunteered to be in the study and therefore had an obligation to take part even if the procedures became unpleasant (Milgram, 1963, 1974).

A more recent partial replication of many aspects of Milgram's original study using virtual reality found many similar findings (Slater et al., 2006). It is of course tempting for the current generation of readers to wonder whether they would act in a similar way to the majority of Milgram's participants. I would like to think that I would not but I do not feel that that is the truthful or honest answer. Without prior knowledge of the study, I think most people (including myself) would act in a similarly destructive and obedient fashion. The vast majority of people seem to act in this way and it would be arrogant to think that we are in some way different from the norm. It might be argued that the results were a product of the time, although this is disputed (see Burger, 2009). Perhaps people were more obedient in the 1960s? Thomas Blass (1999)

reviewed results from various replications of the Milgram study from 1961 to 1985 and found no relationship whatsoever between the results and the dates that the studies were conducted. It seems likely that obedience levels remain stable over time. Indeed it would be surprising if this was not the case because our culture tends to socialise people into obeying figures that we perceive as authoritative, such as police officers, parents and teachers. Society can often work better if people are obedient in this way, providing the authority figures we look to for guidance.

Obedience lessons applied to The People's Temple

Some critics have argued that Milgram's research may have helped tyrannical figures to exploit this new found research knowledge for their own destructive ends. There is little evidence that Jim Jones himself was aware of any of the social psychological literature on destructive obedience, although Jones could hardly have set up a better practical example exploiting numerous powerful and persuasive techniques if he had. Jones managed tragically, but most successfully, to employ numerous psychological techniques to persuade 'normal' people placed in a terrifying situation to commit atrocious acts against both themselves and other people. How did he manage this?

One important element of destructive obedience is the step-by-step corruption of absolute power. Many Temple members at the final 'white night' reckoning probably felt helpless in the face of Jones's absolute power over the situation. The members had sold all their possessions and given up their passports – they were under tremendous pressure to obey. However, it is clear from the documentary evidence that this was not the case when members started to join the movement and that they had had the opportunity to leave before they were so involved. Similarly, there were clearly members who, even during the final suicide act, still maintained their belief in Jones and the People's Temple and committed suicide willingly. For example, one woman's body was found with the words 'Jim Jones is the only one' scrawled in ink on her arm, and one guard's last words were reported to be 'It's a great moment . . . we all die' (Lifton, 1979). A very gradual incremental increase in commitment and loyalty is not as noticeable as an immediate and large commitment. Milgram demonstrated this by only asking participants to increase the shocks gradually by 15 volts each time. Once the first 15 volt 'shock' was given, why not just give another 15v more each time? Surely each participant would have felt it odd to refuse to administer 200v after having just given 185v? Before participants

knew it they were at the 450v level, which they would not have administered without the gradual incremental increase. This was clearly explained by an interviewee who stated 'If you had to push the 450 volt switch first, no one would do it' (Perry, 2012).

Milgram's gradated shock technique still operates with the 'foot-in-the-door' technique beloved of sales people. Freedman and Fraser (1966) demonstrated this when, posing as consumer group employees, they telephoned people at home. Their initial request was that homeowners might answer a few questions about the soap they used. A few days later, they asked the homeowner to allow a team of researchers to visit them to make a full inventory of all their household products. Up to 53 per cent of people who had previously agreed to the smaller request agreed to the second major request compared to only 22 per cent who were 'cold called'. Such techniques are still used by salesmen and women on a daily basis and it appears evident that Jones did the same. Initially small commitments to the movement gradually became larger and larger and exploited people's desire to be consistent in their behaviour to themselves and others.

Imagine the scenario. A few hours given over to the church each week gradually increases to a more substantial commitment. More and more time, effort and money is given to the church. People need to justify to themselves their behaviour. This relates to the notion of cognitive dissonance discussed at length in another chapter (see Chapter 8). When a person behaves in a way that is inconsistent with their beliefs, the inconsistency results in an unpleasant state of tension. A person involved in the movement would need to reduce the feelings of dissonance that membership must have caused. They could rationalise their behaviour, either by leaving the movement altogether (which some did) or by staying and reducing their nagging doubts by convincing themselves ever further of the doctrine according to Jim Jones. Gradually when people had lost all their possessions and had no other option than to stay in the People's Temple, they had to reduce the dissonance they must have been feeling by becoming ever more committed to the cause. If they didn't do this they would have faced the awful prospect of realising what a complete fool they had been. Perhaps it was better to continue with the belief in Jim Jones than realise one's utter stupidity. Jeanne Mills in her 1979 book vocalises this process by writing,

> We had to face painful reality. Our life savings were gone. Our property had been taken . . . we had alienated our parents . . . even our children

were openly hostile towards us . . . all we had now was Jim and the cause, so we decided to buckle under and give our energies to these two.

By justifying their previous actions and commitments to the cause it was a simple step to accept the ultimate act of mass suicide.

Dissonance theory also predicts that another way in which we will try to reduce the conflict is to selectively attend to 'consonant' information: that is, information that supports our decision. Not only will we give more attention to evidence that makes us feel better, we will also selectively interpret any ambiguous information as being consistent with our cognitions. This is known as 'confirmation bias'. This must have been easy for Temple members; with lots of other supporters showing devotion to Jones, one would want to conform to the majority view. The apparent 'miracles' that Jones produced could also appear convincing to an uncritical eye.

Lessons to be learned

One criticism of Milgram's series of obedience studies was that tyrants and megalomaniacs might learn lessons from his research about how easy it seems to get people to obey orders to destructive ends. Some people felt that it was better to believe that only 'evil' or 'stupid' people could be so misled rather than to realise that we are all capable of evil acts given the particular circumstances we find ourselves in. On the other hand, it is worth noting that in subsequent replications of the Milgram studies some people have refused to obey a destructive authority figure, citing the Milgram studies as evidence that people can be manipulated in this way. This suggests that knowledge of the research findings can help people to become disobedient to a dangerous authority figure! In addition, one condition (which was not reported by Milgram) involved people who were intimate with one another paired as the teacher and learner. The defiance levels here were extremely high and leads to questions about whether authority figures can quite so easily turn ordinary people into behaving in an appalling way against people who they initially feel some empathy or friendship towards (Perry, 2012).

Stanley Milgram courted controversy during his career and many people were upset by his ethical procedures, his findings and his subsequent fame. He left Harvard University when he was denied tenure by some of his colleagues and took a professorship at the relatively obscure City University in New York. His untimely death due to a heart attack occurred at the age of 51 on

20 December 1984. His research and writings continue to influence both scientific endeavour and contemporary culture and thought in a way that many of his former Harvard colleagues could only dream about.

Perhaps unknowingly, Jim Jones created the perfect conditions to show how people can be hoodwinked, bullied and controlled to a destructive purpose. It is only to be hoped that people will learn from both the lessons of Jonestown and the series of experiments conducted by Milgram to understand the power of the situation and the need for all of us to take full responsibility and, at the same time, become more self-aware of our actions. It is also important to resist going on 'automatic pilot', to be mindful of situational demands, to engage critical thinking skills, to be ready to admit any error in one's initial compliance and not be afraid to change one's mind.

Stanley Milgram remains one of the true giants of social psychology and it is fitting to end this chapter with his own words:

> When an individual wishes to stand in opposition to authority, he does best to find support for his position from others in his group. The mutual support provided by men for each other is the strongest bulwark we have against the excesses of authority.

Furthermore, "the social psychology of this century reveals a major lesson: often it is not so much the kind of person a man is as the kind of situation in which he finds himself that determines how he will act." (Milgram, 1974). If only the followers of Jim Jones had known this.

References

Blass, T. (1999). 'The Milgram paradigm after 35 years: Some things we now know about obedience to authority'. *Journal of Applied Social Psychology*, 25: 955–78.

Burger, J.M. (2009). 'Replicating Milgram: Will people still obey today?' *American Psychologist*, January, 64(1): 1–11.

Freedman, J.L. and Fraser, S.C. (1966). 'Compliance without pressure: The foot in the door technique'. *Journal of Personality and Social Psychology*, 4: 195–202.

Lifton, R.J. (1979). *The Broken Connection: On Death and the Continuity of Life*. Washington, DC: American Psychiatric Press.

Milgram, S. (1963). 'Behavioral study of obedience'. *Journal of Abnormal and Social Psychology*, 67: 371–378.

Milgram, S. (1974). *Obedience to Authority: An Experimental View*. New York: Harper & Row.

Mills, J. (1979). *Six Years with God*. New York: A and W Publishers.

Perry, G. (2012). *Behind the Shock Machine*. Victoria, Australia: Scribe Publications.

Scheeres, J. (2011). *A Thousand Lives: The Untold story of Jonestown*. New York: Free Press. Simon & Schuster.

Slater, M., Antley, A., Davison, A., Swapp, D., Guger, C., Barker, C., Pistrang, N. and Sanchez-Vives, M.V. (2006). A virtual reprise of the Stanley Milgram obedience experiments. Available at: PLoS ONE 1(1): e39. doi:10.1371/journal.pone.0000039.

Chapter 8

The end of the world is nigh
The case of Dorothy Martin

In September 1954, the *Lake City Herald* newspaper in Salt Lake City, USA, published a story about a suburban housewife called Mrs Dorothy Martin who had received messages that the end of the world was going to happen on 21 December. Martin prophesied that a great flood would submerge an area from the Arctic Circle to the Gulf of Mexico. The newspaper reported that Mrs Martin claimed that she had been sent the messages by superior beings from a planet called 'Clarion'. These beings had visited earth in flying saucers and had noticed fault lines in the earth's crust that predicted the deluge. Furthermore, Martin had attracted a number of followers called The Seekers who believed in her prophecy. On reading the article, Leon Festinger and his fellow psychologists Henry Rieken and Stanley Schachter thought this was too good an opportunity to miss. They decided that they would infiltrate The Seekers in order to study them and observe how they would react when the prophecy inevitably proved incorrect.[1] Their work provided an early exploration of the phenomenon called cognitive dissonance, a term that refers to the mental conflict that occurs when beliefs or actions are contradicted by or in conflict with one another. How would The Seekers react to reduce their feelings of dissonance given their contradictory belief in the end of the world and the clear evidence that they were wrong?

The end of the world

Given the number of doomsday predictions that arise every few years or so it is perhaps surprising that anybody believes such predictions any more. In recent years, we have had doomsday scenarios about 21 December 2012 predicted by the Mayan calendar, and Harold Camping, the founder of the independent ministry Family Radio International predicting that the world would end on

21 May 2011. Camping came to public attention because he advertised the end of the world on 5,000 billboards in the US in order to warn the public of the impending doom, despite the fact that he had previously got his prediction wrong. When the date came and went Camping (again) argued that he had got his dates wrong. It seems surprising that such predictions are often connected to those who have a Biblical belief, bearing in mind that the New Testament writer of the gospel of Mark was fairly unequivocal about such Judgement Day predictions: 'But of that day and that hour knoweth no man, no, not the angels that are in heaven, neither the Son, but the Father' (Mark 13: 32).

One of the most infamous doomsday sects was the so-called Heaven's Gate group based initially in Texas and then later in California. This group were led by Marshall Applewhite who preached that a spaceship would save true believers from the impending apocalypse. At the end of 1996, the sect were listening to a radio programme on which they heard that someone had 'seen' a UFO in the tail of the comet Hale-Bopp, which was visible in the night sky. The group began preparations to board the supposed UFO, and this involved mass suicide in order that their souls could board the craft. When police entered the Heaven's Gate house in the spring of 1997 they found 39

Figure 8.1 Leon Festinger

Source: © Estate Of Francis Bello/Science Photo Library

decomposing bodies all dressed identically in black with purple cloths over their heads and $5 bills on their person suggesting some ritual preparation for the next life. The exact circumstances of their deaths were open to speculation. Despite widespread publicity about this group, doomsday groups continue to evolve and exist.

A major problem with all these doomsday prophecy groups is the lack of information that psychologists can find out about them and their beliefs and actions. Many of these groups are very secretive and therefore keep their beliefs and activities largely to themselves. The one group that psychologists did manage to gain information about through direct observation in the 1950s was The Seekers.

Dorothy Martin aka Marian Keech and The Seekers

Dorothy Martin (to preserve her anonymity Festinger et al. called her Marion Keech) was a 'slight wiry woman with dark hair and intense, bright eyes' and at the time of the events purported she was about 50 years old. Martin reported that she had awoken one winter morning at dawn with a strange numbness in her arm. Without knowing why, she picked up a pen and she began to write in a different style of writing to her own. She realised that someone else was using her hand to pass on a message. Asking the person to identify themselves, Martin realised that it was her deceased father.

Martin had some previous acquaintance with psychic phenomena, practised Scientology and was also fascinated with flying saucers and the possibility of extra-terrestrial beings. Along with many others, her mother scoffed at the idea of her deceased husband contacting her daughter, but this did nothing to deter Martin who spent hours perfecting her 'automatic writing', often waiting days for the next message. Martin claimed to get better at receiving the messages and soon started to get messages from a being she named 'the Elder Brother' and then other beings from planets she called Clarion and Cerus. In mid-April she received messages from Sanada who identified himself as the contemporary identity of Jesus. Martin was reassured by messages from the 'Guardians' that she was the chosen recipient of the messages and that she should spread the message to other people. Martin told some close friends of her experiences and gradually, through word of mouth, she developed a small but loyal band of followers. Messages continued to be heard such as 'We are like the human beings of Earth and have much in common: though there are millions of years difference in our culture, we are still brothers. What we enjoy as natural everyday enjoyments, you of the world cannot imagine' (Festinger et al., 1956: 44), and similarly

> We are coming through your atmosphere and being seen by your astronomers . . . we know no death, as you do. It is as a cocoon turns into a moth – very consciously and voluntarily – when we need or desire the change. We never go back to our Earth body.
>
> (p. 44)

It was suggested that the Guardians were communicating with Martin in order for her to teach humans the 'principles, ideas and guides to right conduct that are necessary to advance the spiritual development of the human race and to prepare the people of the earth for certain changes that lie ahead' (p. 45). Many of the messages suggested that there would be visitations from space and soon there were prophecies of war and a great flood.

One morning on 23 July, Martin received a message that a space craft would land on Langley Airbase at noon. She was told to go there to witness the event. A dozen of The Seekers accompanied her. At midday, no space ship landing occurred, although the party did meet an unknown man who happened along the road. Martin reported him as behaving oddly and possessing a strange look in his eyes. The man refused offers of food and drink and seemed to disappear as quickly as he had materialised. Nothing else happened that day but on 2 August Martin received a message stating that the man had been Sanada disguised as the man. Martin was euphoric since she believed that she had talked and offered hospitality to a disguised embodiment of Jesus. However, not all The Seekers were so convinced and by December, only five of the 12 who had witnessed the non-event at Langley remained as disciples.

Martin revealed that her group of followers were instructed to go to the Allegheny Mountains prior to the flood (due on 21 December) where they were to establish an altar or spiritual community on earth who would then be taken bodily and spiritually via a spaceship to either Clarion or Venus. After an appropriate period of indoctrination they would be safely returned to earth to repopulate it with good people who 'walked in the Light'. During the months leading up to the predicted flood as many as 33 different people attended meetings relevant to the predicted catastrophe. However, only eight members were heavily committed and could be said to have taken direct action consistent with their belief that the flood would occur. These actions varied from publicly telling others about the flood to quitting their jobs, selling possessions or not making any plans beyond the due date. Another seven members appeared more doubtful and were less willing to talk actively about it. The members were of a variety of ages, educational levels and occupations.

From 16 December onwards, many newspapers got hold of the flood prophecy and Martin and the other mainstay of the group, a Dr Armstrong, were confronted by journalists seeking interviews and quotes. Martin and Armstrong largely refused to co-operate and the newspapers published stories ridiculing the group and the flood prophecy. At this point, Martin and her followers were not trying to proselytise despite the frequent opportunities to do so. Festinger et al. wanted to see how they would react when their prophecies started to be disconfirmed. They didn't have long to wait.

Although Martin had believed that the flood would occur on 21 December, she expected flying saucers to land prior to this to help rescue the believers before the damage could occur. Many members of the group had been expecting help from 4 December and had been ready for rescue on 'a 24 hour alert'. Given the ridicule received from the papers, Martin and her followers must have prayed to escape as quickly as possible and on Friday 17th Martin received a phone call from a man who claimed to be 'Captain Video from Outer Space'! He told her that a space ship would land in her garden at 4 p.m. to pick her up. Festinger et al. believed this call actually happened and, although an obvious hoax, Martin and the group did take it seriously and began making plans. This involved removing all bits of metal from their persons – jewellery, watches, buttons with metal backing and even ripping the zips out of their clothing. At 4 p.m., the ones chosen to depart put their coats on and waited in the kitchen looking up to the sky. Martin was in a state of excited euphoria. By 4.40 p.m. the tension was reduced and at 5.30 p.m. everyone gave up and returned to the living room with Martin refusing to discuss the matter. Martin sat with pen in hand waiting for a message to try to comprehend what had happened. Martin received a message saying that Sanada had decided that the chosen ones would be taken up by spaceship but would not need to return to earth again. Martin was happy that the message reconfirmed their importance in the scheme of things. Other members of the group hypothesised that the spaceships hadn't landed because of all the media interest around the house (there was a TV crew outside at 4 p.m.), but it was clear that no-one was clearly convinced by the argument. In the end the group decided that the 4 p.m. arrival had been simply a practice session. When the time was right, they would come!

Figure 8.2 The Seekers group believed that beings from the planet 'Clarion' had visited earth in flying saucers

Source: © Shutterstock

At this point, the newest convert to the group appeared to be having some doubts about the prophecies. She was an 18-year-old girl who had a fervent belief in flying saucers. However, after this first non-event she left the house at 11 p.m. to meet a boyfriend and never returned. The newest member of the group with the least commitment to it had given up. The other members of the group continued with their commitment.

From this point on, Festinger's confederate observers report that Martin, Dr Armstrong and The Seekers made renewed efforts to persuade and convince others of their beliefs. On the face of it this is surprising since they had no new evidence to support their belief; indeed, quite the opposite had occurred. At midnight Martin received another message that a flying saucer was on its way. The Seekers who remained at the house made hurried plans to embark again. Waiting in the wet, snowy, freezing back garden the women removed their bras with metal clasps and one worried about the metal fillings they had in their teeth. After two hours in the cold they went back inside disappointed yet again and went to bed. Rising in the morning, all present decided that it must have been another rehearsal and decided not to tell others of the non-event.

Over the next few days, Martin received phone calls from two young men purporting to be from the planet Clarion. Later, five young men turned up at the house claiming to be spacemen. Dr Armstrong and Martin tested them with a quiz and decided that they were the real thing. The Seekers were content and more convinced by their beliefs – the contact had come on the Saturday night rather than Friday. However, two more followers left the group disillusioned and never returned.

At 10 a.m. on 20 December, Martin received a message stating that the next day at midnight the believers would be taken in cars to a location where a flying saucer would be waiting. The Seekers were relieved to finally get confirmation that their long vigil would be over. Once again, preparations were made such as the removal of metal items on their persons. The tension was evident as they waited in the house at midnight. At 5 minutes past midnight, the Creator announced that the plan still held but that there had been a slight delay. At 2.30 a.m. Martin received a message saying that the group should take a break and have a coffee. The group discussed their disappointment and wondered whether they had got the dates wrong. At 4.45 a.m., Martin claimed that she had got a message saying that the world had been spared because The Seekers had spread so much light during their wait that God had saved the world from destruction. Most of the believers were jubilant to be given a satisfactory explanation for the non-appearance of the spaceship. However, one more member left the group never to return.

There was one more prediction of a visit from a spaceman due on 24 December. Again, five members of the group collected to sing Christmas carols and witness the event. Again, the prophecy was not confirmed. After this last failure of prophecy, some of the group's members began to split up and move away. However, Festinger et al. report that despite the seemingly overwhelming evidence to the contrary, Martin and her closest followers actually started prophesising more after the failure of her predictions.

Cognitive dissonance

Festinger and his colleagues had previously suspected that Dorothy Martin might be even more convinced of her beliefs after the failure of the prophecy. Perhaps this was the one prophecy that did hold true in the entire story! Festinger et al. stated that five conditions must be present if someone is to become a more fervent believer after a failure or disconfirmation (1965: 3–4):

- A belief must be held with deep conviction and it must have some relevance to action, that is, to what the believer does or how he or she behaves.

- The person holding the belief must have committed themselves to it; that is, for the sake of his or her belief, he or she must have taken some important action that is difficult to undo. In general, the more important such actions are, and the more difficult they are to undo, the greater is the individual's commitment to the belief.
- The belief must be sufficiently specific and sufficiently concerned with the real world so that events may unequivocally refute the belief.
- Such undeniable disconfirmatory evidence must occur and must be recognised by the individual holding the belief.
- The individual believer must have social support. It is unlikely that one isolated believer could withstand the kind of disconfirming evidence that has been specified. If, however, the believer is a member of a group of convinced persons who can support one another, the belief may be maintained and the believers may attempt to proselytise or persuade non-members that the belief is correct.

Reading of the behaviour and commitment shown by Dorothy Martin it might seem surprising that she managed to attract any followers, but psychological studies show how the failure of such prophesies has the surprising effect of making the beliefs of their proponents even stronger. This can be explained through a phenomenon Festinger and his colleagues called cognitive dissonance.

Cognitive dissonance theory explains why people become motivated to change their attitudes. Festinger et al. (1956) proposed the theory of cognitive dissonance, which is concerned with the way people change their attitudes when they realise that two thoughts or cognitions that they hold are inconsistent (i.e the end of the world prophecy and direct evidence to the contrary). This conflict between two thoughts or cognitions creates a negative feeling of dissonance or psychological discomfort. People deal with this dissonance either by changing one of the cognitions or adding a new cognition to explain the conflict. For example, to widen the scope, suppose a person who you consider a friend ignores you at a party. Your cognitions about your friend and their behaviour at the party conflict with one another. How could you deal with these conflicting thoughts that result in cognitive dissonance? You could change one of your thoughts. You might decide your friend is rude and actually has never been that nice and isn't really a friend. You might however decide that his or her behaviour was not really that rude. Alternatively you might add a new cognition and blame their new partner for turning them against you. Any of these new cognitions would help to reduce the feeling of cognitive dissonance and produce instead feelings of cognitive consistency. Festinger believed that the need to reduce dissonance is as basic as the need for safety or the avoidance of hunger. It is a drive that compels us to be consistent and the more important the issue and the greater discrepancy between attitude and behaviour, the greater the feelings of dissonance experienced. In terms of the Dorothy Martin case, The Seekers could have disbanded and abandoned their end-of-the-world beliefs or made up some other beliefs in order to reconcile their views. In the Dorothy Martin case this involved a recalculation of the dates or the suggestion that the group's commitment was so exemplary that God decided to save the world.

One key element of cognitive dissonance theory is that it recognises that people do not always think rationally. However, people do try to rationalise their behaviour albeit sometimes in an irrational way! People delude themselves by creating new cognitions that if they thought about rationally must be wrong (Gross, 2005). Smoking would be a case in point. All over the world people seem able to make a case for continuing to smoke although rationally their arguments would not stand up.

Festinger argued that people selectively avoid information that will increase dissonance. Hence a smoker may not read a pamphlet detailing the dangers of smoking. We selectively choose television programmes and read books that confirm our attitudes and behaviour. We also choose our friends on the same basis, which is why many of our friends have similar views to ourselves. Dorothy Martin surrounded herself with believers. People who disagree with us or present differing views are likely to increase the discomfort felt by dissonance processes (Griffin, 1997) and hence are rejected by sects or cults. This selective exposure preference helps to reduce dissonance.

Festinger also stated that there are certain processes that increase the amount of dissonance experienced. The more important the issue the greater the dissonance felt. The longer the delay between choosing the way to behave the greater the dissonance felt. The greater the difficulty in reversing the decision once made, the more the person will agonise over whether they made the right decision. These are sometimes called 'morning after' doubts for obvious reasons (Griffin, 1997). Sometimes once the decision is made people will still continue to look for evidence to support their decision. An additional process is also called the 'minimal justification' hypothesis, which proposes counter-intuitively that the less the external incentive/reward (or justification) to change one's attitudes, the greater the change (shown in the $20/$1 experiment below).

There have been a great many experimental research studies that have investigated cognitive dissonance theory. Many of these are forced compliance studies where participants are almost forced into holding conflicting opinions about something they don't really believe in. Perhaps the most famous is known as the $20 and $1 experiment.

The $20 and $1 experiment (Festinger and Carlsmith, 1959)

Festinger and Carlsmith (1959) wanted to experimentally test two aspects of Festinger's (1956) cognitive dissonance theory:

1   If a person is induced to do or say something that is contrary to their private opinion, there will be a tendency for them to change their opinion so as to bring it into correspondence with what they have done or said.
2   The *larger* the pressure used to elicit the overt behaviour (beyond the minimum needed to elicit it) the *weaker* will be the above-mentioned tendency.

A laboratory experiment was set up and 60 male students took part. They were asked to do some extremely boring repetitive tasks for 30 minutes; some participants had agreed to a payment of $1 and others had agreed to a payment of $20. One task involved turning wooden pegs one at a time on a large board. Once they had completed these boring tasks they were asked to go to the waiting room and greet other participants who were waiting for their chance to participate. They were told that they must tell the waiting participant (who was actually a female confederate who was 'in' on the experiment) that the task they were about to do was extremely interesting. After this, the attitudes of the participants to the task was measured. It would appear to make sense that those paid the most would change their attitude the most. The greater the reward the greater the attitude change. However, that was not what Festinger and Carlsmith had predicted and it was not what occurred. Instead, it was the participants who had only been paid $1 that changed their attitude the most. The $1 participants felt that the tasks had not been that boring whereas the $20 participants had not changed their attitudes towards the tasks at all. So why had this occurred?

Festinger and Carlsmith argued that the $1 group had experienced more cognitive dissonance. There was a large conflict between what they were saying to the next female participant and their attitude to the tasks. In order to reduce this dissonance they had changed or modified their view of the boring tasks (perhaps they weren't that boring after all!). The $20 group experienced much less dissonance. They knew the tasks were boring but could justify their lying (or 'counter-attitudinal advocacy') because they had been paid a decent sum of money to do so! The $1 group couldn't really reduce their cognitive dissonance by using this argument (since $1 was too little for this) so they changed their attitude to the task. They had to create another justification for their compliance (lying). This effect, whereby the smaller the reward or incentive, the greater the attitude change, is known as the 'less-leads-to-more effect' or the 'minimal justification' hypothesis (Gross, 2005).

One of the earliest examples of cognitive dissonance

Aesop's Fables: The fox and the grapes

One hot summer's day a Fox was strolling through an orchard till he came to a bunch of grapes just ripening on a vine that had been trained over a lofty branch. 'Just the things to quench my thirst,' quoth he. Drawing back a few paces, he took a run and a jump, and just missed the bunch. Turning round again with a One, Two, Three, he jumped up, but with no greater success. Again and again he tried after the tempting morsel, but at last had to give it up, and walked away with his nose in the air, saying: 'I am sure they are sour.'

Evaluation of cognitive dissonance (consistency) theory

It has already been mentioned that some of Festinger's conclusions may have been counter-intuitive. The idea that offering a large reward or incentive has less effect on attitude change than a smaller one created a great deal of hostility in social science circles (Griffin, 1997). Many psychologists were affronted that rewards might actually have a detrimental rather than helpful effect on behaviour. However the $20/$1 study (outlined above) does seem to support this idea.

Further examination of the idea of cognitive dissonance led some to state that the theory was conceptually weak. Aronson (reported by Griffin, 1997) claimed that the theory failed to explain under what conditions dissonance occurs. Cognitive dissonance is criticised as a 'never fails' theory. When it is clear that dissonance has led to attitude or behavioural change, the case is supported but when research fails to find attitude or behavioural change, it is claimed that the person did not experience sufficient dissonance to change their attitude or behaviour. Thus cognitive dissonance theory can never be proved wrong. Aronson developed the theory arguing that the amount of dissonance experienced is related to the effort invested in the behaviour. The more effort someone puts in to something, the more they are going to buy into it. The greater the hardship associated with the choice the greater the dissonance and therefore the greater the pressure towards attitude change (this is called the 'suffering-leads-to-liking' effect) (Gross, 2005). An example of this may help. My son wanted to join a local football team. The two best teams invited him for trials. After the first trial, one offered him a place. The other told him it was difficult to say if he would get in but he should keep coming for training. After 3 weeks, they also offered him a place. Which did he accept? He signed for the team for which he had expended the most effort to get in.

The dissonance theory was later expanded in a more complicated way. In the original $20 and $1 study the experimenter's request to persuade the next participant (actually the confederate) was not ostensibly a part of the experiment. Thus participants were free to choose to refuse this request – in other words, they were given freedom of choice over this request. Second, since the confederate had stated that she wasn't going to take part in the experiment until she was told that the experiment was interesting, the participant's lying led to negative consequences for the confederate (Hewstone et al., 1996). Other studies have confirmed that freedom of choice and negative consequences as a result of counter-attitudinal behaviour are important factors in the arousal of dissonance. Thus dissonance change is a complicated theory involving freedom of choice, incentive size and negative consequences as a result of any action.

There have been a number of experiments that support Festinger's cognitive dissonance theory. However, there is a problem in that because we cannot physically observe cognitive dissonance we cannot objectively measure it. Consequently, the term cognitive dissonance is somewhat subjective. There are also individual differences in whether or not people act as this theory predicts. Highly anxious people are more likely to do so. Many people seem able to cope with considerable dissonance and not experience the tensions the theory predicts.

Finally, many of the studies supporting the theory of cognitive dissonance have low ecological validity. For example, turning pegs (as in Festinger's experiment) is an artificial task that doesn't happen in everyday life and as such it may be difficult to generalise the results from such experiments.

Cognitive dissonance and everyday life

If, as Festinger argues, the need to reduce feelings of cognitive dissonance are so important what can we do about these feelings in our everyday life? I guess a lot depends on the amount of dissonance experienced. Dorothy Martin must have felt a large amount of dissonance and hence she acted firmly to persuade others of her beliefs to reduce her feelings that she was the only one who believed in her prophecies. We continually produce 'little white lies' in our social lives ('You look great in that shirt'), which may cause us a little anxiety but helps maintain social relationships. Matz and his colleagues (2008) showed that our personality can help mediate the effects of cognitive dissonance. They found that people who were extroverted were less likely to feel the negative impact of cognitive dissonance and were also less likely to change their mind. Introverts, on the other hand, experienced increased dissonance discomfort and were more likely to change their attitude to match the majority of others in experiments.

It is always worth thinking about the role of cognitive dissonance in your life and considering whether you are ever lying to yourself or whether you are comfortable with your thoughts and behaviour. As Socrates wrote 'An unexamined life is not worth living.' In other words, challenge and be sceptical of any decisions or actions that leave you with an intuitive feeling that something is not quite right.

Cognitive dissonance can also be used as a therapeutic technique to try to change unhealthy attitudes and behaviours. It has been used to change eating disorders, gambling, road rage and other negative behaviours (Becker et al., 2008). With these interventions, people are asked to consider their current attitudes and behaviour and the negative costs associated with these unhealthy beliefs. People have to assess their views and examine how far these may conflict with healthy behaviours. By understanding the role cognitive dissonance plays in most of our lives, we can be on the lookout for its sometimes negative effects.

Participant observation

Another issue in the Dorothy Martin prophecy case involved the use of covert participants to gain data about what the group was actually doing on a day-to-day basis. Most psychological studies involve some observation of behaviour, whether it be observing children playing in a school playground or observing the speed of a person's reaction in a laboratory. Observation can occur as part of a laboratory study. However, when one talks of observational techniques this usually refers to a study where observation is the main research method involving the precise (objective) measurement of naturally occurring and relatively unconstrained behaviour. Moreover, the observation usually occurs in the participant's own natural environment.

There are two main types of observation:

*   Participant observation: this involves the observer becoming actively involved in the activities of the people being studied. Instead of merely observing, the psychologist can experience a more 'hands-on' perspective on the people and the behaviour being observed. They become a 'participant' in the research. Participant observation can either be disclosed (when people are told they are being observed) or undisclosed (participants remain unaware of being observed).
*   Non-participant observation: this involves the researcher observing the behaviour from a distance and they do not become actively involved in the behaviour to be studied.

The distinction between participant and non-participant observation is not always clear cut since it may be difficult for an observer to participate fully in some behaviours (e.g. criminal activities) and conversely a non-participant observer is unlikely to have no impact whatsoever on a situation. Think of the example of a football referee. Are they a non-participant or participant observer of the match? Festinger's observation team never disclosed to Dorothy Martin or her followers that they were carrying out a psychological study of the group. The observation team needed to be well accepted and integrated into the group, but at the same time they needed to avoid any acts of commitment, behaviour or proselytising that would have an undue effect on the course of the movement. There were obvious ethical issues with not disclosing the true nature of their work but to do so would have meant immediate expulsion from the group and it is difficult to imagine any other way that the data could have been gathered. If participants are unaware of being observed, issues of invasion of privacy and informed consent arise. One advantage that occurs when people do not know they are being observed in a psychological study is that there are few problems with demand characteristics. In this case there was also the problem of not influencing the behaviour of the group but not remaining so detached as to arouse suspicions as to the observer's beliefs in the prophecy. This was a difficult balance for the researchers to achieve.

Festinger and his colleagues acknowledged these difficulties in the research. The research team were able to gain an insider's viewpoint of the group and report on a great amount of rich detail that could not conceivably have been gained in another way. However the two main sources of error with such participant observation methods remain. These relate to bias and reactivity effects. All the events were reported through the viewpoint of the observation team. How can we be sure that they were not biased in their reporting of the events? If observers know the purpose of the study, they may see what they want to see. Observers need to produce reliable results. Where there is more than one observer, the observational records of one observer can be checked or correlated against another to see if they are observing in the same way. A comparison such as this is called inter-rater reliability. All the observation team made extensive notes as soon as they could about what they had witnessed – indeed some made notes in the toilet of Dorothy Martin's home during the group meetings. The collaboration of different observers ensured that the data was more likely to be reliable, although we cannot be sure that the observation team did not succumb to some element of subjectivity in their reporting.

Observers, once immersed in a group, can become sympathetic to the group of people being studied or indeed, feel alienated from the group. Either situation can lead to biased reporting. An additional problem is that because the observer is a participant in the activities and events being observed, it is easy to influence other people's behaviour, thereby raising the problem of 'reactivity' – influencing what is being observed. Again Festinger's team were most aware of this issue and tried to avoid this by being as non-committal at group meetings as possible, while at the same time successfully keeping up the pretence of being fully committed group members. There were occasions when this proved to be extremely difficult. An example of this occurred one night in late November 1954, when Dorothy Martin virtually demanded that one of the researchers lead the meeting. Needing to agree to her request, the researcher suggested 'that the group meditate silently and wait for inspiration'. Luckily in the resulting silence another member of the group acted as a medium for the first time, perhaps something that would not have otherwise occurred without the researcher prompting the silence. On another occasion, the author/research team had been informed of an upcoming meeting that they could not have known about without their insider knowledge. When they approached Martin to ask to attend any meeting around that date, Martin treated their 'coincidental' request as evidence of the supernatural.

It remains difficult to know what influence, if any, the researchers had on the group's behaviour. Medin (2013) suggests that the overall effect of the observers was perhaps 'a minor factor in the dramatic increase in proselytising after the prophesised date had come and gone' but that the research team's 'careful, balanced discussion of observer effects' was 'a model of good science'. It could be added that the validity of the reported data could have been checked against other sources of data and Festinger's results did seem to tie in with the few other items of reported material available from journalists who also took an interest in Dorothy Martin's activities at various times.

Still believing . . .

Festinger and his colleagues saw this as a case that would lead to the arousal of dissonance when the prophecy failed. Altering the belief would be difficult, as Keech and her group were committed at considerable expense to maintain it. Another option would be to enlist social support for their belief. As Festinger wrote, 'If more and more people can be persuaded that the system of belief is correct, then clearly it must after all be correct.' The Dorothy Martin case, as reported by Festinger and his colleagues, did seem to provide good evidence for the cognitive dissonance phenomenon.

No doubt disappointed by the failure of the various prophecies and worried by threats concerned with involuntary commitment in a psychiatric hospital, Martin left Chicago to live for a few years in Peru at the Brotherhood of the Seven Rays, a community established by George Hunt Williamson, another person who claimed to be a contactee for alien beings. Martin claimed that Jesus appeared to her there and cured her of cancer. Having been healed by Sanada (Jesus) and using her religious name of Sister Thedra she moved back to Arizona in 1965 and founded The Association of Sananda and Sanat Kumara. During this time, she continued to report messages from the Elders. After a brief flirtation with Mount Shasta, California, the group settled in Sedona, Arizona. On Saturday 13 June 1992, Dorothy Martin died aged 92 but the

Chapter 9

Innocence lost
The story of Genie

One day in early November 1970, a woman called Irene Wiley sought out the services for the blind at her local Los Angeles County Welfare Office. Her 13-year-old daughter accompanied her. Being completely blind in one eye, and with her cataracts causing her 90 per cent blindness in the other, Irene mistakenly led her daughter into the offices for general social services instead. This mistake was to change both their lives forever. As they approached the counter, the social worker stood transfixed staring at the daughter. At first sight, she appeared to be 6 or 7 years old with a stooped posture and an unusual shuffling gait. A supervisor was called immediately and started an investigation. Finally, after 13 years of neglect, isolation and abuse, the world had become aware of a girl who was subsequently known as 'Genie'.[1]

Family background

A key figure in the story of Genie and the person who was to spend the most time with her over the coming years was Susan Curtiss, a linguistics graduate at the University of California. Curtiss wrote and published her doctoral dissertation about Genie, and as she put it: to 'understand this case history, one must understand the family background' (Curtiss, 1977). It was hoped that by exploring Genie's family history, there might be some explanation for the almost unbelievable situation that she had found herself in.

Irene had had an unexceptional upbringing with a working and loving father and a mother who was reported as rather stern and unapproachable. One unfortunate incident in her childhood occurred when she slipped and banged her head on a washing mangle. This caused neurological damage that would later have profound effects. It would cause her blindness in one eye and make it more difficult for her to look after herself and her dependants. In her early

20s, Irene married Clark Wiley who was 20 years older than her. Although they met in Hollywood there was to be no fairytale ending to their union.

At the commencement of the second world war, Clark easily found work and proved himself an invaluable worker in the aircraft industry, so much so that he continued to work in that area after the war. Outwardly, Irene and Clark appeared happy and contented, but at home, Clark was later described by Irene as being overly protective and rather confining. Irene claimed that her life ended on her wedding day. One thing Clark was certain about was that he did not want children. Despite this, after 5 years of marriage, Irene fell pregnant with their first child. During a stay in hospital to treat injuries sustained from her husband, Irene gave birth to a healthy daughter. Within 3 months, the child was dead. The cause of death was said to be pneumonia, although it is suggested that the child actually died of exposure having been left in the garage by Clark because he could not stand her crying. Their second child died of blood poisoning soon after birth and again neglect may have been a contributing factor. Their third child John was born a healthy boy, but due to neglect developed very slowly. John was helped by his paternal grandmother, Pearl. Pearl feared that her son Clark had serious mental health issues and thus often looked after John for months at a time. On 18 April 1957 their fourth child was born. She was called Susan Wiley (soon to be known to the public as Genie). She survived a difficult birth thanks to a blood transfusion but, by this time, Pearl was too old to help with her upbringing. Irene and Clark would have to bring up their little girl as best they could. In her first year, during a routine medical examination, their daughter was described as 'slow' and 'retarded'.

A key incident at this time involved Clark's mother. Visiting her son and his family one day, Pearl was killed by a hit-and-run driver while crossing the road to buy an ice cream for her grandson, John. Clark had been very close to his mother and became very depressed soon after the incident. The guilty driver was given a probationary sentence. Clark was outraged; he believed that society had treated him badly and he started to become more and more isolated. Clark decided that he could do without such a world and that his family could do the same. He quit his job and became a recluse. Clark moved the family to Pearl's house on Golden West Avenue in Temple City, California. No-one slept in Pearl's bedroom and it was left untouched from the day that she died.

Unfortunately, Clark thought that the best way to protect his family was to also keep them at home. Clark used to sit in the evenings with a loaded gun on his lap. He thought he needed to prevent others in an evil world from exploiting their vulnerability. They were, indeed, vulnerable and they were to remain his virtual prisoners for the next decade. Neighbours reported hardly ever seeing the family. Perhaps Clark never realised that he didn't protect them from his own villainy. An evil far worse than any they might have experienced in the outside world.

Isolation

On discovery, it was found that Genie had spent virtually her entire life in a small bedroom in the house in Golden West Avenue. For most of that time she had been restrained on an infant's potty seat attached to a chair. She had a calloused ring of hard skin on her bottom from sitting on the potty for days on end. She could not move anything except her fingers and hands, feet and toes. Sometimes at night she was moved to another restraining device, ostensibly a sleeping bag that had been altered to act as a straitjacket. Genie was then placed in a wire cot with a wire cover overhead for the night.

Genie was actively discouraged from making any sounds and, indeed, her father beat her with a stick if she made any. Clark would only make barking sounds and often growled at her like a dog might. Genie's brother John, under instruction from his father, rarely spoke to her. Indeed, elsewhere in the house, her brother and mother usually whispered to each other for fear of annoying their father. Genie heard hardly any sounds in her isolation. Unsurprisingly, Genie learned to keep silent. Her visual sense wasn't stimulated either. The room had only two windows, both of which were taped up except for a few centimetres at the top to let in a little light. She could only see a glimpse of the sky in the outside world.

Occasionally, Genie was allowed to 'play' with two plastic raincoats that hung in the room. Sometimes, she was also allowed to look at edited TV pages with any 'suggestive' pictures having been removed by her father. Empty cotton reels were virtually her only other toys.

Genie was given very little to eat. She was given baby food, cereals and very occasionally a hard-boiled egg. She was fed quickly in silence by her brother so that contact with her was kept to a minimum. If she choked or spat out food, it was rubbed into her face. It's hard to imagine a more cruel and deprived existence for a young child. This regime was maintained by Clark. Soon after Genie's birth a doctor had told Clark that Genie was retarded and wouldn't live very long. He told Irene that if Genie lived for 12 years

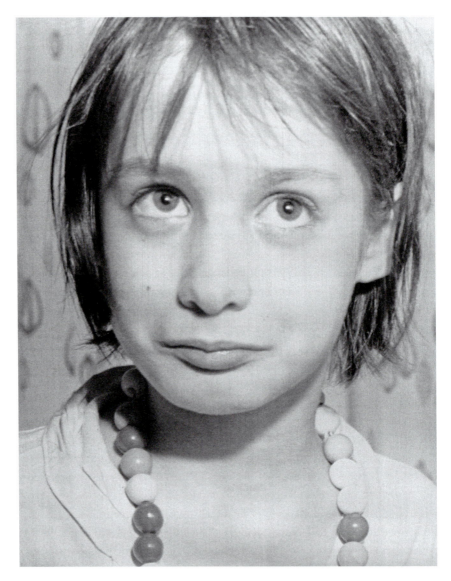

Figure 9.1 Rare photo of Genie, Susan Wiley
Source: © Bettmann/Corbis

they would seek help for her. Perhaps miraculously, Genie did live that long and when Clark refused Irene's requests for help, she decided to do something about it. After an horrendous fight during which Clark threatened to kill Genie, Irene took Genie and left home to stay at her parent's home. A few days later they ended up at social services seeking help for her visual impairment and welfare payments for Genie. Genie had been discovered at last.

Placed in care

During the ensuing investigation, Genie was taken into care in the Children's Hospital in California. Her parents were charged with wilful abuse of a minor and were due in court on 20 November 1970. On that morning, Clark took his Smith and Wesson and fired a bullet clean through his right temple. He had laid his funeral clothes out on the bed, with $400 for John and left two suicide notes – one explained where the police could find his son, the other simply read: 'The world will never understand. Be a good boy, I love you.' Irene was already in court when she heard the news. She pleaded not guilty on the grounds that she had been forced to act the way she did by an abusive husband and her plea was accepted. It seemed that, at last, Genie and Irene could begin life again. However Irene agreed that Genie should become a ward of the state.

Genie was examined at the Children's Hospital of Los Angeles and treated for severe malnutrition. She was actually 13 years old and she weighed only 59 pounds (26 kilos) and was only 54 inches tall. She was incontinent and couldn't chew solid food. She couldn't swallow properly, salivated excessively and constantly spat. Her clothes were often covered in spit and she often urinated when excited. This meant that she often smelt badly. In addition, she could not focus her eyes beyond 12 feet. What need was there for her eyes to focus beyond the distance of the world she had known in her bedroom? She had two sets of teeth and her hair was extremely thin. She walked with great difficulty and could not extend her limbs properly. She did not seem to perceive heat or cold. She never cried and could barely talk. Although she could understand some words such as 'Mother', 'blue', 'walk' and 'door', she could only say a few negatives, which were rolled into one word, such as 'stopit' and 'nomore'.

Testing times

James Kent was the Children's Hospital psychologist and he began an assessment of Genie's cognitive and emotional abilities. He stated that 'she was the most profoundly damaged child I've ever seen ... Genie's life was a wasteland' (Rymer, 1993: 40). Due to her lack of speech, it was incredibly difficult to assess her intellect. She seemed capable of expressing only a few emotions: such as fear, anger and, surprisingly, laughter. However, her anger was always expressed inward, she would scratch her face, urinate, but never make a sound.

Genie made rapid progress. Even by the third day, she was helping to dress herself and using the toilet. A few months later, she made hitting gestures at a girl in the rehabilitation centre who was wearing a dress that she had previously worn. Her observers were pleased to note that this was the first instance of her directing anger outward. Genie was hoarding various objects such as books. She seemed to be developing a sense of self. A month later, when James Kent was leaving after one of their sessions, she held his hand in order to stop him. She seemed to be developing friendships with some of her adult helpers.

Genie was subjected to various intelligence tests and she showed amazing improvements over the first few months. In some areas, she gained a year in development over a couple of months. She was able to bathe herself to the same level as a 9 year old and yet her chewing of food was at the level of a 1 year old. There was a 'scatter' in her development; some things she did well, others badly. Her level of language acquisition remained extremely poor. But she had started to engage in play with others and no longer shrank from physical contact.

She enjoyed going on day trips from the hospital. To Genie, everything was new and exciting. Generally the people she met were very friendly. She was given things by complete strangers. Curtiss hints that she felt that Genie was a powerful non-verbal communicator. Indeed, Curtiss became convinced that she was witnessing in Genie unspoken communication – a kind of telepathy.

Genie particularly liked shopping and collected 23 plastic beach buckets of different colours. She kept these by her bed. Anything plastic was coveted. It is believed that this obsession dated back to the two plastic raincoats in her bedroom. These were a major source of play; perhaps she continued to associate plastic with play.

Genie had also developed the idea of object permanence: the concept that something exists even when it remains unseen. According to Jean Piaget, children develop this at the end of the sensori-motor stage of development at about the age of two. She was also capable of deferred imitation, that is, the ability to imitate behaviour that has been seen before. She showed this by once barking like a dog that she had seen earlier in the day. Genie was also becoming less egocentric. That is, she was beginning to understand that other people could see things from another viewpoint: her way of thinking was not the only possible way of thinking. This ability characterises Piaget's 'pre-operational stage' of development from 2–7 years.

The prize

Jay Shurley, a psychiatrist and acknowledged expert on the effects of isolation was also invited to visit Genie. He described her as having suffered the most long-term social isolation of any child ever described in the literature. Rather worryingly he noted that because such cases didn't come along that often, a contest had developed among the professionals interested in Genie as to who would conduct treatment and research with her. Far from being a neglected child that no-one took any interest in, Genie had become a prize. She became the centre of a political battle among the researchers.

The researchers argued about Genie. Should her therapeutic interests be paramount above those of the scientific research? It was argued that any scientific findings could help benefit deprived children in the future.

Occasionally, Genie stayed overnight at the home of Jean Butler, one of her teachers from the rehabilitation centre. During one of these stays, Butler contracted rubella and in the interests of all concerned, Genie was quarantined at home with her teacher. Butler became very protective of Genie and began to disagree with other members of the 'Genie team' (as she referred to them). There were heated arguments as to the best way to proceed. Butler felt that Genie was being experimented on too much and that the research was intruding on her rehabilitation. The research team felt Butler wanted to become famous as the person who had rescued Genie from her isolation. Butler asked for Curtiss to be removed from the team and to no longer have access to Genie.

At this time, Butler applied to be Genie's foster parent. In the end this was rejected on the grounds that it was against hospital policy for patients to be placed in staff homes. With no obvious alternative foster parent, David Rigler, a professor and chief psychologist in the hospital's psychiatry division agreed to take Genie for a short period. The hospital policy about staff–patient relationships was overturned. Genie stayed with the Riglers for 4 years.

Unsurprisingly, Genie was not the ideal houseguest. She defecated in Rigler's daughter's waste basket, took the other children's possessions and continued to spit frequently. However, she did take a great interest in music. Curtiss played the piano and Genie loved it. She became transfixed by the music but only if it was classical. Rigler discovered that during her isolation, a neighbour

Figure 9.2 Genie was transfixed by the sound of classical music
Source: © Tetra Images/Alamy

used to have piano lessons and perhaps this was Genie's only regular source of sound as a child.

Genie was enrolled in a nursery school and then a public school for the mentally retarded where she could interact with other children. She appeared to be blossoming at the Rigler's. She showed a good sense of humour, she learned to iron and sew. She enjoyed drawing. Sometimes her drawings allowed her to depict her thoughts when her language failed her. On Gestalt drawing tests, which involve seeing the organisation behind a scattered scene or the whole picture from numerous parts, she scored higher than anyone in the literature. One day in the summer of 1972, Genie was out with Curtiss shopping. She seemed overjoyed with her experiences. Genie turned to Curtiss and said 'Genie happy'.

Meanwhile, her mother, Irene, had had her eyesight restored due to a cataract operation and had moved back to her house on Temple Avenue. She continued to visit Genie. Unfortunately, she didn't feel welcome at the Rigler's and was only invited there three times in four years. She began to distrust the scientists looking after Genie and felt that they looked down on her. She never accepted any part in the abuse of Genie, whereas many of the scientists questioned her passive role. Irene still maintained a friendship with Jean Butler who also questioned the 'scientific pursuit' of Genie. Butler claimed that Genie had actually declined in the Rigler's care.

After 4 years, a research grant that the Riglers applied for to continue to study Genie was refused. There had been little progress in Genie after the initial few months and very few academic papers had been produced. Rigler argued that the 'anecdotal' nature of his research was at odds with those of the accepted scientific community. He no longer had the funds to look after, or study, Genie. Within a month, Genie was on the move yet again.

Rather surprisingly, she was allowed to move back home to be with her mother. Here she returned to the scene of her abuse. This was not a success. Her mother could not cope and social services again moved Genie to another foster home. This was a disaster. The new parents ran their home in a military fashion quite at odds with Genie's experiences at the Rigler's and not in accordance with her needs. In response to her new home Genie regressed. Like her father, she turned inward and shut out the world. She wanted to control her life and she felt the only way to do this was to withhold her faeces and her speech. She became constipated and refused to speak at all for five months. The new foster mother became exasperated by this and once tried to extract her faeces with an ice cream stick. The abuse had started again and she had to endure a stay of 18 months with this family. Genie's life was falling apart as was the academic research.

During this time, Curtiss was the only professional to visit her. She was no longer receiving a grant for the work, but had obviously developed a warm and caring relationship with Genie. Eventually, Genie ended up malnourished and Curtiss persuaded the authorities to re-admit her to the Children's Hospital.

Financial wrangles threatened to make matters worse. Rigler presented a bill for psychotherapy he had given during the time Genie had resided with him and this amounted to more than the small inheritance Genie had been left from her father's estate. The case went to court. Although Rigler won a partial award, he claims that he never saw any of the money. He later stated that he took these legal steps merely to prevent the state from taking her inheritance. However, when Irene became Genie's legal guardian again and took over her estate, the money awarded was missing.

That was just the beginning of a series of court cases surrounding Genie. Irene became upset that Curtiss had included the label 'wild child' in the title of her book. She objected to private conversations being published without her consent. She accused the scientists of testing Genie too often in an insensitive way. She claimed that testing took 60 or 70 hours per week. Curtiss denied this and claimed that Genie enjoyed the tests, many of which were very informal. Both Rigler and Curtiss believed that Irene's friend, Jean Butler, was the real instigator of the legal suit.

After much legal wrangling, in March 1979 the court case was settled out of court for an undisclosed sum. Irene agreed that scientists might have access to Genie for particular research. Genie was to receive all income from such research and all the royalties from Curtiss's 1977 book. Indeed, Curtiss had already set up a trust fund for Genie to this effect. Virtually all the scientists involved in her case appeared to realise that they had failed Genie. The 'Genie team' broke up and went their separate ways. Many of them became disinclined to talk of their experiences. Most accepted that although their intentions had been honourable, their methods may have been flawed. Jay Shurley went further. He stated that Genie was exploited by the researchers, of which he was one. He believed that Genie was an exceptionally difficult, unique case and no-one really knew how to act for the best. There was no manual to follow.

Irene 'hid' Genie away in a home for mentally retarded adults. She never allowed scientists any further access. Curtiss, in particular, was devastated by this and to this day misses Genie. Genie visited her mother for weekends each month. In 1987 Irene sold her house in Golden West Avenue and left no forwarding address. It is believed that Irene Wiley died in 2003 in California. To all intents and purposes, Genie had vanished once more. In 2008 John Wiley gave an interview to the American news network ABC.[2] John Wiley was 56 and lived in Ohio earning a living as a painter and decorator. He had also been deeply affected by the abuse he had experienced as a child. Aged 18, John had finally run away from home when Genie had been discovered. He had been interviewed by the police in order to provide details of the case but had been largely ignored by the authorities and had never received any counselling or care from the authorities. No-one blamed John for his lack of action over his sister's abuse. Indeed, it was recognised that he was also a victim of his totalitarian father's iron will. Indeed, John was frequently beaten by his father with a wooden board. However, John stated that he did put Genie out of his mind because of the shame he felt. After leaving home, John led a troubled life including brushes with the law, a discharge from the navy and a failed 17-year marriage. His marriage produced one daughter.

John reported that he had found out that Genie was being well cared for in a good private institution in Southern California. Genie could speak some words and had relearned much of the sign language that she had been taught by earlier researchers. John has not visited Genie since 1987. There have been subsequent reports of her life inside the institution. Jay Shurley visited her on her 27th and 29th birthdays. He reported her as being chronically institutionalised, very stooped and without eye contact. She didn't speak much and appeared to be depressed. He describes her as someone who was isolated, then lived and experienced the world and all that it offers for a while, and was then was placed back in isolation again. The scientific alias given to her was more apt than the researchers could ever have imagined.

In the interview in 2008, John Wiley noticed some comparisons between the Genie case and that of Austrian Josef Fritzl who kept his daughter and other members of his family incarcerated in the cellar of his home for up to 24 years. When finally discovered, some of the family were physically malnourished with stooped statures and suffered from language deficits after years of isolation. It would be refreshing if the psychologists responsible for their future welfare could avoid some of the pitfalls that befell Genie.

Neurology

From early neurological investigations, it became obvious that Genie performed well on so-called right hemisphere tasks and extremely poorly on left hemisphere tasks. Usually, language is a task that is mainly associated with left hemisphere processing. Each hemisphere of the brain controls the opposite side of the body. This is called contra-lateral control. For example, a stroke in the left hemisphere is likely to lead to some disability on the right side of the body and vice versa.

In a dichotic listening task, people are asked to listen through a set of head-phones to two different messages, one being played to each ear. In this circumstance, the sounds presented to each ear get processed almost entirely by the opposite hemisphere. Using this technique, Curtiss could present information to a specific hemisphere. Curtiss wanted to find out what processing was occurring in Genie's brain. Curtiss found that Genie's brain was processing language on the right hemisphere, whereas usually there is a marked preference for the left. Indeed, Genie's performance on language presented to her left hemisphere was the same as children whose left hemisphere has been surgically removed. Curtiss concluded that our brain development is determined by our environment, more specifically, by our encounter with language before puberty.

Language acquisition: The unnatural experiment

The way in which humans acquire language has been a matter of much debate among both linguists and psychologists. There are, broadly, two competing schools of thought: nativists who place the emphasis on innate factors or 'nature' and empiricists who place an over-riding importance on the effect of experience or 'nurture'. Thus, language acquisition plays a part in the nature/nurture debate. One way of resolving these arguments might be to take a child and allow them to hear no language at all. Would they still develop some kind of language based on their innate abilities? Pinker (1984) later stated that language acquisition is such a robust process that 'there is virtually no way to prevent it from happening short of raising a child in a barrel' (p. 29). Of course, it is obvious that no experiment of this type could ever be conducted, but with Genie researchers felt that they might have found a 'natural' experiment. One in which the suggested manipulation of the environment had 'naturally occurred'. Her unnatural upbringing meant that researchers might be able to test out many of their hitherto untested hypotheses.

The most well-known proponent of the nativist position is Naom Chomsky. Chomsky (1965) proposed that language acquisition cannot be explained by simple learning mechanisms alone. Chomsky argues that some portion of language is innate to humans, and independent of learning. Empiricists, on the other hand, argue that language can be learned without any intrinsic or innate ability.

Nativist linguistic theorists believe that children learn language through an innate ability to organise the laws of language, but that this can only occur with the presence of other humans. Other people do not formally 'teach' the child language but the innate ability cannot be utilised without verbal human interaction. Learning undoubtedly plays a significant role since children in an English-speaking family learn English and so on. But nativists also claim that children are born with an innate language acquisition device (LAD). The major principles of language are already in place, and certain other parameters are set dependent on the particular language that they learn. On being exposed to a language, the LAD makes it possible to set the appropriate parameters and deduce the grammatical principles underlying the language, whether it be English or Chinese.

This nativist approach to language acquisition remains extremely controversial. There is evidence to support this view. For a start, all children appear to go through the same sequence of language development. A 1 year old speaks a few isolated words; a 2 year old can say a few two- or three-word sentences; and a 3 year old can produce many grammatically correct sentences. By the age of four, a child sounds very much like an adult. It's suggested that this consistency across cultures suggests an innate knowledge of language. At the age of 13, it was estimated that Genie had the language development of a 1 year old.

In addition, there is the evidence of a universal grammar structure to all languages. Indeed, languages are similar in a number of different respects. Furthermore, there is evidence that profoundly deaf children with no exposure to sign language or oral language develop manual systems of communication that mirror many of the features of spoken language. Brown and Herrnstein conclude 'one irresistibly has the impression of a biological process developing in just the same way in the entire human species' (1975: 479).

Like other innate behaviours, the acquisition of language has some critical periods. Lenneberg (1967) states that the crucial period of language acquisition in humans ends around the age of 12 years (remember, when Genie was found she was 13 years old). After puberty, the brain's organisation is complete and it is no longer flexible enough to learn language. Lenneberg claims that if no language is learned before puberty, it can never be learned in a normal and fully functional sense. This is known as the 'critical period hypothesis'. Lenneberg never took any interest in studying Genie, believing that there were too many confounding variables in her case to be able to draw any firm conclusions.

The concept of a critical period in nature is not new. Imprinting is a good example. Ducklings and goslings, given the correct exposure, can adopt chickens, people or mechanical objects as their mothers if they encounter them immediately after hatching.

Human infants less than 1 year old have the ability to distinguish the phonemes of any language (a phoneme is a category of speech sound such as /b/ for 'boy'). This ability is lost by the end of the first year. For example, Japanese children lose the ability to distinguish /l/ from /r/ (Eimas, 1975). Any child not exposed to any language prior to puberty would provide a direct test of the critical period hypothesis. Genie was one such case. Given a nurturing and enriched environment, could Genie learn language despite having missed out on the critical period of acquisition? If she could it would suggest that the critical period hypothesis was wrong; if she couldn't it would suggest that it was correct.

Many psychologists and speech therapists spent years trying to teach Genie to speak. Despite all this work, Genie never really developed language in the normal way. Although her vocabulary developed rapidly she was unable to learn syntactic constructions despite very clear instructions from her teachers.

On initial assessment at the Children's Hospital, Genie scored the same as 1 year olds; she seemed to recognise her own name and the word 'sorry'. However, she showed great delight in discovering the world around her and rapidly began to increase her vocabulary. Beginning with one-word utterances like toddlers do, she soon progressed to put two words together in ways that she would not have heard, such as 'want milk' or 'Curtiss come'. By November 1971 she sometimes put three words together such as 'small two cup' or 'white clear box'. She seemed to be showing encouraging signs of acquiring language. Genie even reported the phrase 'little bad boy' about an incident earlier in the day where a child had fired a toy gun at her. She was using language to describe past events. This continued with horrific phrases such as 'Father take wood. Hit. Cry'; 'Father angry'. She repeated such phrases over and over again. Children who reach this stage of language then experience 'a language explosion' where, within a few months, their speech develops rapidly. Unfortunately Genie did not experience this explosion.

Curtiss suspected that Genie was lazy, always shortening words or combining them. Genie earned the nickname of 'The great abbreviator'. Her speech did progress beyond simple phrases such as 'no eat bread' to 'miss have new car'. This shows she could use verbs occasionally and according to some of her speech therapists, she was acquiring some of the rules of grammar. But she never asked questions, she had great difficulty with pronouns ('you' and 'me' were interchangeable and reflected her egocentrism) and her development was painfully slow. This, in spite of intensive training using the most advanced methods. Indeed, from this point on her language acquisition stopped and levelled out.

The evidence remains inconclusive but Genie provides some evidence for the 'critical period hypothesis'. Her case suggests that language is an innate capacity of human beings that is acquired during a critical period between the ages of 2 years and puberty. After puberty, it becomes more difficult for humans to learn languages, which explains why learning a second language is more difficult than learning a first one. However, Genie did acquire some language so she showed that some language could be acquired after the critical period. Genie never managed to cope with grammar and it is this aspect that Chomsky argued distinguishes human language from animal language. From this viewpoint, Genie failed to develop language after having missed the critical period. In many respects, the argument boils down to what we count as 'language'.

The methodological problem with the study of Genie is that she wasn't *merely* deprived of opportunities to practise and hear language. She was also abused in numerous other ways. She was malnourished and suffered from a lack of visual, tactile and social stimulation. Given the crucial role of language in human interaction and development, it is almost inevitable that anybody deprived of early language stimulation would also be deprived of other opportunities for normal cognitive or social development. Genie most certainly was. How could psychologists disentangle these effects? This proved impossible to do. In the case of Genie there was also the lingering doubt as to whether she had been born with some biological or congenital retardation. Her father emphasised this throughout her early life and the paediatrician who examined Genie as an infant did mention some early problems. However, Irene stated that Genie had started to make babbling sounds and produce the odd word prior to her father placing her in isolation. This suggests that she might have been developing language at a normal speed prior to the abuse. Of course, this is anecdotal evidence and as such, cannot necessarily be relied upon. In addition, Curtiss believed that Genie was not retarded. She scored very highly on spatial tests and she developed the ability to see something from another perspective.

Susan Curtiss regarded Genie as a case that strongly refuted Lenneberg's critical period hypothesis, that natural language acquisition cannot occur after puberty (Curtiss, 1977: 37). Genie did acquire some 'language' after puberty and Curtiss claimed that Genie also acquired language from 'mere exposure' (p. 208). However, subsequently it has been reported that Curtiss appeared to change her mind fairly radically about linguistic nativism. She suggested that Genie did not provide real evidence of true language development after puberty. Separately, both Sampson (1997) and Jones (1995) detail the way in which Curtiss's discussions of Genie in later publications contradicted what she wrote in her earliest book, although no fresh evidence was available to her and no explanations for the contradictions were ever given.

Nature/nurture?

What can we say about Genie? Certainly, her father failed her, the system set up to protect children from such abuse failed her, arguably even after her 'discovery' the professionals who set out to care for her failed her. Although Genie became perhaps the most famous case study in psychology, she did not provide conclusive evidence for or against the critical period hypothesis of language acquisition. She did become a focus of debate about the ethics of psychological research and the potential conflict between the demands of the scientist and the participant. With no definitive answer as to whether she was 'retarded' at birth, she was never going to help clarify the nature/nuture debate.

Ultimately, Genie's story can be seen as a catalogue of unfortunate or mis-guided mistakes. Indeed, she might be seen as the product of man's inhumanity to man. However, her story can also be seen in a different light. Despite the abuse, the lack of care and love, despite all the suffering, mistrust and disinterest she experienced, Genie still reached out to people, touched their hearts, became fascinated in life and showed us the true depth of human forgiveness. In her own special way, Genie remains an inspiring example to us all.

Notes

1   'Genie' was a scientific alias given to protect her true identity. It was felt to be an appropriate choice since she appeared to have come from nowhere. However, even at the time of the court case newspapers reported names and addresses of those involved. It is now also so widely reported on the Internet that there would seem little potential harm in revealing her real name to be Susan M. Wiley. Indeed, her brother John gave an interview to ABC News in 2008 giving further personal details of the case. Material in this chapter has been drawn from Rymer (1993), unless otherwise indicated.
2   The interview took place on 19 May 2008. Available at: http://abcnews.go. com/Health/story?id=4873347&page=1

References

Brown, R. and Herrnstein, R. (1975). *Psychology*. Boston, MA: Little, Brown.
Chomsky, Noam (1965). *Aspects of the Theory of Syntax*. Cambridge, MA: MIT Press.
Curtiss, S. (1977). *Genie: A Psycholinguistic Study of a Modern-day 'Wild Child'*. New York: Academic Press.
Eimas, P. (1985). 'Speech perception in early infancy'. *Scientific American*, 252: 46–52.
Jones, P. (1995). 'Contradictions and unanswered questions in the Genie case: A fresh look at the linguistic evidence'. *Language and Communication*, 15: 261–80.
Lenneberg, E. (1967). *Biological Foundations of Language*. New York: John Wiley and Sons.
Pinker, S. (1994). *The Language Instinct*. New York: William Morrow and Company.
Rymer, R. (1993). *Genie: A Scientific Tragedy*. New York: HarperCollins.
Sampson, G. (1997). *Educating Eve*. London: Cassell.

Chapter 10

The boy who was never a girl
The story of David Reimer

Bruce Reimer was born on 22 August 1965, the eldest of twin boys. Eight months later while undergoing a routine circumcision, his penis was accidentally burned off. After consulting a world renowned sex researcher, Dr John Money of Johns Hopkins University in Baltimore, the boy's parents decided it was in the best interests of Bruce to raise him as a girl, to be called Brenda. This involved a proposed surgical sex change and a 12-year programme of social and mental readjustment. The case was reported in the scientific literature as an unqualified success and unbeknown to Bruce he became one of the most famous case studies in medical and psychological literature. The so-called 'twins' case allowed for a greater exploration of gender identity and the classic nature versus nurture argument.[1] Infant sex reassignments, where a child is born with ambiguous genitalia, continue to this day based, in part, on the evidence from this case. In reality, the experiment had been a total failure. On being told of his past, 'Brenda' had chosen to resume his life as a man and soon after began a new life with his wife and family in Winnipeg, Canada.[2]

Background

Ron and Janet Reimer grew up with similar rural backgrounds near Winnipeg, Canada. They were both descended from families of Mennonites, a strict religious sect rather similar to the Amish. As teenagers Ron and Janet felt restricted by their religions and in their late teens they both went to live in the city. Janet got a job as a waitress, Ron in a slaughterhouse. Honest jobs for honest hardworking people. They married on 19 December 1964 and dreamed of having twins. Just 9 months later, the dream came true. They named the twin boys Bruce and Brian. Although identical twins, Janet and Ron could distinguish between them and they found that Bruce was, by far, the more active child. The family looked forward to a contented, simple and happy life.

When the twins were about 7 months old, Janet noticed that they seemed to be distressed while urinating. She took them to the doctor and they were diagnosed with a condition called phimosis, a condition in which the foreskin is too tight and which is easily rectified by circumcision. Janet arranged for both of their circumcisions to take place on 27 April 1966. On the day of the operations, the usual doctor could not perform the surgery, so Dr Jean-Marie Huot, a general practitioner stood in. A nurse was sent to collect one of the twins for the first operation and, purely by chance, she picked up Bruce.

Confusion surrounds the exact details of the operation but it appears that an artery clamp was applied to Bruce's foreskin. Then, rather than using a scalpel to remove the foreskin, a Bovie cautery machine was used. This uses an electric current allied to a sharp cutting device to burn the edges of the incision and thus seal the blood vessels to prevent bleeding. It was unnecessary to use both a clamp and the cautery machine and, indeed, dangerous since the clamp could have conducted the electric current onto the penis. When the needle failed to cut first time, the current was increased. This time, the effects were devastating. The penis had been burned right up to the base. Bruce was fitted with a catheter and Brian's operation was cancelled.

Within 2 weeks of the operation, bits of Bruce's burned penis had dried up and flaked off until virtually nothing was left. There was no possibility of restoring the organ to its original state. Ron and Janet were told by their local hospital that the best course of action was for Bruce to have an artificial phallus fitted prior to him starting school. Phalloplasty, in the 1960s was in its infancy and so they were informed by an eminent psychiatrist that in the future Bruce would have to realise that 'he is incomplete, physically defective and that he must live apart'.

Ron and Janet returned home with the twins in a state of shock. Adding to their distress was the realisation that Brian's phimosis had cleared up of its own accord – Bruce had not even needed the circumcision in the first place. The botched operation had a devastating effect on the family. Ron told a couple of close friends at work about the operation but they joked about it and so Ron and Janet made the decision to try to keep details of the operation secret. They believed this would protect the family from ill-meaning gossip, but it also had the effect of isolating them. They became prisoners in their own house since they didn't even want to risk any childminder finding out the truth when they changed Bruce's nappy.

Figure 10.1 David Reimer
Source: © Reuters/Corbis

A possible solution?

Ten months after the operation, Ron and Janet sat down to watch a current affairs program on television little knowing that what they were about to watch would be the catalyst for an even worse chain of events. On the programme that night was Dr John Money from Johns Hopkins University in Baltimore. Money was one of the world's leading sex researchers and a charismatic and persuasive academic. On the show he announced that his group were successfully conducting transexual surgery. He argued that it was possible for an individual to successfully change gender. He claimed that assigned sex was the best indicator of an individual's future gender, far better than chromosomal, hormonal or gonadal sex. A transexual appeared on screen and stated that she was now far happier and more accepted in society as a woman. The program moved to the topic of intersex children, that is, children who are born with ambiguous genitalia. Money explained that through surgery and hormone replacements children could be raised successfully in whatever sex was assigned to them. He stated that genetic sex does not have to correspond with psychological sex (gender) (Diamond and Sigmundson, 1997; Le Vay, 1991).

Ron and Janet were mesmerised by Dr Money and they immediately wrote to him giving details of their situation. Money, realising the unique nature of the case, wrote by return of post.

Money knew the importance of this case. He had long argued that an intersex child's gender identity was not determined at birth. Money proposed the theory of 'gender neutrality' at birth. He believed that in intersex cases, surgeons should choose the most appropriate gender at birth and then through a combination of surgical operations, socialisation and hormonal treatments, the child could successfully adapt to whichever gender they had been assigned. Critics argued that this theory could only apply to a small sub-group of the population, namely, children born with ambiguous genitalia or hermaphrodites. On the contrary, Money believed that his theory of gender neutrality could be applied to *all* children (Money and Ehrhardt, 1972). Bruce provided him with a unique opportunity to 'prove' his theory. Furthermore, as an identical twin, there would be a perfectly matched control in Brian. If a normal male child could be successfully reared as a girl, it would surely show that sexuality is, indeed, undifferentiated at birth in *all* children. It would help make a major contribution to the long-running nature/nurture debate in psychology. Are we what we are because of our genetic inheritance or are we what we are because of our upbringing and environmental experiences after birth? If Money could resolve this debate in terms of sexuality, he would become one of the world's most famous and respected academics. Money couldn't believe his good fortune, it was too good an opportunity to miss.

Money immediately invited the Reimer family to Johns Hopkins University to discuss the case. At about the same time, a young graduate called Milton Diamond started his postgraduate career examining the effects of hormones on human behaviour. Diamond was working at the University of Kansas and wasn't so convinced by Money's theory of neutrality. Indeed, he believed that gender specific behaviour was pre-programmed in the womb. The Kansas team tested this by creating hermaphrodite guinea pigs by injecting pregnant females with testosterone. The resultant female guinea pigs were born with clitorises the size of penises. The key question was whether these female guinea pigs would demonstrate male or female behaviour. The answer was that the testosterone treated females acted like males by attempting to mount unaffected females. Diamond believed that they had shown that pre-birth experiences determine subsequent gender specific behaviour. In other words, in guinea pigs at least, masculine behaviour could be programmed before birth regardless of the actual sex of the guinea pig. This seemed to directly contradict the theory of gender neutrality at birth but their findings had only been tested on animals. It was unclear whether their findings were applicable to human behaviour. Diamond however was adamant that Money was wrong. He unequivocably argued that pre-birth factors were of over-riding importance for gender identity and that socialisation plays a subsidiary role. Diamond believed that while it might have been true that hermaphrodites could be successfully steered into one gender or another, the theory of gender neutrality could not apply to all 'normal' newborns. Diamond even threw down the gauntlet to Money, suggesting that to support his theory he would have to provide an instance of a normal male successfully raised as a female. The 'twins case' meant that Money could do this and unfortunately Diamond's views would be largely ignored for years to come.

From boy to girl?

When the Reimers first met John Money they immediately felt that he was someone they could work with. He was a respected and confident academic with great persuasive powers. Janet and Ron Reimer regarded him as a god and were happy to place their complete trust in him. Money explained that Bruce could be successfully raised as a girl and develop successfully as a woman. He would be able to have sexual intercourse as a woman and be attracted to men. Ron and Janet were unaware that Money was recommending a course of action that had never been attempted before with a child born as a fully functioning male. Money was impatient for the go–ahead from Ron and Janet since he believed that the gender reassignment had to take place prior to the child's second birthday. After considerable deliberation, Ron and Janet came to their decision. They believed it would be easier for Bruce to be raised as the 'gentler' sex and that the problems he would have suffered as a man without a penis would be too hard to bear. On 3 July 1967 Bruce was surgically castrated and, choosing a name with the same initial, Bruce became Brenda. The Reimers returned home with strict instructions from Money about how to bring up their daughter and they slavishly followed his advice from that moment on. They immediately let Brenda's hair grow, dolls were bought and no mention was ever made about the tragedy that had occurred. To all intents and purposes, the Reimers had two non-identical twins, a boy and girl.

To look at the twins, strangers saw two beautiful looking non–identical children. Brian with his short brown hair and Brenda with her shoulder length wavy hair. However, this difference disappeared as soon as Brenda moved or spoke. In everything Brenda did she was masculine. She would never play with the toys she had been given as a girl, she would always borrow Brian's. She would play physical games, want toy guns, play soldiers and use a toy carpentry set that Brian had. According to Brian, she would walk like a boy, sit with her legs apart and would usually win the fights that the twins had. Indeed, Brenda was described as the 'male' leader of the pair. For Brenda, this was confusing and for Brian it was also somewhat upsetting. Money dismissed all these facets of Brenda's behaviour as 'tomboyism' and continued to insist that Ron and Janet bring Brenda up as a girl.

There were other more obvious clues as to Brenda's past. Brenda would insist on standing up facing the toilet when urinating. Her kindergarten teacher noted that she was more of a boy than a girl and of course, her fellow students also noticed such differences. Brenda started to have behavioural and emotional problems at school. Despite her delicate looks (and Janet always dressed her in the most feminine of clothes) she would often end up fighting with the boys and come home covered in mud. Brenda had been given an IQ test by Money and had scored 90, placing her slightly below average intelligence, but her performance at school was much worse. Ron and Janet had never informed the school of Brenda's troubled history but to avoid her being placed one year behind her peer group they finally informed her teachers.

The struggle Brenda was experiencing at school was in marked contrast to the academic success that John Money was now enjoying. Since the 1950s, Money had argued that post-birth environmental factors were of over-riding importance for gender identity. He had cited evidence on intersex twins who had been brought up successfully as different genders and now he produced the 'twins' case to support his argument. Here, Money had two identical boys whose experiences pre-birth followed the normal male pattern and one was now living successfully as a girl. Money made no mention of Brenda's problems beyond the comment that she did express some tomboyish traits as a result of copying her brother. To Money's eager audiences around the world, the argument was over. The ultimate experiment had shown that boys and girls are made, not born.

The 'twins' case was an immediate sensation. Scientific textbooks were rewritten advocating that evidence showed that nurture was of over-riding importance in gender identity. At this time in psychology, behaviourism was the pre-eminent paradigm and Money's ideas seemed to fit well with this approach. The Women's Rights movement took up the argument suggesting that biological differences no longer explained gender differences. Surgeons and parents who had for years wondered what to do when faced with an intersex child more readily agreed to immediate genital surgery. After all, if a male child could be brought up successfully as a girl, an intersex child should have even fewer problems. The ramifications from the 'twins' case were far-reaching and Money basked in it all.

There was at least one dissenting voice in the wilderness. Diamond was still not convinced by the gender neutrality argument. He argued that the 'twins' case merely highlighted the wonderful adaptability of human behaviour, but that biology still played a central part in sexual identity. Diamond could not believe that biology did not play a key role and, indeed, there were some cases where male children born with micro-penises had been surgically reassigned as girls only to later revert back to being male at adolescence. In addition, methodological problems with Money's research were highlighted (Diamond and Sigmundson, 1997). A paper outlining these was almost prevented from being published due to Money's insistence and far-reaching influence. When these concerns were published they were virtually ignored. Money was a world famous academic and the 'twins' case was regarded as the final conclusive proof of his theory of gender neutrality. Money advocated sex reassignment surgery at birth for children born with ambiguous genitalia and this procedure was adopted in every major country in the world with the exception of China. The 'twins' case should forevermore serve as a reminder of the dangers of blindly accepting an expert's view, particularly one who is viewed as pre-eminent in their field.

Research doubts

As part of Brenda's reassignment, the family made annual visits to Johns Hopkins University in Baltimore to visit John Money. Brenda reacted with horror and fear to each visit. From the age of four, she fought, hit and kicked anyone who wanted to perform any test on her. Brian was also required to accompany Brenda and he also found the visits extremely upsetting. Gradually, it dawned on the twins that something was amiss. Why did they have to undertake such visits? Visits that none of their friends undertook. Brenda could not understand why most of the questions focussed on sex and gender. On being asked to undertake the standard 'Draw a person' test, which is supposed to help identify a child's gender identity, she drew a stick figure of a boy. When asked whom she had drawn she simply answered 'Me'. Gradually, Brenda and Brian began to realise what answers were required of them. 'Demand characteristics' refer to a situation in which a participant guesses the purpose of a study and adjusts their behaviour accordingly. This is exactly what the twins began to do and thus results reported by Money may have been contaminated by this bias. Of course, Money was aware of such methodological problems and tried to probe the twins' answers, but it must have been increasingly difficult for him to remain objective since he began to obtain the answers that he was hoping for.

One incident stands out in this respect. Money asked Brenda about a trip to a local zoo. He asked her which type of animal she would like to be if she could be changed into one. Brenda suggested a monkey. When Money asked her whether she would prefer to be a boy monkey or a girl monkey, he reports she replied 'a girl'. This was taken by Money as evidence of Brenda's gender preference (reported by David Reimer, BBC interview, 2000). However, years later David argued that he had said 'a gorilla' in answer to the question. Ignoring any deliberate misreporting by Money, this can be taken as evidence of a researcher hearing answers that they want to hear.

The twins later reported that Money presented himself in very different ways during these sessions. When Ron and Janet were present, he presented an image of the 'friendly uncle' but when they were absent he could be quite threatening towards them. It is reported that he asked the 6-year-old twins to perform simulated sex with one another. On other occasions, he showed them sexually explicit pictures to try to reinforce their gender identities. These details were later denied by Money although Money has written that such pictures can form a useful part of a child's sex education (BBC, 2000). Ron and Janet were entirely unaware of all such instances. They had to offer bribes, such as trips to Disneyland, to get the twins to continue the visits.

When Brenda was 7 years of age, Money started to talk about the possibility of having further vaginal surgery. Money argued that many of Brenda's problems occurred because she was aware that she was different to other girls. Brenda was, indeed, aware of this and could not apparently even bring herself to look between her legs. Money enlisted the help of Ron and Janet to keep up with their 'homework assignments'. These involved talking to Brenda about her genitalia and the surgery. Brenda was particularly upset since she felt that her parents were now working with John Money and against her wishes. Nevertheless, Brenda remained adamant that she would not undertake any surgery. Under extreme pressure from Money and constantly unhappy at school, Brenda eventually had a nervous breakdown.

Family doubts

At around this time, Ron and Janet were beginning to have doubts as to their original decision. They could see how unhappy Brenda was and that the reassignment did not appear to be working. But they trusted John Money; they had put their faith in him and they could see very little option but to continue with the path set out for them. Their situation was intolerable. Brian was also having behavioural difficulties. He was jealous of all the attention Brenda got and was caught shoplifting at a local store. In desperation and in need of a new start, the Reimers sold their house and moved west to British Columbia. Rather than starting afresh, the move was a disaster. Brenda became even more isolated in school, Ron became engrossed in his work at the sawmill and hit the bottle on returning home each day and Janet fell into bouts of serious depression. Janet swallowed a bottle full of sleeping pills but was saved by Ron's timely intervention. The family decided to return to Winnipeg. Brenda believed that many of the family problems were directly attributable to her and vowed to try to save her parent's marriage by becoming more feminine. However, her efforts were made more difficult by various physiological changes that emphasised her masculinity. These included a deepening of her voice and the development of more muscular features.

Brenda continued to have problems in school. She was shunned as a misfit, but managed to join a group of tomboys and develop some tentative friendships. Other classmates ridiculed her and called her 'cavewoman'. She was eventually banned from using the girl's toilet when she was caught urinating standing up. She had to sneak out to a quiet side street to go to the toilet. Brenda became increasingly troubled. Local psychiatrists were assigned to her case and became perplexed to try to reconcile the reality of Brenda with the academic reports of her that they had read written by John Money. Nevertheless, none questioned the original decision to rear her as a girl. They realised that it was now too late to do anything. They needed to persuade Brenda to take oestrogen, the female hormone, to facilitate the effects of female puberty. Brenda resolutely refused to take any such medication. The last thing she wanted was to become more feminine. Given no choice, Brenda did start to take the medication around her twelfth birthday. Even so, when the opportunity arose, she flushed the pills down the toilet. Brenda immediately began bouts of binge eating in a desperate desire that her increasing weight would disguise the effects of the oestrogen.

The local psychiatrists discussed Brenda's case. Brenda reported that she knew that she was physiologically different to 'normal' and that she had been told by her father of 'some mistake'. On further questioning, Brenda said that she thought that her mother might have beaten her between her legs. This statement appeared to fit in well with Freud's theory of psychosexual development. Freud hypothesised that boys have a sexual desire for their mothers (1905). This he called the Oedipus complex after the Greek tragedy whereby a young man unknowingly slays his father and then marries his mother. Boys realise that they are competitors with their fathers for their mother's affection. When they realise that their fathers are far more powerful than them, they suffer from 'castration anxiety', that is, the worry that their fathers will emasculate them. To avoid this, but still to impress their mothers, they adopt the behaviour of their father. That is why boys turn out like their fathers. Freud argued that girls, on the other hand, experience the Electra complex. According to Freud, when girls realise they lack a penis they suffer from 'penis envy' and place the blame for this absence on their mother. Indeed, it could be interpreted that this is exactly what Brenda had done – she placed the blame for her lack of a penis on her mother. In order to try to possess a penis, girls choose their fathers as their primary love object. Symbolically, in having sexual relations with her father, the girl may repossess the penis. According to psychoanalytic therapy, it is beneficial to recognise and try to resolve many of these issues. Of course, one of the problems with psychoanalytic theory is that any number of other possible interpretations can be placed on the situation. When Janet was told that Brenda wondered whether she had abused her, Janet was horrified. Something had to be done and Janet asked Brenda whether there was any point in continuing with their annual visits to see Money. When Brenda said no, their trip was cancelled. To the relief of everyone in the family, they never visited Baltimore again.

What was my name?

In 1979 the BBC sent an investigative team to Winnipeg and Baltimore to study the twins case as part of a film on gender identity. They contacted Brenda's psychiatrists and also spoke to Money. Although Money initially welcomed their interest, the reporters mentioned that they had spoken to other academics who were questioning the success of the case. The main critic cited was once again Milton Diamond. On being told this, Money immediately threw out the BBC reporters and wrote a threatening letter to the director general of the BBC warning of legal action and compensation claims for any harm caused to the Reimers. Ignoring this, the BBC programme was aired but did not have the expected impact among the academic community. Despite obvious criticisms, Money's reputation remained intact and his evidence on the twins case unquestioned. With no further access to Brenda, Money's direct public pronouncements on the case ceased after 1980. Money explained his reluctance to publish any follow-up on the case as due to the inappropriate intrusion of the media on the case.

The months rolled by with Brenda increasingly displaying a boy's persona. She became more and more boyish in her words, dress and actions. Brenda's local psychiatric team believed that the time was right for Brenda to be told the truth about her birth. The Reimers agreed. One day, Ron picked up Brenda from the local psychologist and offered to buy her an ice cream. Brenda feared the worse since bad news often accompanied a trip to get an ice cream. Ron started telling Brenda of her birth and the accident that followed. While Ron cried, Brenda remained dry eyed, staring straight ahead. Brenda experienced a myriad of different emotions; disbelief, incredulity and anger, but most of all, relief. At last there was an explanation, however horrific, for all the difficulties she had faced. Brenda asked one question of her father: 'What was my name?'

Immediately, Brenda decided to revert to her biological sex. The main problem was deciding how this was to be done. After all, it's not something that you can change as simply as your clothes. Such a decision was bound to attract unwelcome comment and Brenda was well aware of the hurt that gossip and innuendo can cause. Brenda did not want to revert to her former name 'Bruce' since she didn't like it. Eventually she chose David, after King David, since the name was associated with overcoming difficulties of Goliath proportions. One week after his fifteenth birthday, David made his first public outing at a family wedding. He began to have testosterone injections as a replacement for the oestrogen he had been taking and underwent a painful double mastectomy. Just before his sixteenth birthday, he had further surgery to construct an artificial penis.

The twins concocted a story that Brenda had died in a plane crash and that David was Brian's long lost cousin. The story seemed to convince some whereas others didn't want to ask exactly what was happening. Although David was far happier as a boy, there were still painful experiences for him. David couldn't stop thinking of the doctor who had performed the botched circumcision and decided to seek his revenge. He bought a second-hand gun and found out the name and place of work of Dr Huot. He went to the hospital and found his room. David entered the room with the gun in his pocket. On recognising David, Dr Huot started crying. David asked him whether he realised the hell he had put him through and left. David threw the gun into a local river where he himself went to cry.

Becoming a man

When David turned 18, he was eligible for the money that he had been awarded in an out of court claim settled by St. Boniface Hospital 16 years earlier. With a small part of his $170,000 David bought a van, which was (ironically) nicknamed 'The shaggin' wagon'. David always made excuses to girlfriends to refrain from actually having sex and often pretended to pass out as a result of too much alcohol. On one occasion, he did actually pass out and in the morning it was obvious that his girlfriend had discovered his secret. Unfortunately, having been told his full life history, she couldn't stop telling others and once again, David was the object of gossip, ridicule and innuendo. Soon after, David was discovered unconscious by his parents having taken an overdose and Janet remembers asking Ron if they ought to leave him to die in peace having suffered enough. Without waiting for Ron to answer, Janet rushed him to the local hospital to have his stomach pumped. During his recovery, David withdrew into himself and spent long periods isolated in a log cabin in a forest near Lake Winnipeg where he developed a love of nature.

The final tragedy

Near his twenty-second birthday, David had another phalloplasty and was delighted with the results. Brian's wife knew a young woman called Jane who had three children but was now a single parent. A blind date was arranged between Jane and David. The two of them were friends from the moment they met. Jane had already been told of David's troubled history and it seemingly made no difference to her feelings for him. On 22 September 1990 David and Jane were married and got on with their family life. At this time, David was described as possessing a keen sense of humour, a self-assured man who enjoyed both his work and his young family. He enjoyed outdoor pursuits such as fishing and camping and was an ardent Elvis fan. He was quoted as having accepted his past but not forgotten it. He was at last settled and able to enjoy a normal family life, one that included sexual intercourse with his wife.

David particularly resented his surgical castration, which ensured that he was unable to have children of his own. Up to 1990 David was never actually aware of how famous he was as an academically cited case study. He certainly never believed that people thought his case had been a success. On discovering this, David dropped his anonymity to try to publicise the circumstances of his case. He wanted to try to act as a warning to others who found themselves in similar situations. He went public with his story, appearing on the Oprah Winfrey show. In 2000 David even wrote to John Money asking for a meeting and an apology from him. Rather against the combative nature of the man, John Money refused to meet him.

Unfortunately, tragedy was going to strike the Reimer family once again. In 2002 Brian, who was suffering from schizophrenia, died. He had died alone in his flat and his body had lain undiscovered for three days. Although, it was suspected that suicide may have been the cause, Janet Reimer insisted that the real cause of death was a brain haemorrhage. Losing his identical twin in such circumstances had a profound effect on David. He withdrew into his grief, visiting his brother's grave virtually every day and suffered long bouts of depression. Despite a history of mental illness in the family, David seemed to blame himself for his brother's death. Brian had always received less attention than his brother and, of course, had also been lied to by his parents regarding the exact circumstances of his brother's birth. He had also been traumatised by the annual visits to see John Money and had been teased by workmates when David went public with his story. Irrationally, David blamed himself for all this. Continuing his downward spiral, David lost his job and separated from his wife Jane and, in turn, lost the close contact he had had with his stepchildren who had started to call him 'Dad'. In a disastrous business decision, David had also lost $65,000 that he had received as part of a film deal of his life from a film production company. A book about his life written by the award winning journalist John Colapinto (2000, and which much of this chapter comes from) had been a success and Colapinto had generously shared the royalties with David. However, Colapinto wondered whether these funds had enabled David to avoid getting a job and ensured that he brooded more and more about his life circumstances. Given such circumstances and taking account of his life history, it was perhaps no great surprise that early on 4 May 2004 David Reimer (38 years old) committed suicide. He drove to a local supermarket car park and then shot himself with a sawn off shotgun. Janet Reimer laid the blame for both her sons' deaths on the unusual circumstances of their upbringing.

A spokesman for Johns Hopkins University issued a statement on John Money's behalf reiterating his policy to not comment on the twins' case.

Research fall-out

Although John Money made no direct reference to the twins' case after 1980, he continued to promote the theory of gender neutrality and the success of gender reassignment surgery. This continued despite the fact that a researcher in California had shown that testosterone injections could increase penis size in children born with micro-penises. In the early 1990s Milton Diamond set out determined to find the truth about the twins' case. It remained the most influential piece of research into gender identity and fuelled rumours that all was not as reported by Money. Prof. Diamond was by now Professor of Anatomy and Reproductive Biology at the University of Hawaii. In 1994 he contacted the treating psychiatrist at Johns Hopkins University (Dr Keith Sigmundson) and discovered that Brenda had been living as a male since the age of 14.

With the help of the BBC, Diamond eventually tracked down David and (with David's consent) wrote a paper presenting evidence that David had not accepted his sex of rearing (Diamond and Sigmundson, 1997). An indication of Money's continuing pervasive influence is shown by the fact that it took two years for Diamond to secure publication for this explosive paper. Many people were upset and disbelieving of its findings and conclusions. In the paper Diamond appeared to effectively demolish many of the arguments put forward by Money. Diamond argued that individuals are not psychosexually neutral at birth and that psychosexual development is not determined by genitalia or upbringing. That is, you cannot change a child's genitalia and upbringing and expect them to successfully adopt the chosen gender. As David puts it, 'If a woman lost her breasts would you turn her into a guy?' (BBC, 2000).

Diamond cites other studies that suggest a strong neurological basis for sexual behaviour (Reilly and Woodhouse, 1989; Reiner, 1996). It is suggested that the most important organ in determining gender identity is actually the brain, not the genitals. Indeed, there have been other case studies that have reported that boys with micro-penises never doubt their correct assignment as males (Le Vay, 1991) and the case of a girl who, after declaring herself to be a boy at 14, subsequently found herself to be chromosomally male (Swaab and Fliers, 1985). An increasingly influential group called the Intersex Society of North America (ISNA) comprised of 400 intersex individuals also advocates the abandonment of genital reassignment surgery for infants. Such individuals continue to call for this change despite the fact that this causes them more distress since they are implicitly criticising their parents' decisions of many years before.

Diamond concludes that there is no known case where a chromosomal male has 'easily and fully accepted an imposed life as a female regardless of physical and medical intervention'. He suggests that chromosomally normal males should be raised as males and that surgical intervention should conform to this decision despite the greater difficulties with this type of surgery. Immediate surgery and sex reassignment as a female appears a more favourable and easier, immediate solution but it is unlikely to be so in the long term. Despite such arguments, many of Money's ideas are still followed and sex reassignment at birth continues today.

Subsequently, Money published an article detailing the reasons why David's case should not be taken as evidence for the failure of the gender neutrality theory. Despite, at one time, arguing that David provided the classic test for his theory, Money later argued that the special circumstances of the case mean that little can be concluded from it. Initially, it was thought that if a child born male could be brought up successfully as a girl this would prove the case. Now it is argued that because David was born a normal male his case can have no bearing on the thousands of intersex children born each year. It is estimated that sex reassignment surgery for intersex cases accounts for about 1,000 operations per year on a worldwide basis. Diamond questions these procedures and declares that the evidence is not there to support this. He suggests a conservative approach whereby gender assignment should follow the sex chromosomes of an individual and that surgery should be delayed until the gender preference of the child is clear. Infants should still be assigned a gender at birth but no surgery should be performed until a clear gender identity is established. Money argues that a child cannot remain an 'it' until the gender preference is clear and that gender reassignment at birth is preferable. The case did impact on Money's academic career – he took early retirement from Johns Hopkins University and died on 7 July 2006 aged 84 from complications arising from Parkinson's disease. He was briefly married in the 1950s and had no children. In his later years he refused to discuss the case, but close friends are quoted as saying that he was horrified by the turn of events.

Many parents still favour gender reassignment and give permission for surgical procedures to commence soon after birth. Parents tend to feel that they would be placing an untolerable burden on their child by leaving them with ambiguous genitalia. Money echoes this by arguing that Diamond's advice would actually wreck the lives of unknown numbers of intersex children by causing them profound psychological harm during their early years.

The tide appears to be turning in favour of more conservative treatments with intersex children and there is little doubt that had the accident occurred today Bruce would have been brought up a boy. Nevertheless, while academics continue to debate the best course of action, the life of David Reimer 'the ultimate case study' serves as a poignant reminder as to the crucial importance of the debate.

Notes

1   Much of this chapter is taken from Colapinto (2000), a fascinating book on this case, written with David Reimer's consent.
2   Although, sex and gender are often used interchangeably in the literature, here sex will refer to biological or genetic sex whereas gender will refer to which sex a person feels themselves to be.

References

BBC (2000). David Reimer's interview with BBC Horizon programme.

Colapinto, J. (2000). *As Nature Made Him: The Boy Who Was Raised a Girl*. New York: HarperCollins.

Diamond, M. and Sigmundson, H. (1997). 'Sex reassignment at birth: A long term review and clinical implications'. *Archives of Pediatric and Adolescent Medicine*, 151: 298–304.

Freud, S. (1958) [1905]. 'Three essays on the theory of sexuality'. In J. Strachey (ed. and trans.), *The Standard Edition of the Complete Psychological Works of Sigmund Freud*, 7. London: Hogarth Press.

Le Vay, S. (1991). 'A difference in the hypothalamic structure between heterosexual and homosexual men'. *Science*, 253: 1034–7.

Reilly, J.M. and Woodhouse, C.R. (1989). 'Small penis and the male sexual role'. *The Journal of Urology*, 142: 569–72.

Reiner, W.G. (1996). 'Case study: sex reassignment in a teenage girl'. *Journal of American Aademy of Child and Adolescent Psychiatry*, 35: 799–803.

Swaab, D.F. and Fliers, E. (1985). 'A sexually dimorphic nucleus in the human brain'. *Science*, 228: 1112–15.

Chapter 11

The 'Wild boy of Aveyron'
The story of Victor

On 9 January 1800 a young boy aged about 11 or 12 appeared from the woods surrounding the village of Saint Sernin in Southern France. He walked erect but could not speak and made unintelligible cries. He wore only a tattered shirt and was completely unworried by his nakedness. He entered the garden of the local tanner intent on digging some vegetables to eat when he was caught. As is the norm in such small rural villages, word quickly spread about the capture of the 'wild savage'. So began the story of the 'Wild boy of Aveyron' as he was to be known – the story of a wild child that would soon become the talk of Europe.[1]

Discovery

It was quickly discovered that the boy was not housetrained – he squatted to urinate and defecated standing up wherever he happened to be. He chose to eat only potatoes, which he would throw onto an open fire and then eat them scorching hot, usually burning himself in the process. It became clear to all that visited him in the early days (and there were many curious onlookers) that he had lived wild in the woods for quite some time and was completely devoid of any of the usual social niceties. After two days, the boy was taken to the local orphanage in Saint-Affrique where he was named Joseph.

Immediately, Joseph seemed to turn inwards and suffer from some kind of depression since it was reported that he didn't make a sound for the next two weeks. He refused virtually all food with the exception of potatoes and would only drink water. He tore up any clothes he was given to wear and would not sleep in a bed. He was described as being 4½ feet tall, having white (but tanned) skin, a roundish face, a pointed nose, dark brown matted hair and hundreds of little scars covering his entire body. In addition, he had a

41mm scar across his throat. These scars led to speculation that he had been mistreated as a younger child and/or had had his throat cut before being abandoned. His right leg was bent slightly inward, which ensured he walked with a very slight limp. All his senses appeared intact but he paid little attention to anything, with the exception of his food and sleep. The director of the orphanage realised that he had a unique case on his hands that would fascinate scholars and lay people alike. He called the boy a 'phenomenon' and wrote to Parisian newspapers suggesting that the boy be studied and taken care of by the government. The story of the 'enfant sauvage de L'Aveyron' became the talk of Paris. Here was a chance to test the philosophical theories of Jean Jacques Rousseau. In his early writing, Rousseau argued that man is essentially good, a 'noble savage' when in the 'state of nature' (the state of all the other animals, and the condition man was in before the creation of civilisation and society), and that 'good' people are made unhappy and corrupted by their experiences in society (Rousseau, 1992). He viewed society as 'artificial' and 'corrupt' and believed that the development of society results in the continuing unhappiness of man. The discovery of the 'wild child' gave people the opportunity to fully test these ideas and view a child who had grown up as nature intended without the 'unnatural' influences of society.

At this time in Paris, there was a famous institute for deaf-mutes, which was run by Roche-Ambroise Cucurron Sicard, a respected academic and an acknowledged expert in the education of the deaf. Having read about the case, Sicard wrote two letters requesting custody of the boy for scientific study. One of these letters was to Lucien Bonaparte, Napoleon's brother, who was minister of the interior in the new Republic. With such powerful friends, it was perhaps inevitable that the boy would eventually find himself the subject of intense scrutiny in Paris.

Nevertheless, the local commissioner suggested that the boy remain in the local vicinity for a short period so that the story could be checked for authenticity (there were fears it was a hoax) and that local parents who had missing children could come and see if he was their own child. During this time, he began to gradually expand his diet, eating peas, green beans, walnuts and rye bread. After 4 months he started to eat meat but appeared indifferent to whether it was cooked or raw. He used to take any leftovers out into the garden and bury them in the ground, perhaps saving them to eat later.

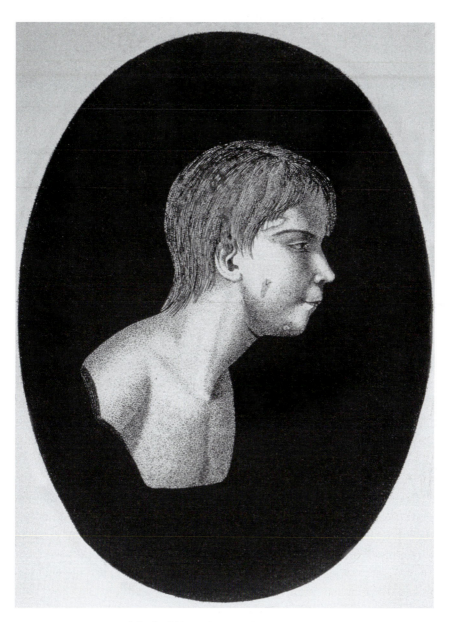

Figure 11.1 Engraving of the 'Wild boy of Aveyron'

Source: CCI Archives/Science Photo Library

The years of isolation

Further details were sought about the case. There were many intriguing questions to answer. Was the boy a child of nature? Was he a real wild child or was he an imbecile who had been abandoned a few weeks earlier in the woods? Could he care for himself in the wild? How long had the boy lived wild? Where had he lived and how?

Reports identified that a naked boy had been seen in an area around Lacaune approximately 70 miles to the south of Saint Sernin for at least the previous 2 to 3 years. He survived on roots and acorns and ran away whenever anybody tried to approach him. He was occasionally spotted moving on all fours, but was later found to only do this when very tired. The lack of marked callouses on his knees suggests that for the most part he walked upright. Apparently, peasants living in the area were aware of his existence and regarded him merely as a curiosity to be ignored. There were reports that he had once been captured in 1798 and put on show in the village square, but he had escaped and was not subsequently sighted for at least a year. However, in June 1799, three hunters accidentally came upon him and captured him. A local widow looked after him for a few weeks and taught him how to cook potatoes and gave him a shirt to wear – the same tattered shirt that he had been found in months later. After the kindness shown by the widow, the boy appeared to seek out more human contact and was frequently spotted by local farmers. He would often approach isolated farms and wait nearby for food to be given to him. One particular farmer always gave him potatoes that he would cook in the fire and then pick out and eat burning hot. After being fed, he would disappear once again into the hills to hide out in the most isolated of spots.

In effect, the farmers treated him as one might a wild animal or bird who visits occasionally. Although they recognised him as human they did not feel they should try to capture him or clothe him. He was causing them no harm and so they felt no reason to try to tame him. In those days, people were more familiar with the idea of village idiots roaming among them and the wild boy must have come into some such similar category of humanity. The boy could probably have continued to live such an existence but for some reason chose to move north up to Saint Sernin. The people there were less familiar with his presence and thus his capture was far more likely. The local commissioner spent some weeks trying to find out what had happened to the boy in the first place but there was no reliable evidence to explain how he had ended up living abandoned in the forest. Subsequently there have been many far-fetched tales associated with him having being brought up by wolves and such like, but these remain pure conjecture.

In order to further test whether he was a hoax or not, 'Joseph' was tested on a number of rather crude experiments. For example, he was given a mirror to see what his reaction would be. He saw the image of a boy but apparently did not recognise it as himself. Indeed, he tried to reach out and grasp the potato that he saw in the mirror.

There were also doubts as to whether he could have survived the harsh winters found in that area of France. Although the summers in the area were hot, winters were cold with many nights below freezing accompanied by frequent snowfalls. Furthermore, the boy seemed to dislike the cold since he chose to spend many hours curled up by the fire. To test his tolerance to cold, the boy was stripped and led by the hand outdoors on a freezing evening. He showed no hesitation and even seemed to enjoy his naked foray in the cold. It was concluded that much like a cat or a dog, he was largely indifferent to the cold but given the choice would prefer to spend time warming himself by the fire.

Further study in Paris

After 5 months in the local district, the boy had made little real progress. The people responsible for his care were discouraged and suggested that he was still more of an animal than a human. It was decided that the best solution would be to send him to Paris for further training. Unfortunately he caught smallpox on the journey to the capital and this delayed his arrival, but eventually his stagecoach arrived outside the Institute for Deaf-Mutes sited in the Luxembourg Gardens on 6 August 1800. He was immediately handed over into the charge of Sicard. For the first two weeks, Sicard was so busy with other work that Joseph was virtually abandoned once more. Joseph had grown quite fat by now, loved to be tickled and was often found laughing, although no-one could be sure what he was actually laughing at. However, these apparent signs of progress were tempered by less promising behaviour. Joseph would still not use a toilet but would go outside and perform his bodily functions without any modesty. He was interested almost exclusively in eating and sleeping. Indeed, it was reported that 'his entire being was focused in his stomach'. He paid virtually no attention to anything around him and took no interest in anything either; he had become almost completely apathetic. He actively avoided other children at the institute but was never mean or nasty towards other people.

There are conflicting reports at this time as to whether Joseph was allowed free rein in the Institute. Some reports suggest that he was left almost entirely to his own devices and that he never tried to escape (which must have been possible for him), and others report that he was frequently chained around the waist in order to prevent his escape attempts. Whichever was the case, nothing seems to have been done for Joseph for 3 months, during which time his condition deteriorated. He began soiling his bed again and started to self-harm and bite and scratch his helpers. He was often visited by curious members of the public who managed to bribe the attendants in order to view 'the wild child'. Joseph was continuously pestered by these onlookers and wandered the corridors and garden in the institute in a pitiful state. Sicard the great educator appears to have ignored his charge. From being the talk of the nation, Joseph became a forgotten and abandoned child once more. It is surmised that Sicard decided that Joseph was a hopeless case beyond help and that by attempting to treat him he risked ruining his own great reputation. A further commission was set up to systematically measure and ascertain Joseph's abilities. Its conclusion was the same as Sicard's. Joseph was an 'idiot', reduced to animal instincts from his time in the woods and nothing could be done for him.

If such a child was discovered today (as in the case of Genie in Chapter 9) the child would be the subject of a whole battery of psychological tests to try to work out what deficits they had and what the possible causes were. There might have been an 'organic' cause, in which the deficits occur due to a physical cause such as brain injury, or a 'functional cause' where there is no obvious physical cause. A functional explanation would suggest that environmental circumstances resulted in the deficits whereas an organic cause would suggest a deficit at birth. In many respects, these differences mirror the nature/nurture argument discussed in relation to the case of Genie. Was Joseph born with an 'organic' problem or were his problems the result of his restricted upbringing? Given the scarcity of reliable information in the case, there can be no definitive answer to this. However, apart from the scar on his neck, which suggested that he had either scratched himself very severely in the wild or that someone had tried to cut his throat before abandoning him in the wild, there were no signs of physical injury. In 1967 Bruno Bettelheim examined this case and concluded that Joseph probably suffered from a form of autism, although it was impossible to establish whether he was born with the condition (and that this contributed to his abandonment) or whether he developed it during his years of isolation. However, other distinguished experts in the field consider it unlikely that either an autistic boy or an idiot would have managed to survive alone in the woods for 5 or 6 years. Indeed, it could be argued that a pre-adolescent boy who managed to survive alone in the woods for that many years must possess a remarkably *high* level of intelligence (it is, of course, recognised that autistic individuals can be very intelligent).

Hope

With his life going nowhere, hope arrived for Joseph in the autumn of 1800 in the shape of a new doctor who was recruited to the institute – his name was Jean-Marc Gaspard Itard. Itard immediately took an interest in Joseph and began to watch his behaviour closely. Itard obviously saw some promise in the boy that the other academics had not and started a programme of assessment and training with him. Itard secured an apartment within the institute that enabled him to work ever more closely with Joseph. Itard was an enthusiastic and young doctor who was open to new ideas and innovative methods of treatment. With no family of his own, he devoted his entire life to his work and eventually on his death left his money to benefit future generations of deaf-mutes at the institute. Itard unofficially became Joseph's foster father and devoted more and more time to the boy. In some respects, Itard was challenging the diagnoses of his mentors. In contrast to Sicard, Itard believed there was some hope for Joseph and to Sicard's credit he was willing to allow Itard the chance of proving him wrong. Itard believed that people were the product of their environment and so assumed that it was possible to re-educate Joseph given the appropriate circumstances. If this could be done, then the 'blank slate' or 'tabula rasa' theory of human development would gain support. This theory suggests that infants are born with very few innate capabilities and that development occurs almost exclusively as a result of environmental influences. It is very much the 'nurture' side of the traditional nature/nurture philosophical argument.

Itard recognised that he couldn't devote all his time to Joseph. He felt it was essential to secure help from another adult who could also become a surrogate parent. Madame Guerin lived with her husband at the institute. Her husband worked on the gardens and they both lived in a small apartment near the kitchens that happened to be directly below the room allocated to Joseph. The Guerins were both in their 40s with grown-up children who no longer lived with them. Madame Guerin was a kindly and sympathetic person with great compassion who was entirely undaunted by Joseph's strange behaviours. She was recruited as another surrogate parent by Itard and, remarkably, devoted the next 27 years of her life to Joseph. Joseph began to spend most of his time with Madame Guerin; she fed him, clothed him, nursed him, took him on trips out of the institute and looked after every one of his often unique needs. Given such a close relationship, any credit for the improvement in Joseph's behaviour was shared by both Itard and Madame Guerin.

Rehabilitation

Itard designed a therapeutic program for Joseph with the express purpose of improving both his physical abilities (speech and thought) as well as his social interactions with others. Together Itard and Madame Guerin started to improve the care that Joseph had experienced since arrival at the institute. They gave him a freer rein in his activities. He loved to go for walks in the surrounding fields, particularly in bad weather, and he always chose to go to bed when it got dark. Often during the night of a full moon he would stand and stare at the countryside for hours on end out of his bedroom window. Like many so-called 'wild children' he also enjoyed snow. One morning he showed his pleasure at finding snow on the ground by going and rolling in it while laughing joyously.

During his first miserable months at the institute, Joseph had shown little interest in anything except food, he had never responded to any sounds except those connected with food and despite his wretched life he had never been known to cry. Itard decided that just as young children benefit from water play with a daily bath, Joseph should have a hot bath on a daily basis. The regime seemed to have an immediate effect. He appeared to look forward to the baths and enjoyed pouring water over himself. Gradually he began to refuse to get into a bath if it wasn't hot enough and thus appeared to have learned a dislike of the cold. This had two effects; first, he stopped wetting his bed at night and he began to put on warm clothes to suit the temperatures found in mid-winter Paris. Other improvements were immediate. Joseph began dressing himself and started using a spoon to get his favourite food, boiled potatoes out of the hot pan. Itard suggests that his sense of smell started to develop and, remarkably, he saw Joseph sneeze for what he believed was the first time ever. Although Itard could not have been certain of this, the startled response from Joseph supports the idea that he had never sneezed before. Joseph also started to become quite fastidious about his food. After years of living wild in the most filthy manner imaginable, Joseph became somewhat obsessive about dirt.

He refused plates of food if he thought there was anything even slightly amiss with them. Joseph also started to catch colds and other minor ailments and Itard declared ironically that the civilising process was working!

Itard also set about developing Joseph's mental faculties. As was the case with Virginia Axline and her treatment of Dibs almost 200 years later (Chapter 13), Itard placed a great deal of importance on the role of play in developing Joseph's intelligence. However, Itard was disappointed by Joseph's lack of interest in many of the toys he was given and, indeed, Joseph often hid or destroyed them when given the chance. One game he did enjoy involved hiding objects under upturned cups and then mixing up the cups to see which one contained the object. Initially, to gain his interest, Itard used a chestnut that Joseph would then eat. Joseph soon became extremely skilled at following the moves, again suggesting that an untapped level of intelligence lay beneath the surface.

One day, Itard took Joseph out into the countryside on a two-day trip in a horse drawn carriage. In marked contrast to his lack of interest in the views on his trip to Paris some months previously, Joseph seemed ecstatic to be out in the woods and fields once again. He jumped from side to side soaking up the images of the countryside as it fled past. Itard was so worried by this re-found interest that precautions were made to prevent his escape back into the wild. On his return to the institute, Itard reported Joseph as being more troubled than ever and vowed to never take him back into the countryside again. Madame Guerin continued to take him on daily walks in the next door garden of the observatory and Joseph settled down again to some routine approximating family life. Madame Guerin reports that he was generally happy.

Learning to communicate

Of course, Joseph still did not communicate with anyone. Despite being able to hear, he paid no real attention to any sounds bar the occasional response to an unexpected noise or strange tone of voice. He made no real sounds beyond some suppressed cries, but he did laugh. Itard knew that Joseph could hear because if he heard voices he could quickly work out where they were coming from and run away in the opposite direction to hide. He also seemed particularly responsive to the sound 'O'. For that reason, Itard proposed renaming Joseph with a name that ended in this sound. From then on he was called Victor (pronounced *VicTOR* in French with the emphasis on the second syllable) and whenever he was later called by name he did acknowledge it.

Despite some improvements in hearing there was no noticeable improvement in Victor's speech. After various experiments, it was concluded that he was capable of producing speech and that his slit throat had not affected his vocal chords. Itard spent many frustrating months trying to encourage Victor to speak. Victor would mainly drink water (*eau* in French) and milk (*lait*) so every time he was given water or milk they pronounced the appropriate word over and over again hoping that he would associate one of his favourite sounds with the drink. After hundreds of such trials, Victor did indeed articulate the word *lait* when milk was poured but despite Itard's efforts he never said the word *before* he received milk only on *presentation* of the milk. Itard concluded that Victor never really grasped the word's true meaning; he had simply associated the sound with the drink. Despite Itard's disappointment, Victor did make some progress with spoken language. He began to copy Madame Guerin's common saying 'Oh God' (*Oh Dieu*), at least to the extent that it was recognisable as such. Itard also proposed that Victor's actions were so highly expressive by this time that he had little need for speech. Victor had little difficulty in expressing his wishes: pointing to the outside meant he wanted to go for a walk and getting out his cup meant that he wanted milk. If visitors bored him Victor would go and get their gloves and hat to hasten their departure. Which words could be clearer than that!

Despite housing about 100 deaf-mutes who used sign language to each other on a daily basis there is no evidence that Victor was given any training in this 'action' language. Modern speech therapists have argued that Victor might have readily responded to such teaching. Itard gave no indication why this path was not chosen but instead developed another method of teaching that involved hanging objects beneath simple line drawings representing them. Itard would then take down the drawings and Victor would replace them beside the appropriate object. Victor soon managed to learn what was required of him even if the objects were moved around the room. Victor was definitely developing the capacity to 'compare and contrast' objects and drawings. The next stage was to get Victor to distinguish colours and shapes using a similar procedure in which coloured pieces of paper of various shapes were fastened round Victor's bedroom. Again, Victor quickly managed to group the paper cut-outs by both shape and colour. Itard pressed on, making the tasks more difficult day by day. Rather than finding it a challenge to be overcome, Victor appeared to get increasingly frustrated by this. It became almost a battle of wills between the two of them, with Itard forcing the pace and Victor becoming ever more frustrated at being asked to perform tasks that he clearly thought were beyond him. Victor's usual response was to fly into a rage and throw objects around the room. Eventually one day Victor became so enraged at the task he was asked to do that he started to bite the fireplace, throw burning coals around the room and have an epileptic fit, which resulted in him losing consciousness. At this point, Itard backed off from these tasks, but this resulted in Victor having more frequent attacks at the slightest frustration. Itard became very worried for Victor. He wondered whether Victor was beginning to have the fits as a remedy to any frustrations. The fits were becoming a learned habit as a form of self-protection. Itard decided to take drastic action. One day when Victor was just beginning to show the initial signs of having a 'fit', Itard grabbed him by the hips and dangled him out of the fifth floor window head first. After a few seconds he pulled him back inside and Victor stood there trembling, pale and in a cold sweat. Itard made him pick up his work that he had thrown around the room and then Victor lay down quietly on his bed and cried. It was the first time Itard had seen him cry. This threat from Itard had a remarkable effect and the now 'tamed' Victor continued with his work with far less resistance and his full-scale tantrums never returned.

Over the next few months, Itard reports that Victor learned to spell simple words and to understand that words stood for 'objects'. Sometimes he even carried around letters with him to spell out his needs. Itard was excited by the progress shown by Victor. Itard developed a mantra 'education is all', arguing that with love, patience and understanding and the systematic use of rewards and punishments human beings are capable of quite remarkable feats. Psychologists might compare some of Itard's methods to 'operant conditioning' techniques, which, put simply, means 'learning through the consequences of one's actions'. But Itard predominantly adopted a sympathetic, humane approach that recognised the individual needs of Victor. Perhaps a more appropriate comparison of his individually tailored learning methods would be to what we now call 'special education'.

Victor obviously valued both Madame Guerin and, perhaps to a lesser extent, Itard. There are some stories that tell how Victor cried for long periods when he knew he had upset her. Itard also reports going to his bed before he was asleep and being welcomed by hugs, laughter and kisses before being invited to sit on the bed with him. It had taken Itard nine painstaking months to get to this stage; but he had certainly made some noticeable progress with Victor against all the perceived wisdom at the time.

Figure 11.2 One of Victor's greatest achievement was his ability to spell out the word *lait* on presentation of milk

Source: © Shutterstock

Development of other faculties

Itard decided to continue to try to develop some of Victor's faculties, including his hearing, speech and taste. Itard developed a method whereby he blindfolded Victor to see if he could discriminate different musical sounds and words. Despite Victor's ability to make such discriminations and the fact that his hearing was intact, after months of teaching, Victor had only managed to make minimal progress. This involved learning a few simple monosyllabic words to identify anger or friendship. Itard became dispirited and began to reassess Victor's progress. Victor had gained the ability to spell out the word *lait* on presentation of milk and this was hailed as his greatest cognitive achievement. However, Itard noticed that he only used the word on *immediate* presentation of milk. As with his speech, he could not detach the word *lait* from the presence of milk; in other words, he couldn't use the word *lait* to indicate that he wanted milk. Itard concluded that without this Victor could not be said to possess real language capacity. Itard also discovered that Victor could not imitate. He set up two blackboards side by side and tried to get Victor to copy his movements, Victor found it impossible. This inability to imitate must have severely affected his learning capacity and also tells us something of his capabilities. Many non-human animals can imitate behaviour successfully and yet Victor could not.

However disheartened Itard was over this discovery he did not give up on his teachings with Victor. He began sending Victor out of the room to fetch objects that he had put in other rooms. After a lot of training, Victor could go to another room and collect as many as four objects, which Itard had shown him on cards. This was reported as a clear sign of the development of cognitive ability, but later Itard sent Victor to a room and asked him to collect a book. Despite the room having many books in it Victor could not link the word 'book' with *any* book, only the *specific* book that he had associated the word with in the first place. He could not generalise the words on the cards presented to him with any object, only one specific object. Again Itard reports this as an incredibly dispiriting result, so dispiriting in fact that Itard called him a useless being. Despite not understanding a word that he said, Victor must have sensed the tone of the message, closed his eyes and started sobbing. Itard went and hugged Victor as any father might and he reports that this physical moment of contact between boy and man helped their working relationship in the months to come. Eventually, Victor did learn to generalise that one word could represent many similar objects and, in fact, started generalising too much confusing the word 'brush' for 'broom', 'knife' and 'razor'. Despite setbacks, progress, albeit slow, was being made.

Victor began to learn more and more nouns (room, person) and started to combine them with simple adjectives (such as big, small) and also verbs (such as touch, drink). Victor even managed to write simple words that were legible, and Itard reported that by the end of 1803 he could communicate through writing and reading in a very basic and crude way. By this time, Victor had learned to imitate behaviour, so Itard spent months trying to get him to form the shapes of sounds with his mouth in order to facilitate his speech. Itard spent months trying to do this but in the end he abandoned any such attempts and concluded that he would never be capable of spoken language. Itard had to accept that no amount of training could overcome his early deficits and led Itard to question whether environmental influences (5 years of training in this case) could overcome either nature or early environmental influences.

Civilised or wild?

So was Victor now a civilised, mute child or was he still basically the wild child that had been found all those years ago near Saint Sernin? Victor never lost his immense enthusiasm for the beauty of nature – the sight of a full moon on a still summer evening could leave him in raptures and he continued to adore his daily walks with a fierce passion. Such behaviour could be interpreted in different ways – were these responses an indication of the remains of the wild child within him or did he now recognise, as a result of the civilising process, the beauty of nature?

Victor continued to live with the Guerins and seemed keen to contribute to the running of the household. He made himself useful by performing small chores such as chopping wood and laying the table. One day, Monsieur Guerin fell ill and a few days later died. The day he died, Victor set his place at the table as usual. On seeing this, Madame Guerin burst into tears. Realising that his actions had caused the tears, Victor removed the table setting and never laid it again. Such actions suggest that he was developing emotional maturity – he could understand another's feelings and empathise with them. Soon after Monsieur Guerin's death, Madame Guerin became ill and could not look after Victor. As a direct result of this, Victor escaped from the institute and was found by local police in a nearby village. It took 2 weeks for him to be identified and returned to the institute. On being reunited with the now recovered Madame Guerin he was ecstatically happy – he was reported as being like a son being returned to his affectionate mother.

Soon after this incident, Itard decided to test Victor's sense of justice. Rather cruelly, he decided to punish Victor unfairly as a test of his understanding of right and wrong. One day after Victor had been working well at his books for quite some time, Itard suddenly rubbed out his writing, grabbed him and started to drag him over to a wardrobe where he occasionally confined him as a punishment. Victor immediately physically resisted the punishment and indeed bit Itard's hand so hard that it left toothbites. Itard had never known Victor to resist in such a way given that on all previous occasions the punishment had been justified. Itard was delighted – he reports that the pain from the bite brought joy to his heart – the act of legitimate retaliation was proof that Victor understood and had a sense of justice and injustice – right from wrong. To Itard this was evidence of a civilising effect and a sign of Victor changing from a boy to a man. Victor was so sure of his sense of right or wrong that he would go so far as to challenge the authority of his teacher.

At this time, Victor was approximately 17 years old and Itard was anticipating a marked change in his behaviour due to puberty and an interest in all matters sexual. Victor had led a life of isolation away from the other children in the institute and had had no peers in which to guide his sexual conduct. Given no such guidance from Itard or Madame Guerin he must have been at a complete loss at what to make of his developing sexual desires. It was reported that he caressed women, hugged them and sometimes grabbed them to his neck but these behaviours must have been extremely embarrassing affairs for the women concerned and confusing for Victor. Indeed, he often fell into foul moods as a result of such interactions. Itard and Madame Guerin arranged special diets, cold baths and lots of exercise to ease the effects of puberty and after some time it seems that Victor gave up with his efforts towards the opposite sex.

The end of his training

By 1805 Itard had been training and teaching Victor for 5 years. It is probably fair to surmise that both Itard and Victor were fatigued by their efforts and they needed a break. Madame Guerin was given official charge of Victor in 1806 and a salary of 150 francs a year to look after him. In 1810 Sicard wrote a report about Victor detailing that his original diagnosis of 'complete idiocy' had been correct and that virtually no progress had been made in the case. This seems unfair to both Itard's and Victor's efforts and achievements and also to have hastened Victor's exit from the institute. By 1811 the institute had become an all-male establishment and the administrators felt that Madame Guerin should leave her residence within the grounds and find a house nearby. They also believed that Victor was a hopeless case and was a disturbing influence to other children. Madame Guerin was given an additional 500 francs to facilitate their move and she moved with Victor into a small house on the Impasse de Feuillantines just around the corner from the institute. One purpose of this was to be close by so that Itard could continue to work with Victor if he wished. However, for reasons that are not clear, this did not happen and Victor became a forgotten man once more.

There are very few reports about Victor's or Madame Guerin's lives after leaving the institute. We know that Victor continued to live with Madame Guerin and there is no record of him causing any problems or scandals. It is reported that people recognised him by his limp. We don't know what he did with his life or whether he managed to earn any living. Being mute, this would have been a difficult task but Madame Guerin's annual salary would have kept them from being penniless. Victor died in 1828 at the age of 40, not an old age even in those days. There are no documents that detail his cause of death or place of burial. Victor Hugo lived just four doors away for 2 years but there are no clear-cut references in any of his writings to the wild boy's existence, suggesting that he kept himself very much to himself. The fact that he continued to live in the back streets of Paris suggests that he did not miss his former life in the deepest countryside.

Itard continued to work at the institute and developed a number of teaching techniques used successfully with deaf-mutes, which were evolved from his work with Victor. Itard pursued a successful career and became a respected and acknowledged expert with the deaf. At the end of his career, he worked with an up and coming academic called Edouard Seguin. Seguin was hugely impressed by Itard's approach and later on developed special education programmes for the mentally retarded. Maria Montessori, an Italian psychiatrist, was, in turn, influenced by Seguin and founded Montessori schools, which even today use cut-out shapes and letters in the classes in a similar way to Itard with Victor. Both Montessori and Seguin acknowledge their debt to Itard (Lillard, 2011). There have also been criticisms of Itard's approach (Kanner, 1967). Although he did not do it deliberately, Itard placed Victor in an isolated environment away from his peers. This excluded him from a potentially vital form of peer learning and an important form of social interaction. It seems Victor was destined to spend his entire life in some form of restricted isolation. It is also argued that Itard should have attempted to teach Victor sign language. It is unclear whether this would have been successful, but it has been so in other subsequent, but less profound cases.

Success or failure?

So what can we conclude from the case of Victor? Case studies of wild children such as Victor should make an important contribution to the nature/nurture debate. But as has been found with other subsequent case studies, there is always the confusion as to whether deficits were present at birth or as a result of their period of isolation. In Victor's case, there are conflicting views. The idea that Victor was born an idiot (to use Sicard's description) incapable of showing any real progress can be largely discounted. Victor did make progress with Itard and to survive alone in the woods for the period of time he did without capture would surely have required a ready and quick intelligence.

Alternatively, Victor may have suffered from some psychological deficit or abuse prior to his abandonment and his physical and mental capabilities may have been affected as a result of his years of isolation. It remains unclear which of these two explanations holds the most weight. Itard believed in the latter and spent almost 5 years of his life trying to surmount the effects of the isolation. It remains a contentious judgement as to whether he was successful or not since we cannot imagine, let alone prove, what the effects of 7 years of living alone in the wild would do to a young child. Additionally, with no base level of assessment of Victor's abilities it is impossible to measure the actual improvement. Evidence suggests that Victor was not born an 'idiot' but that he may have had some special needs, such as a form of autism. There are many different types of autism but generally it is a developmental disability that significantly affects both verbal and non-verbal communication and social interaction. The period of isolation certainly had a profound effect on his physical, emotional and social development. It is clear that childhood is a critical period for the learning of many skills, not least language, but that some of these deficits can be overcome as a result of intensive training later. The story of Victor is one of the most famous case studies (along with Genie) of a deprived child.[2] There are many other children recovered from the wild, girls as well as boys, and these individuals provide further evidence of the effects of a deprived childhood and the lack of normal socialisation. They range from a child brought up by dogs (found as recently as 2004 in Siberia), to a boy who was found living with ostriches in 1945![3]

Many of these case studies have fuelled the debate about what it is to be 'human'. Although all of us are born and could be categorised as 'homo sapiens', there is something more that is required before one can be really said to possess all the characteristics of what we mean by the term 'human being'. Babies are born with great potential but need a nurturing environment in order to learn to be 'human'. Children who are deprived of this through early isolation and abuse find it extremely difficult, if not impossible, to overcome the effects at a later stage. The story of Victor illustrates this all too clearly.

A postscript of the success (or otherwise) to the 'Wild boy of Aveyron' case was penned by Itard himself 20 years later (Itard, 1962). Itard reported that

> a large proportion of my days for six years was sacrificed to this demanding experiment. The boy . . . did not gain from my attentions all the advantages I had hoped. But the numerous observations I was able to make, the instructional procedures . . . was not entirely lost, and later I put them to

more successful use in dealing with children whose muteness arose from less insurmountable cases.

Notes

1   Material in this chapter has been drawn from the two most comprehensive (and recommended) books devoted to this single case study: Shattuck (1980) and Lane (1976). The latter includes detailed verbatim accounts of the case.
2   The case of two girls called Amala and Kamala found living with wolves in India in 1920 is perhaps equally famous and is reported in Candland (1993).
3   Further amazing stories about wild children can be found on the comprehensive website http://feralchildren.com

References

Bettleheim, B. (1967). *The Empty Fortress*. New York: Free Press.
Candland, D.K. (1993). *Feral Children and Clever Animals: Reflections on Human Nature*. Oxford: Oxford University Press.
Itard, J.M.G. (1962) [1801, 1806]. *The Wild Boy of Aveyron*. Trans. G. Humphrey and M. Humphrey. New York: Appleton-Century-Crofts.
Kanner, L. (1967). 'Medicine in the history of mental retardation'. *American Journal of Mental Deficiency*, 72(2): 165–70.
Lane, H. (1976). *The Wild Boy of Aveyron*. Cambridge, MA: Harvard University Press.
Lillard, P.P. (2011). *Montessori Today: A Comprehensive Approach to Education from Birth to Adulthood*. London: Knopf Doubleday Publishing Group.
Rousseau, J.-J. (1992). *Discourse on the Origin of Inequality*. Trans. D.A. Cress. Indianapolis, IN: Hackett Publishing Co.
Shattuck, R. (1980). *The Forbidden Experiment*. London: Quartet Books.

Chapter 12

Two little boys

The story of Little Albert and Little Peter

The history of psychology is littered with academics contesting the merits of their respective theories with which they seek to fully explain all facets of human behaviour. One such academic, called J.B. Watson, proposed a scientific, objective psychology of behaviour called 'behaviourism' (Watson, 1913). Watson argued that learning should be studied without any reference to internal mental processes. He rejected the idea of introspection and put the focus on observable behaviour and how an organism (human and/or animal) learns through adaption to their environment. The emphasis was placed very much on 'nurture' in the classic nature/nurture philosophical argument. Ivan Pavlov in Russia had already shown the effect of conditioning on simple behaviours such as the salivation response in dogs, but Watson suggested that more complex human behaviours might also easily be conditioned (Asratyan, 1953). In order to test this hypothesis, he decided to take an 11-month-old infant and try to condition a fear response in the child, one evoked from a previously neutral stimulus. So began one of the most cited case studies in the history of psychology: the testing of Little Albert.

Background to the study

John Broadus ('JB') Watson originally started his research into learning in (non-human) animals but by 1916 had turned his attention to human infants. Initially interested in the use of conditioned reflexes as a method of testing the senses in infants, he started to write about the conditioning of human fears. He had noticed his children's seemingly unlearned fear of thunder and lightning and began to consider methods by which he might condition such fears in a laboratory experiment. His first attempts to inhibit a child's reaching response to a lit candle had taken over 150 trials (mainly, he argued, because he had to stop the child burning their hand severely), and thus this was not a particularly exciting demonstration of the power of conditioning.

Although no-one is certain exactly when the Little Albert study took place it seems clear that it took place around the Christmas of 1919; publishing his results in 1920 with his assistant Rosalie Rayner (Watson and Rayner, 1920), Watson suggested that the complex range of human emotions shown by adults must be the result of learning through one's environment. They set out to demonstrate this in an experimental demonstration with an 11-month-old infant they named 'Albert B.'. Albert was described as a 'normal' child, well developed for his age with a phlegmatic character described as 'stolid and unemotional'. He had been chosen by Watson and Rayner for the study because he was readily available for study (his mother was a wet-nurse at a local home for invalid children) and because being such a strong and stable character, they felt he would come to 'relatively little harm' as a result of the study. The use of such phrases suggest they were aware at the outset that *some* harm might befall him.

At the age of 9 months Albert was put through a battery of emotional tests. He was also shown a white rat, rabbit, dog, monkey, face masks, cotton wool and a burning newspaper to see his reactions. His responses to these stimuli were filmed and at no time did he show fear in any of the situations. During the testing, it was noticed that he very rarely cried. Watson and Rayner needed to test his fear reaction and thus had to devise a method of inducing fear in him. Possibly drawing on his own children's reactions to thunder, Watson developed a technique in which one of the researchers, without warning, struck a hammer on a 4-foot long steel bar suspended just behind and out of Albert's view. This procedure had the desired effect. Albert immediately showed distress to this unanticipated unpleasant sound; his breathing became stilted, his hands were flung upwards and his lips trembled. By the third stimulation, 'the child broke into a sudden crying fit'.

Questions to consider

In their journal article, Watson and Rayner state that they then spent 2 months hesitating over the procedure to adopt in their study. They were clearly worried about the possible effects of their experiment on Albert. Nevertheless, they decided that many of the fear reactions they were going to induce may have occurred naturally in the normal 'rough and tumble of the home'. So with Albert, now aged 11 months and 3 days they began their series of groundbreaking experiments.

The questions that they set out to test were: could they condition fear of an animal by visually presenting it at the same time as striking the steel bar? Would any such conditioned emotional response transfer to other animals? How long might such a response last? And further, what methods might be devised for removal of the response if it did not extinguish immediately?

As a test of the first question, they presented Albert with a white rat from a basket. Showing no fear, Albert reached out for the rat with his left hand and just as he touched the rat, they struck the steel bar with the hammer behind his head. He jumped violently and buried his face in the mattress. After a short period of time, he again reached out for the rat and the procedure was repeated. Albert fell forward and began to whimper. Watson and Rayner reported that 'in order not to disturb the child too seriously, no further tests were given for one week'. Exactly 7 days later the rat was presented without sound. With Albert making no attempt to reach for the rat, they moved it closer. Albert instantly withdrew his hand. It was clear that Albert's behaviour had been modified after only two presentations and that this effect had lasted a week. They gave Albert building blocks to play with to check that he had not been conditioned to fear any such objects given to him and he showed no fear, playing with them in the usual way. The blocks were then cleared

Figure 12.1 Watson and Rayner used a white rat in their conditioning of Little Albert
Source: © Shutterstock

away and five presentations of the rat and sound were conducted with Albert showing various amounts of distress on each occasion. After these presentations, when the rat was presented to him with no sound, Albert cried, turned sharply and crawled away at great speed. So fast in fact that they barely had time to catch him before he fell off the edge of the table on which he was sitting! As Watson and Rayner described it, it 'was as convincing a case of a completely conditioned fear response as could have been theoretically pictured'. This had taken just seven joint presentations (rat and sound) over a 7-day period. They had found the answer to their first question. It is possible to condition fear of an animal by visually presenting it along with an unpleasant, unexpected and unexplained sound.

It seems clear that Albert had acquired a conditioned (or learned) emotional (fear) response. Before the conditioning trials, he showed no fear of the rat; this represented a neutral stimulus. The banging of the steel bar was an unconditioned stimulus (US) since it naturally provoked a fear response (an unconditioned response or UR) in Albert. With repeated presentations of the rat and the unpleasant sound, the sight of the rat alone became a conditioned stimulus (or CS) and produced a learned, fear response (conditioned response or CR) in Albert. This classical conditioning procedure is summarised in Figure 12.2 below).[1]

Another 5 days later, Little Albert found himself back in the experimental room. He played happily with his building blocks, which showed there had been no transfer of fear to other objects such as the room, the table or the blocks. The rat was presented and he showed the conditioned fear response. To test whether there had been any transfer to other animals, a rabbit was now presented. Albert reacted at once, he leaned as far away as possible and

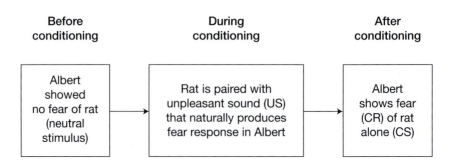

Figure 12.2 The classical conditioning of Little Albert

started to whimper and cry. When the rabbit was placed next to him, he crawled away as he had done from the rat. After a period during which he was given his building blocks to play with, a dog was presented. Albert's reaction was described as not being as pronounced as his reaction to the rabbit, but it still resulted in him crying. Other objects were tested. These included a fur coat made of seal skin (crying and crawling away); cotton wool (markedly less shock and fear shown); a Santa Claus mask and one of the researchers also put his head down to see if he would show fear of his hair (an aversive response was obtained from the mask but less so to the presentation of the hair). Watson and Rayner had found the answer to their second question: the conditioned fear response did transfer or generalise to other animals and, indeed, some similar-looking objects.

Yet again, after a period of 5 days, Little Albert returned to the small, experimental room to be placed on the mattress on top of the table. Watson and Rayner decided to strengthen his fear reaction to the dog and rabbit so paired the presentation of these animals with the striking of the steel bar. Albert was then taken to another larger room lit with natural sunlight. They wanted to test whether Albert's reactions would be the same in a different situation from the original experimental setting. They presented Albert on separate occasions with the rat alone, the rabbit alone, the dog alone. On each presentation, they reported a slight fear reaction but as they describe it, it did not seem as marked as those in the original experimental setting. The experimenters then decided to 'freshen up the reaction to the rat' by pairing it with the sound. After a single presentation of the rat and sound in this new environment, Albert showed a fear response to presentations of both the rat and the rabbit separately. On initial presentation of the dog, Albert did not show such a marked fear reaction but when the dog was only about 6 inches from Albert's face, the previously mute dog barked very loudly three times. Watson and Rayner noted that this produced a marked fear response in both Albert (immediate wailing) as well as all the experimenters present! Watson and Rayner concluded that emotional transfers do take place and are not dependent on the experimental setting. They next set about testing how long such a response might last.

Watson and Rayner stated that they knew that Albert was due to leave the hospital in 1 month's time and therefore this was the longest period by which they could test how long the response would last. During this month, Albert was given no further conditioning trials, although he was given weekly developmental tests such as those concerned with handedness (testing left- or right-hand preferences). Twenty-one days after his first birthday, Albert was re-tested on his emotional responses to the previously conditioned stimuli. On presentation of the Santa Claus mask he withdrew from it and on being 'forced to touch it', he whimpered and cried. To the presentation of the fur seal coat, he withdrew his hands immediately and also began to whimper, when it was moved closer to him, he tried to kick it away. Next, he was presented with his building blocks, with which he happily played again showing discrimination or the ability to differentiate among stimuli. Albert then allowed the rat to crawl towards him while keeping completely still. When the rat touched his hand, he withdrew it immediately. Watson and Rayner then placed the rat on his arm and Albert began to fret, they let the rat crawl across his chest and he covered his eyes with both hands. Albert's reaction to the presentation of the rabbit was very muted at first. But after a few seconds he tried to push it away with his feet. However, as the rabbit came nearer, he reached out to touch the rabbit's ear but when it was placed in his lap, he started to cry and at one point characteristically sought comfort through thumb sucking. When presented with the dog, Albert began to cry and covered his face with his hands. Watson and Rayner concluded that these experiments 'would seem to show conclusively that directly conditioned emotional responses as well as those conditioned by transfer persist, although with a certain loss in the intensity of the reaction, for a longer period than one month' (p. 6).

Watson and Rayner were also planning to test the removal of the conditioned emotional responses from Albert but this proved impossible since they report 'unfortunately Albert was taken from the hospital the day before tests were made'. They concluded that the emotional responses that they had conditioned in Albert would persist indefinitely unless an accidental method for removing them was encountered. Nevertheless, Watson and Rayner outlined how they would have attempted to remove Albert's conditioned responses. They suggested that they would have constantly presented the conditioned stimulus (e.g. rat) without the presentation of the unconditioned stimuli (the sound) and that with repeated trials the child would have habituated to the stimuli. Alternatively, they would have tried a form of reconditioning in which they might have paired pleasurable sensations with the fear-inducing stimuli. They suggested these might have included feeding Albert sweets just as the rat was presented or by 'simultaneously stimulating the erogenous zones (by touch) . . . first the lips, then the nipples and as a final resort the sex organs'.

In their original 1920 report, Watson and Rayner added further observations about the study. They discussed the fact that when emotionally upset Albert would often resort to thumb sucking as a form of comfort. They noted that while thumb sucking, Albert was impervious to the fear-producing stimulus. To prevent this, the researchers had to continually pull his thumb out of his mouth.

The lessons from Little Albert

So what can we make of this case study? Did Watson and Rayner manage to demonstrate the acquisition of a phobia (an exaggerated, illogical fear of an object or category of objects) through classical conditioning? Should it be cited as a piece of classic, groundbreaking research into the effects of classical conditioning on behaviour or are there justifiable areas of concern regarding the ethical treatment of the participant and further methodological criticisms that cannot be ignored?

One problem with the Little Albert study is that there are so many discrepancies and myths that have evolved from the study. Indeed, it has been claimed that

> most accounts of Watson and Rayner's research with Albert feature as much fabrication and distortion as they do fact. From information about Albert himself to the basic experimental methods and results, no detail of the original study has escaped misrepresentation in the telling and retelling of this bit of social science folklore.
>
> (Harris, 1979)

It has been demonstrated that numerous textbooks have made serious mistakes about the exact details reported in the original 1920 article. This is attributed to many factors. The most likely source of confusion and, perhaps the most surprising, is Watson himself. Watson wrote a number of articles in subsequent years detailing the Albert case study and often seems to have (mis)reported various important details that do not concur with the original (Watson and Watson, 1921). For example, Watson subsequently failed to mention that they were aware that Albert would be leaving the hospital and that they knew the reconditioning of Albert would thus become impossible. Did Watson deliberately omit this important detail in order to make this omission appear less heartless?

Examples of textbook errors include conditioning of different stimuli such as a man's beard, a cat and a teddy bear. Many texts change the ending to report that Watson and Rayner did remove (or recondition) Albert's fear. Possible reasons for the errors are the desire to tell ethically pleasing stories and the desire to make the evidence fit in with everyday explanations of how organisms act – in essence to make the findings more readily believable. It is also thought that such changes help to portray the study and Watson's role in it in a far more favourable light. Any criticisms of the study would be seen as a criticism of both behaviourism and its leading and most influential exponent.

So are these errors just slips of the pen or are they more serious than that? On closer inspection, there are also a number of serious methodological criticisms that can be made of the original 1920 study. Watson and Rayner's procedure of removing Albert's thumb from his mouth on various occasions in order to obtain the fear response; Albert being forced to occasionally touch some (but not all of the stimuli); and the decision to periodically 'freshen up the (fear) reaction a bit' suggests that the experimental procedures were not standardised. The lack of detail regarding such behaviours brings into question the precise experimental techniques used. These are serious criticisms of the research and particularly ironic given Watson's emphasis on objective, scientific methods. Another problem with the study is that subsequent researchers have been unable to replicate the Albert study – surely a prerequisite of science and a further indication that 'the (conditioning) process is not as simple as the story of Albert suggests (Hilgard and Maquis, 1940: 293). Why did Watson not replicate his Albert study with other infants? Indeed, Watson had spent his earlier career testing animals and he had never previously relied on a single participant. Many books suggest that Watson was unable to do this because he resigned his position at Johns Hopkins University very soon after the original study. Again, such stories may reflect the desire to make the account more believable since, in fact, he did continue at the university until September 1920, well over 6 months after the Albert study was published. In addition, Watson continued to play an active part in behavioural research projects for many years to come and would certainly have had the opportunity to supervise a direct replication of the study.

There is also some question as to exactly how much of a fear reaction was induced in Little Albert (Harris, 1979). It has been suggested that Albert did not develop a phobia to rats nor even a consistent or pronounced fear of them or any other animals. Even in the original paper, the description of Albert's reaction to the rat after eight conditioning trials over a 10-day period revealed that although he did try to crawl away 'there was no crying, but strange to say, as he started away he began to gurgle and coo'. There are further descriptions such as 'fear reaction slight . . . allowed the rat to crawl towards him without withdrawing' . . . 'reached out tentatively and slowly and touched the rabbit's ear with his right hand, finally manipulating it'. All of these responses seem at odds with the strength of feeling that one would normally associate with a marked fear or phobia. How many people with a phobia of a spider would willingly reach out and touch one?

Given all these inconsistencies it is no surprise that the study 'could not have become enshrined as the paradigm for human conditioning on the basis of its hard scientific evidence' (Samuelson, 1980: 621). Even Watson himself described the study as being 'in such an incomplete state that the verified conclusions are not possible; hence this summary, like so many other bits of psychological work, must be looked upon merely as a preliminary exposition of possibilities rather than a catalogue of concrete usable results' (Watson and Watson, 1921). This quote is in direct contrast to the one mentioned above where Watson and Rayner (1920) describe the Little Albert study as 'as convincing a case of a completely conditioned fear response as could have been theoretically pictured'. So which version by the same authors are we to believe and why has this study become such a 'classic'?

Academic debate

At the end of their journal article, Watson and Rayner ridiculed the Freudian analyst who might one day find themselves treating Albert's phobia. They stated:

> The Freudians twenty years from now, unless their hypotheses change, when they come to analyze Albert's fear of a seal skin coat − assuming that he comes to analysis at that age − will probably tease from him the recital of a dream, which upon their analysis will show that Albert at three years of age attempted to play with the pubic hair of the mother and was scolded violently for it. (We are by no means denying that this might in some other case condition it). If the analyst has sufficiently prepared Albert to accept such a dream when found as an explanation of his avoiding tendencies, and if the analyst has the authority and personality to put it over, Albert may be fully convinced that the dream was a true revealer of the factors that brought about the fear.
>
> (Watson and Rayner, 1920: 7)

The inclusion of this paragraph suggests two things. First, it confirms that Watson and Rayner believed that Albert's phobia might persist into adulthood and it suggests a rather uncaring or flippant attitude towards this state of affairs. Whatever one's opinions of Freudian interpretations, it seems incredible that Watson and Rayner felt they could use Albert's misfortune (brought about entirely by their own actions) to poke fun at the Freudian therapist's views of phobic acquisition.

Ethical issues

Watson and Rayner's research would never have been allowed to go ahead within today's ethical guidelines. Some people might argue that it is unfair to impose current ethical standards on a piece of research that is over 80 years old. Indeed, the ethical techniques used by Watson and Rayner did not seem to attract open criticism at the time (Gross, 2003), and this cultural change is an interesting subject in itself, but would certainly not be allowed today. In 1920 psychologists did not have a set of written ethical guidelines to follow. There is little doubt that at least one of today's key ethical issues, namely, protection of the participant from both psychological and physical harm, was broken. Albert certainly appeared to suffer a great deal of distress and this may have continued beyond the duration of the study. Watson and Rayner wrote that it was unfortunate that Albert was removed from the hospital before they had a chance to recondition him. Their subsequent writings hint that they were taken by surprise by his departure but a closer reading of the original report makes clear that they knew a month in advance of his departure. In any case, exactly how difficult might it have been to locate Albert at a later date and offer his mother the chance for them to recondition Albert? The question of how hard they tried to minimise any permanent harm suffered by Albert remains unanswered. Watson and Rayner discuss the possibility of harm being caused but stated that they decided to go ahead in the belief that many of the conditioned emotional reactions that they were planning might have been acquired by Albert in his everyday life, in 'the rough and tumble of the home'. This may have satisfied both Watson and Rayner but it is surely questionable as to how many of the reactions might have been encountered. Many might well encounter rabbits but not usually when an unexpected and unpleasant noise sounds behind their head. Indeed, most children probably have very positive initial encounters with rabbits and dogs. These positive associations lead many children to want to keep their own pets from an early age. Although it is clear that a small minority of children do, through circumstances, naturally develop phobias, say of dogs, this does not justify the deliberate infliction of one.

It may be that it was fortunate for Albert that Watson and Rayner did not manage to 'recondition' him since the techniques they were suggesting were dubious in the extreme. It is often reported that they were planning to recondition him by pairing the rat (by now the conditioned stimulus) with a pleasurable stimuli such as sweets to try to reverse the effects of the unpleasant noise association. But they also suggested that they would have used other methods, including tactual stimulation of the lips, then the nipples and, as a last resort, the sex organs. This is far less readily reported and yet these outrageous methods would surely be regarded today as a form of child sexual abuse.

Further studies: Little Peter

Watson did, indeed, supervise and advise on further studies that involved young children and their fears and phobias. These experiments, although supervised by Watson, were actually conducted by Mary Cover Jones (Jones, 1924a). The goal of the research was to systematically study the best method for the elimination of children's fears. Children (aged 3 months to 7 years) from a local care home who already had a fear of certain situations, such as the dark, sudden presentation of a rat, a rabbit, a frog and so on, were the participants. Jones tried many different methods of elimination including, finally, direct conditioning.

The child in the 'direct conditioning' case was named 'Peter' (Jones, 1924b). The case of 'Little Peter' is widely recognised as the sequel to the Little Albert case study and gave Watson and Jones the chance to test the principles of 'reconditioning', which they did not implement with Albert. Peter was 2 years and 10 months old and intensely afraid of various things such as rats, rabbits, fur coats and cotton wool. Initially, they tried to lessen his fears using 'modelling' techniques, whereby he was allowed to observe and interact with children who played happily with a white rabbit – one of his feared objects. The rabbit was moved closer to Peter each day and this gradual technique seemed to have a positive effect, to the extent that he could eventually pet the rabbit on the back. Unfortunately, Peter then contracted scarlet fever and during the ensuing 2 month delay he was scared by a large dog. This event, they report, meant that his fears of various animals, including the rabbit, recurred. A new technique was devised. This involved presenting food (an unconditioned pleasant stimulus) simultaneously with the rabbit (the conditioned stimulus). The rabbit was gradually brought closer to Albert in conjunction with his favourite food. Peter grew more and more tolerant of the rabbit (presumably associating it with his liking for the food) and was able to touch it without fear. When his fears spontaneously returned they used a similar counter-conditioning method in which he was allowed to play while the rabbit was gradually brought closer and closer to him over a series of sessions. Eventually Peter was able to play happily with the rabbit. This is thought to be the first case of behavioural therapy and laid the foundation for Joseph Wolpe's later work into systematic desensitisation (Wolpe, 1958). Although Wolpe is generally credited with developing the technique, he acknowledged his debt to Mary Cover Jones. As a result of the 'Little Peter' study and subsequent research, Mary Cover Jones gained the informal title of the 'mother of behavioural therapy'.

What happened to Little Albert and Watson?

In October 2009, three researchers attempted to track down the identity and fate of Little Albert using hospital records of wet nurses employed at the Harriet Lane Home at the time of the original study (Beck, Levinson and Irons, 2000). They concluded that the boy was probably Douglas Merritte, who died at the age of six. It is not known whether his fears persisted during his lifetime or were extinguished over time perhaps due to habituation or through some form of counter-conditioning. We can be more certain of what happened to Watson. During the Little Albert study Watson was having an extra marital affair with his co-author Rosalie Rayner. The scandal that ensued when this became public knowledge meant that he was subsequently forced to resign his academic appointment just as his ideas were gaining more acceptance in the wider scientific community. There may have been no set of ethical guidelines to protect research participants like Albert in the 1920s but there were strict moral standards that academics were expected to follow. Bitterly disappointed, Watson took his knowledge of psychology and human behaviour and applied it in the far more financially lucrative area of advertising. He pioneered the use of classical conditioning techniques in advertsing campaigns. Watson was convinced that successful advertising was not entirely dependent on the quality of the product but on the emotional responses that consumers would associate with each product. To this end he exhorted advertisers to 'tell him something that will tie him up with fear, something that will stir up a mild rage, that will call out an affectionate or love response, or strike at a deep psychological or habit need' (Buckley, 1982: 212).

Nowadays, thanks in no small part to Watson, classical conditioning is used in a glut of advertisements. The idea is to produce an advert (the unconditioned stimulus) and make sure that it elicits a positive response (unconditioned response) in the viewing public. The product being advertised thus becomes the conditioned stimulus. The next time someone is shopping they associate the positive feeling they had for the advert with the product. The positive feeling they have to the product is now the conditioned response that the advertisers hope will lead someone to purchase the product in order to prolong the response.

Using such techniques, Watson helped to create advertising campaigns for among others, Maxwell House Coffee, Pond's Cold Cream, Johnson's Baby Powder, Odorono (one of the first deodorants) and Pebeco Toothpaste. In the baby powder advertisements he played on the fears that young mothers have about looking after their children. In the Pebeco toothpaste campaign, he associated the brand with sexually arousing cues. A seductively dressed young woman was pictured smoking a cigarette with the words 'You can smoke and still be lovely if you'll just use Pebeco twice a day.' Here the attractive woman was the unconditioned stimulus and the toothpaste was the conditioned stimulus. It has been claimed that Watson was the man that put the 'sex' into the phrase 'sex sells'.

Watson also placed a great deal of emphasis on empirical marketing research by stressing the importance of knowing the consumer through scientific study (Schultz and Schultz, 2011). Watson viewed the process of selling as a laboratory for advertising and he made frequent comparisons between the consumer and experimental participants. In the same way that he had manipulated Albert's behaviour, he believed that, with the appropriate reinforcers, advertisers could manipulate consumer's buying behaviour. To this end, Watson developed marketing research techniques and was one of the first to study the idea of brand loyalty – a subject still studied by advertisers today.

Watson's success in advertising ensured that by 1924 he had become vice president of the J. Walter Thompson Advertising Agency – one of the largest agencies in the world. His personal life was less successful. After divorcing his first wife, he married Rosalie soon after. Their marriage produced two children but unfortunately Rosalie died of complications caused by dysentery aged just 35. Watson retired from advertising in 1945 and burned all his unpublished works shortly before his death in 1958.

One of the most memorable (and most cited) quotes from Watson put forward the case for environmental influences on behaviour:

> Give me a dozen healthy infants, well-formed, and my own specified world to bring them up and I'll guarantee to take any one at random and train him to become any type of specialist I might select – doctor, lawyer, merchant-chief, and yes, even beggarman and thief, regardless of his talents, penchants, tendencies, abilities, vocations, and race of his ancestors.
>
> (Watson, 1924: 82)

But the sentence that followed is less cited. He added: 'I'm going beyond my facts and I admit it, but so have advocates of the contrary and they have been doing it for thousands of years' (p. 82).

One of the lessons to be learned from the Little Albert case study is the way that (questionable) experimental evidence can be inadvertently misinterpreted and re-evaluated. These second-hand myths get taken as 'facts' and they, in turn, help confer the study with the status of a 'classic'. There is no doubt that the case study of Little Albert remains a 'classic' in psychology but the question remains as to whether it deserves its place on the basis of its experimental findings alone. Perhaps it deserves its 'classic' status on the basis of the influence (deserved or otherwise) it had on thinking at the time and which continues to this day.

Note

1   The most famous of behaviourist psychologists, B.F. Skinner, called this type of learning 'respondent conditioning' because in this type of learning, one is responding to an environmental antecedent.

References

Asratyan, E.A. (1953). *I.P Pavlov: His Life and Work*. Moscow: Foreign Languages Publishing House.

Beck, H., Levinson, S. and Irons, G. (2009). 'Finding little Albert: A journey to John B. Watson's infant laboratory'. *American Psychologist*, 64(7): 605–14.

Buckley, K.W. (1982). 'The selling of a psychologist: John Broadus Watson and the application of behavioral techniques to advertising'. *Journal of the History of the Behavioral Sciences*, 18: 207–21.

Gross, R.D. (2003). *Key Studies in Psychology* (4th edition). London: Hodder and Stoughton.

Harris, B. (1979). 'Whatever happened to Little Albert?' *American Psychologist*, 34(2): 151–60.

Hilgard, E. and Maquis, D. (1940). *Conditioning and Learning*. New York: Appleton-Century.

Jones, M.C. (1924a). 'Elimination of children's fears'. *Journal of Experimental Psychology*, 7: 381–90.

Jones, M.C. (1924b). 'A laboratory study of fear: The case of Peter'. *Pedagogical Seminary*, 31: 308–15.

Samuelson, F. (1980). 'J.B. Watson's Little Albert, Cyril Burt's Twins and the need for a critical science'. *American Psychologist*, 35(7): 619–25.

Schultz, D. and Schultz, S. (2011). *A History of Modern Psychology*. Boston, MA: Cengage Publishing.

Watson, J.B. (1913). 'Psychology as the behaviourist views it'. *Psychological Review*, 20: 158–77.

Watson, J. B. (1924). *Behaviorism*. Chicago, IL: University of Chicago Press.

Watson, J.B. and Rayner, R. (1920). 'Conditioned emotional reactions'. *Journal of Experimental Psychology*, 3(1): 1–14.

Watson, J.B. and Watson, R.R. (1921). 'Studies in infant psychology'. *Scientific Monthly*, 13: 493–515.

Wolpe, J. (1958). *Psychotherapy by Reciprocal Inhibition*. Stanford, CT: Stanford University Press.

Part 4

Individual differences

Chapter 13

The boy who needed to play
The story of Dibs

Dibs stood alone in the middle of the playroom. The 5 year old stared straight ahead, seemingly unaware of the children playing all around him. His hands swung lifeless by his side and he remained completely motionless. His only movements were made when anyone approached him; he would hit out wildly and try to bite or scratch them. Eventually, he went and laid under a table with his head bowed, where he remained for the rest of the session. It was obvious to anyone who met Dibs that he had severe behavioural problems. Although the teachers had a warm affection for Dibs, they found it impossible to work with him. His mother declared him mentally abnormal and retarded at birth. Echoing the case of Genie, psychologists were invited to study and treat him. Enter Virginia Axline, a practising clinical psychologist, who decided to use a technique known as 'play therapy' with Dibs. Ten years later, Dibs underwent a series of developmental attainment tests. He was, indeed, abnormal. In fact, he was a genius.[1]

'No go home'

The story of Dibs begins at school. Unlike most children of his age, Dibs appeared to hate school. In fact, he appeared to hate life. He often stood for minutes on end with his head buried in his arms leaning against a wall. He sometimes sat in the same place all morning, not moving and not saying a word. He would sometimes snuggle up in a ball and lie there till it was time to go home. Outside in the playground, he usually sought out a far corner, crouched down and scratched the dirt with a stick. He was a silent, withdrawn and unhappy child. Despite this strange behaviour, the teachers recognised that he actually liked school. When it was time to leave, his chauffeur would appear and Dibs would shout and scream, bite and kick and shout 'No go home' over and over again. These temper tantrums never occurred on his way in to school.

Dibs never spoke to anyone who addressed him and he never made eye contact with anyone. He was an unhappy child, alone in what seemed to him to be an unfriendly world. Despite this behaviour, his teachers had a genuine fondness for him. The force of his personality had touched them all. His behaviour was certainly erratic – most often he appeared to be mentally retarded but occasionally he would do something that suggested a ready intelligence. He loved books and always accepted them when offered and during story time would often lurk under a table near enough to hear what was being said.

The school received many complaints about Dibs's disruptive and aggressive behaviour and the staff arranged for him to have some psychological tests. The psychologists failed to assess him since he refused to participate in any of their tests. Was he mentally retarded? Was he autistic? Did he have some mental illness? After 2 years of this behaviour, when Dibs was 5 years old, his nursery school teachers called in a clinical psychologist. This is how Dibs first met Virginia Axline. She was to provide the stimulation and prompting necessary for Dibs to overcome his problems.

The door begins to open

Dibs's mother agreed to let him attend a series of play therapy sessions with Axline. These consisted of a 1-hour session every Thursday. Play therapy is a specific form of psychotherapy for children. It uses the therapeutic powers of play to help children prevent or resolve various psychological difficulties. Children are given the chance to express or act out their experiences, feelings and problems by playing with dolls, toys and other play materials under the guidance or observation of a trained therapist. Through such a process children can, sometimes, be helped to achieve their full potential. Play therapists believe that play can be a means of acting out 'blocked' feelings and emotions. It can also help to address self-esteem issues, anger management and feelings of inadequacy, and allow for emotional release.

There are two broad types of play therapy. Non-directive therapy involves allowing the child a free rein in the playroom. They can play with anything that interests them. The therapist listens or records all the behaviour. This is often done on video from behind a one-way mirror. The therapist uses factual comments on the behaviour such as 'So you're going to play with the father doll today' to allow the play to develop. The therapist is a supportive presence but does not become too involved in the play process. This is the method that Axline favoured with Dibs. It is also commonly referred to as client-centred therapy for obvious reasons.

Directive therapy, on the other hand, involves the therapist taking a more active role in the play. Often they will make suggestions as to appropriate games to play and will use the sessions for specific diagnostic purposes. Therapists will often set up role-playing scenarios that might symbolise the child's own life experiences and then work on possible solutions. For example, animal glove puppets may be used in play fights that symbolise arguments between parents that a child might have witnessed.

Since 5 year olds lack the cognitive maturity to benefit from talking through their problems, it was felt that play could give Dibs a necessary sense of empowerment. Dibs was given the chance to take charge of the sessions and direct the play activities himself. Through play, Dibs would be given the opportunity to overcome any negative feelings and symbolically triumph over the upsets and traumas that had stolen his sense of well-being. Furthermore, he could do this in his own safe and accepting environment. But the question remained 'How would Dibs cope with this new situation?' The key to this healing process would be his own imagination and creativity.

The play therapy room used by Axline consisted of a doll's house with numerous dolls, toy cars, sand pit, watercolour and finger paints, drawing paper and materials and an inflatable doll that bounced upright when hit. During his first session, Dibs merely walked around the room naming each toy in a monotone voice. Axline encouraged this vocalisation by confirming what each object was. On reaching the doll's house, Dibs sobbed urgently 'no lock doors . . . no lock doors'. He repeated this over and over again. The therapeutic process was beginning.

A boy of exceptional courage

On the next visit, Dibs took a marked interest in the easel and paints. He went over to them and, after staring at them for a long time, arranged six of them in the order of the spectrum. He picked up one particular brand of paint and said that he thought they were the best you could buy. Axline realised that Dibs was reading the labels. He sat down and started painting. As he painted, he called out the name of each colour. He could also spell each colour. It was immediately obvious that Dibs was not mentally retarded.

Figure 13.1 Play therapy is a controversial technique of therapy
Source: © Shutterstock

Axline's non-directive therapeutic technique allowed Dibs the freedom to direct the play himself. She would respond to his questions and promptings but it was Dibs who set the pace of the interaction and decided on the play activity. Axline was going to try to be the catalyst for Dibs to uncover his true self. She hoped to give him the chance to work through his feelings in a non-threatening environment. Axline told Dibs that the playroom was his special place to have fun in. A place where no-one could hurt him. A place where he could step 'out of the shadows and into the sun'.

Axline knew that the therapeutic process would take a great deal of time and effort with no guarantee of success. However, she hoped that Dibs would reveal more and more of his true self as he began to feel more secure in her company. When the time came to end the sessions, Axline often had difficulties with Dibs. He would continue to recite 'no go home' through his sobbing breaths. Occasionally he would scream and kick out in protest when his mother came to collect him. During these tantrums, Axline did not try to comfort Dibs with affection. More often, she walked away. She realised that he had to be independent of her. After all, Dibs would only see her for 1 hour a week. It would have been more upsetting for Dibs to become more emotionally attached to someone who could only see him weekly. His strength had to come from within. Although the therapy was important Axline ensured that it did not become a dominant part of Dibs life. There is a danger that patients can become over-reliant on their therapists. She wanted to prevent this happening with Dibs. Sometimes, Axline would stop halfway down the corridor and, however reluctantly, Dibs would continue the walk towards his mother. By this simple act, Axline was showing that she had confidence in Dibs. Axline realised he was a boy of exceptional courage.

'The rapy'

On one visit, Dibs noticed the sign on the door to the playroom. He recognised and read aloud 'play' and looked at the other word. He was trying to work out what this unfamiliar word was. 'The rapy', he said.

During the play sessions, Dibs frequently chose to play with the doll's house and the sand pit. He often asked for the doll's house doors to be locked up. As part of the therapy, Axline merely prompted Dibs to carry out his own suggestions. For instance, when Dibs asked for the house to be locked up, Axline would ask whether he wanted the house locked up. If he said that that was his wish, she would suggest that he did it, not her. When Dibs declared that the house was locked, she would congratulate him on his success.

Axline tried to avoid asking direct or probing questions of Dibs. This helped to avoid any suggestion of confrontation and helped his feelings of security. She recognised her desire to ask straightforward questions but believed that no-one ever answered them accurately during therapy and thus considered them to be of limited use. Instead, Axline always tried to ask open questions that allowed Dibs to express himself further. She often rephrased what he had said to give him more time to identify his thoughts. For example, when Dibs offered to give her a painting he'd done, rather than accept it with a simple 'Thank you', she would ask 'Oh, you want to give it to me do you?' This technique allowed her to keep open the communication and allowed Dibs to add more if he wished. It also helps to slow down the process and not to impose her standards of behaviour on the interaction. With such subtle techniques, Dibs was gradually coming out of his shell. He was beginning to reveal his true self. He was taking control and beginning to enjoy his new-found confidence and freedom. He started to make eye contact with Axline and, more frequently, a smile could be found framed by his curly black hair.

Every week has a Thursday

Axline felt that Dibs was making progress. She had little contact with the parents or, indeed, his school and so was unsure whether this progress was evident beyond the play therapy room. Nevertheless, Dibs continued to have profound difficulties. When upset, he would often pick up a baby's bottle and suck on it seemingly using it as a method of reassurance. Axline also noticed that Dibs used one of two defensive strategies whenever he discussed his emotions and feelings. Sometimes, his language would become very basic and rudimentary and on other occasions he would change the subject by demonstrating his undoubted intellectual ability in writing, reading, counting and so forth. Axline recognised that Dibs felt the need to disguise his true feelings and emotions. Axline believed that Dibs was more comfortable demonstrating his intellectual abilities. Perhaps he also hid his true ability on occasions because he felt upset that people placed too high a value on them.

One day during a session, Dibs picked up a soldier and identified it as 'Papa'. He stood it up standing as he put it 'so stiff and straight like an old iron railing from a fence' and then proceeded to knock it down. He repeated this several times and then buried it in the sand. Dibs left it there for the week. Axline noticed the obvious message in the play and, at the same time, was amazed by his creative and impressive use of language. Given time and space, Dibs would work through his feelings for his father.

It is easy to see the symbolic significance of much of Dibs's play. For example, the locked doll's house could represent all the locked doors that he had faced in his short life. The locked door of his playroom at home and the locked door to his parent's love. Such interpretations were never suggested to Dibs and were not a required part of the therapy but it seems reasonable to suggest that they may have represented such things. Only Dibs could know for sure.

As each week went by, it became obvious that Dibs was enjoying the sessions. He would rush to the playroom and enter with a ready smile. He told Axline how much he enjoyed the sessions. He told her 'I come with gladness into this room and I leave it with sadness.' He appeared to count the days till his next session. He worked out which day next Thursday was, whether it be George Washington's birthday or the day after the Fourth of July. He always knew what date Thursday was. Wednesday always seemed a long day before his session with 'Miss A', as he liked to call her.

So much to say

During these sessions, Axline had had very little contact with Dibs's parents. One day, Dibs's father came to collect him and Axline went to introduce herself. Dibs interrupted their greeting by telling 'Papa' that Independence Day that year would be on a Thursday in 4 months and 2 weeks' time. His father was obviously very embarrassed by Dibs and snapped at him to stop his senseless jabbering. He called Dibs an idiot. Dibs looked completely crestfallen and left in silence. Later Dibs screamed at and kicked his father, shouting how much he hated him, so much so that he was locked in his playroom to calm down. Strangely enough, this incident was a key turning point in the relationship between Dibs and his parents.

Dibs's parents were scared. They had never really discussed their feelings and emotions with one another. This incident forced them to confront their fears and worries about Dibs. They realised that they had failed with Dibs. They had spent their adult lives using their intelligence to protect themselves from emotional reactions and unwittingly Dibs had done the same. Perhaps his parents had also been brought up in emotional wastelands. In their own ways, all three of them had tried to use their intelligence as a form of protective behaviour and it had made them more vulnerable than ever. Dibs's mother and father resolved to do something about it.

Next morning, Dibs's mother rang to arrange an appointment with Axline. On arrival, his mother was obviously ill at ease. She confessed that she had 'so much to say' and that she had carried a great burden about Dibs. This was her chance to unburden herself. Apparently, her husband wanted the therapy to stop. He believed that the therapy was making Dibs worse. Indeed, Dibs had seemed to be more unhappy over recent weeks. Axline was amazed. Was the obvious improvement she had noticed in Dibs not evident outside of the playroom? Through her tears, Dibs's mother described the bitter disappointment of falling pregnant. She had been a gifted surgeon and her career was thwarted. Her husband was a brilliant, but remote, scientist and he also resented the intrusion into their lives that came with the birth of Dibs. Furthermore, they were embarrassed by the fact that Dibs was not normal. They themselves were brilliant and yet their son appeared to be mentally retarded. They both felt totally humiliated and ashamed. When a neurologist found nothing wrong with Dibs, they believed he might be schizophrenic. However, the one psychiatrist who examined them declared Dibs's behaviour to be perfectly normal, but the result of severe emotional neglect. He recommended psychotherapy for Dibs' parents, not Dibs.

Axline asked about Dibs's behaviour at home. His mother actually reported a marked improvement in his behaviour. He was talking more (admittedly still to himself), didn't suck his thumb anymore and his tantrums were a thing of the past. Dibs's mother described the incident with his father as a rational protest to his father's insensitive remark. Dibs would continue with his therapy. The family had turned a corner and were beginning to face up to their problems. Axline noted that many therapists do not undertake therapy without the agreement of active participation from the parents. In Dibs's case, this only came at a later date and illustrates that therapy can be successful even without the initial involvement of the parents.

The leaf

During one session, Dibs told Axline a story about a tree that grew outside his bedroom window. Their gardener, Jake, was told by his father to prune the big elm tree. Dibs leaned out of his window and asked Jake to leave the branches that he could touch from his window. Jake agreed and left the branches uncut. However, Dibs's father noticed them and again asked for them to be cut. Jake explained that Dibs liked to reach out and touch the branches but his father ordered them to be cut, adding that he didn't want Dibs hanging out of the windows. Jake had to cut the branches but gave the tip of the branch to Dibs as a present. A part of the tree he could keep *inside* his bedroom. Dibs treasured the branch tip and kept it secretly.

Jake often told Dibs made-up stories about the garden. He told Dibs a story about his elm tree. In spring, the leaves became green due to the showers of rain and in summer the leaves provided cool shade. But in winter, the wind blew all the leaves away in order for them to travel all round the world. The last leaf on the tree was always very lonely but the wind noticed this and blew again and the little leaf was taken on the most wonderful adventure ever. However, the little leaf missed Dibs and so the wind blew it back to the same old elm tree. Jake found the leaf one day under the tree and also gave it to

Dibs. Dibs mounted and framed the leaf and every time he looked at it he imagined all the wonderful things present in the world. All the amazing things that he had read so much about. Dibs reported his feelings about Jake: 'I like him very, very much. I guess, maybe, he is a friend?'

During play therapy children are encouraged to tell stories about their life experiences. Stories may represent a real incident in the child's life (as here) or a made-up one. This can help to highlight areas of concern and may enable them to make sense of a troubling or upsetting experience. Through the retelling of the story the child has a chance to work through the fear and anger that accompanied it.

'Mother, I love you'

Over the coming weeks Dibs became more confident and relaxed. He reported how much he liked himself. He told of happy day trips out to the seaside with his parents. Dibs still withheld his speech when he wanted to. He knew how much it upset his father and was his way of coping with any criticisms that came his way. One day after a therapy session, he ran down the corridor, jumped into his mother's arms shouting 'Oh mother, I love you'. His mother left in floods of tears.

Dibs was looking forward to the summer holidays with his family. He seemed to recognise that the therapy had run its course. He was happy and content. His mother visited Axline once more. This time she came to thank her for her efforts. She also confided in her that she always knew that Dibs wasn't retarded. She was sure that Dibs could read at the age of two. She had systematically taught him from a remarkably early age. She reported that at the age of six he could recognise hundreds of classical symphonies and that his drawings had an amazing sense of perspective. She had painstakingly pressured him to achieve. She thought she was helping him, developing his innate abilities, but this was at the expense of his emotional well-being. Perhaps his mother was unsure about how to relate to Dibs and had concentrated on the areas she felt comfortable with – the intellectual side – to hide her inability to become emotionally close to her son.

At his last session, Dibs was relaxed, out-going and happy. All his behaviour was spontaneous. He said a final goodbye to 'the lady of the wonderful playroom'. A week later, a clinical psychologist administered an intelligence (IQ) test to Dibs. This is a standardised test used to establish an intelligence level rating by measuring a person's ability to form concepts, solve problems, acquire information, reason, and perform other intellectual operations. The average IQ score of the general population is 100. Dibs had an astoundingly high IQ of 168. Less than one person in a thousand would score as high. He did not finish the reading test since he grew bored but he had already achieved a score far in advance of his years. He was an intellectually gifted individual who was thriving in all respects. Dibs had come to terms with himself and so had his parents.

It is very difficult to evaluate the success of play therapy. After all, what kind of measure of success might be employed? The therapy with Dibs certainly appeared successful, but what were the ingredients that brought this about? Was it the play activities, the toys, the warm relationship with Axline, the one-to-one contact or merely developmental maturation that helped Dibs? It may indeed have been some subtle combination of them all. This is one of the criticisms of play therapy – that it lacks experimental rigour. After all, it would be impossible to take another child with exactly the same problems and deny them therapy merely to try to determine whether they would have shown any improvement over the same time.

The chance meeting

Two-and-a-half years later, completely by chance, Dibs's family moved into an apartment building near to Axline. They met in the street one day. Dibs recognised her immediately. He said that his last therapy session was 2 years, 6 months and 4 days come Thursday. He had ripped out the date of his last session from his calendar and had it framed on his bedroom wall. It was a special day. Dibs told Axline that she had been his very first friend. Dibs was excelling at his new school for gifted children. His parents were happy and so was Dibs.

Dibs's family moved home again and Axline lost contact. However, a teacher friend of hers who knew of her interest in courageous children showed her a letter written by a 15 year old in their school newspaper complaining about the school's treatment of a fellow pupil. The letter contained a series of convincing and eloquent arguments. The teacher admitted that the school was probably going to follow the suggestions it contained. The teacher knew the boy to be a brilliant and sensitive boy that his peers admired. Axline noticed that the letter was written by Dibs.

During his therapy, Dibs once said that every child should have a hill all of his own to climb. Dibs had had a higher hill than most, but through hard work, patience, commitment and guidance, he had reached the top and was enjoying the view. He had found his sense of 'self'.

Note

1 Material in this chapter has been drawn from the fantastic book by Virginia Axline (1986).

Reference

Axline, V. (1986). *Dibs: In Search of Self.* New York: Ballantine Books.

Chapter 14

The man who was turned on by prams and handbags

This case study involves a married man who had developed a particularly strange sexual perversion, which meant that he became sexually excited by prams and handbags. This perversion had become so marked that he had been arrested on numerous occasions charged with causing malicious damage to prams and/or handbags.[1] A pre-frontal leucotomy was suggested as a suitable form of treatment but a severe form of aversion therapy was employed prior to such a drastic, irreversible procedure. The procedure is often characterised as a form of brainwashing and has echoes of those portrayed in the Anthony Burgess book (and subsequent film) *A Clockwork Orange* (Burgess, 1962).

The problem

This is arguably a less well-known case study than the others in this book but people often find this one of the most fascinating of all, probably due to the bizarre sexual fetish that is involved. The patient was a 33-year-old married man who was registered as an outpatient at a psychiatric hospital. He was being assessed for a pre-frontal leucotomy, a brain operation that involves the surgical cutting of the nerve tracts to and from the frontal lobes. The operation was intended to relieve severe intractable mental or behavioural problems but often resulted in noticeable cognitive and/or personality changes. In the history of psychosurgery (first devised in 1935) it was used for patients who were so psychotic that almost any change was thought to be for the good. Operations for such reasons are unheard of today.

The patient's problem involved a bizarre sexual attraction to prams and handbags. This strange behaviour seems to have started at the age of 10 when he showed impulses to attack and damage prams and handbags. Sometimes this involved little more than scratching his thumbnail down the side of a handbag or pram but there had been occasions when the attacks had been far more serious. One attack involved him following a woman pushing a pram and smearing it with engine oil. He had occasionally cut and damaged prams and, indeed, had cut and set on fire two empty prams he once found at a train station. During this time he deliberately rode his motorbike towards a pram that had a baby in it, but swerved at the last minute and narrowly avoided injuring the child within. He also liked to try to drive through muddy puddles and splash any person pushing a pram along the pavement. He had been convicted for careless driving over such incidents. The police were called to a further 12 incidents and he was again charged with driving without due care and attention. He also admitted five other attacks where he had cut or scratched prams and he was convicted of causing malicious damage.

Figure 14.1 The patient's problem involved a bizarre sexual attraction to prams and handbags

Source: © Shutterstock

The patient's history revealed that he had undergone a number of years of psychiatric treatment. He admitted that he had been interested in prams since the age of 12 and often made several attempts per week to attack either prams or handbags. With regard to handbags he was usually satisfied to just scratch them with his thumb nail, and since this could be done often without notice he had only once got into trouble with the police for doing this. Rather than being sent to prison, he was sent on probation to a mental hospital and transferred to a neurosis unit. There, psychiatrists decided he was unsuitable for psychotherapy and was potentially dangerous and should therefore remain in a mental hospital. However, after a period of time he was discharged and carried on with his career of damaging prams.

The patient had undergone many hours of psychoanalytic treatment in the hope that reasons for his strange behaviour might be uncovered. During this treatment, it was suggested that his behaviour might originate in an incident during childhood when he was playing with his toy yacht at the local boating lake. He had accidentally bumped against the side of a pram with his model yacht and 'had been impressed by the feminine consternation' shown by the mother of the child in the pram. Another incident he reported involved one in which he had, for some strange reason, become sexually aroused in the presence of his sister's handbag. The patient accepted the possible significance of these events and ascribed sexual symbolism to both prams and handbags. Perhaps in Freudian terms, both of these 'containers' usually used by women may have represented either a desire for his mother or, more generally, female genitalia?

Obviously in such a case there are a number of difficult problems to resolve. If there had been no danger to children or prams then it may have been possible to just leave the patient to continue with his rather bizarre fetish. If he was doing no harm then there would not necessarily have been any treatment required, unless he himself had felt that it was having a serious detrimental effect on his life. Indeed, the patient in this case was married with two children, and his wife said that he was actually a very good husband and father. However, he had occasionally attacked his own pram and his wife's handbag, and therefore his wife was well aware of the problems that he had.

Possible solution?

So what can psychologists offer such a patient? Although, it was the prams and handbags that were the primary focus of his interest, the patient was worried that he might injure any child who happened to be in a pram that he attacked. He was once more admitted to a psychiatric hospital for 18 months but on release continued with his bizarre behaviour. After further trouble with the police, he was again placed on probation on the understanding that he accepted appropriate medical treatment. It was at this stage that psychosurgery was considered. However, before this irreversible and drastic treatment was employed, psychologists suggested that he might be a suitable case for aversion therapy. Aversion therapy is a form of behavioural therapy. Behaviour therapy was defined by Wolpe (1958) as 'the use of experimentally established laws of learning for the purposes of changing unadaptive behaviour'. Aversion therapy reduces undesirable behaviour by pairing it with an undesirable or aversive stimulus. Most commonly this is drug-induced nausea or pain from an electric shock. Through this conditioning, the aversive stimulus becomes associated with the undesirable behaviour and thus, in turn, the undesirable behaviour is suppressed. In the not so distant past, it was used for a variety of behaviours considered undesirable, including homosexuality.

The aim of the treatment in this particular case was to try and alter the patient's attitude both to handbags and prams by using conditioning techniques. This involved teaching him to associate handbags and prams with unpleasant sensations instead of the evidently pleasurable, erotic ones. The patient was initially very sceptical about the treatments proposed, but he said that he was willing to try anything; by this time he had noticed that even adverts in newspapers and magazines for handbags and prams turned him on!

The principles of aversion therapy are based on classical conditioning first described by Russian physiologist, Ivan Pavlov (1849–1936). During his work on the digestive systems of dogs, Pavlov noticed that the dogs salivated at the mere sight of the person who fed them (Asratyan, 1953). He called the dogs' salivation in response to the actual taste and smell of meat an 'unconditioned' (unlearned) response because it occurred naturally without any prior training (the meat was thus called an unconditioned stimulus). He realised that a normally neutral act, such as the ringing of a bell, could become associated with the appearance of food, thus producing salivation as a 'conditioned' response (in response to a conditioned stimulus). This process is shown in Figure 14.2 below.

In later research, Pavlov found that in order for the conditioned response to be maintained, it had to be paired periodically with the unconditioned stimulus or the learned association would be forgotten (this is known as extinction). Classical conditioning can be applied to human behaviour and

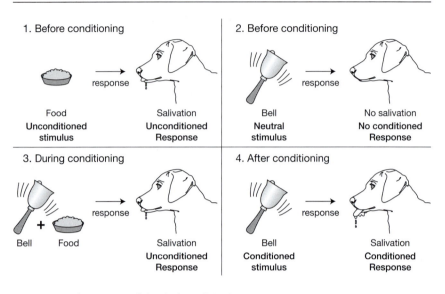

Figure 14.2 The process of classical conditioning

account for such complex phenomena as a person's emotional reaction to a particular song or perfume based on a past experience with which it is associated. Classical (also called Pavlovian or associative learning) conditioning is also the basis for many different types of fears or phobias, which can occur through a process called stimulus generalisation (a child who has a bad experience with a particular dog may learn to fear all dogs) (see Chapter 13). Classical conditioning principles have been developed into a variety of therapeutic techniques. One such is aversion therapy, in which the goal is to make the desirable stimulus unpleasant.

The conditioning treatment proposed in this case involved the injection of a drug called apomorphine, which produces sickness or nausea. The prams or handbags were produced soon after the drug was given, when the nausea occurred. The prams and handbags thus represented the conditioned (learned) stimuli and the nausea represented the unpleasant response with which the conditioned stimulus was to be associated. The treatment regime was tough. The treatment was given every two hours, day and night, and no food was allowed. At night-time amphetamines were used to keep him awake. At the end of the first week, treatment was suspended and the patient was allowed home. After 8 days he was brought back into hospital to continue the treatment and he reported jubilantly that he had been able to have sexual intercourse with his wife without any of his old fantasies involving handbags or prams. His wife also said that she had noticed a marked change for the better in his behaviour. Despite this improvement, treatment was re-commenced but a different emetic (nausea inducing drug) was used when the effect of the apomorphine became less pronounced. After another 5 days the patient reported that the mere sight of prams and handbags made him feel sick. He was confined to bed and given prams and handbags to play with and the treatment then continued at irregular intervals. On the evening of the ninth day he rang his bell and pleaded with the nurses to take away his prams and handbags. They refused to do this. However, a few hours later during which he had cried continuously a doctor removed the prams and handbags and gave him a glass of milk and a sedative. The following day the patient opened up his overnight bag and gave up a number of photographs of prams to the doctor saying that he had carried them for a year, but felt that he would no longer need them.

The patient left hospital, but continued to attend as an outpatient. After 6 months the doctors decided to re-admit him for a booster treatment course. He reluctantly agreed to this. The psychologists produced a film of women carrying handbags and pushing prams in the 'arousing and provocative' way he had previously described. Before the film was started he was given the emetic, which made him feel sick. He was also given handbags to play with. After this course of treatment no further treatment was given. Eysenck reports that the patient was subsequently followed up over a period of years and progressed well. He no longer fantasised about prams and handbags. His wife said that she was no longer worrying about him falling foul of the police, and that their sexual relations had improved greatly. His probation officer also reported that he was making good progress. He never got into further trouble with the police and gained promotion at work. Eysenck reports that the treatment had been remarkably successful, both for the patient, for his wife, for his family and society at large.

Treatment issues

This case and the use of aversion therapy raises a number of serious problems that need to be addressed. The first issue involves the actual treatment methods used. Many people would argue that aversion therapy is not a very understanding or humane form of treatment. The treatments often seem very mechanical and a lot of people (including many psychologists) find it distasteful for human beings to be treated in this way. After all, there is no doubt that the treatment involved a great deal of pain and discomfort. Many believe that this is a kind of brainwashing – a degrading process in which human beings are viewed as a simple box of conditioned reflexes. It is argued that the use of aversion therapy devalues the individual with its premise that all humans learn in the same way and therefore can be treated and conditioned in the same way. However, Eysenck argues that the alternatives to aversion therapy have to be considered in any such argument. The first alternative was to use some other form of psychotherapy, perhaps psychoanalysis? However, there is some evidence (particularly that reported by Eysenck himself) that this form of talking cure does not have any real positive benefits. Indeed, Eysenck has even reported that Freudian psychoanalysis can have a detrimental effect. Of course, a patient might be left to simply get better over time – this effect is called 'spontaneous remission'. However, it has generally been shown that disorders of this particular type do not show a high rate of spontaneous remission.

In addition, the patient had already received a great variety of psychiatric treatment prior to the aversion therapy without any success whatsoever. Eysenck suggests that it was unlikely that any other form of talking cure would have succeeded. The other alternative would, of course, have been to sentence him to a lengthy prison sentence. This would have obviously amounted to a punishment for his actions. But again there is little evidence that this form of punishment has any long-lasting beneficial effect on future actions, particularly in the case of sexual perverts. Indeed, some people have argued that prison merely has the effect of making such people far more careful in the future.

Of course, one of the other alternatives would have been to let him go free or put him on probation. After all, many of his behaviours were fairly minor and often involved little more than scratching the side of a pram with his thumb nail. Yet surely members of the public do have a right to be protected from such individuals? Although the patient professed that he had no desires to harm children, this was an unfortunate possible side-effect of his strange desires towards prams. In addition, some of his attacks on women's handbags had also had a very upsetting effect on the women involved. Looking at all the options available, Eysenck argues that there is a choice to be made between asking the patient to submit to a method of treatment, which is uncomfortable and unpleasant, but not for very long (although to the patient it may seem interminable), sending him to prison, allowing him to go free or asking him to submit to a lengthy, expensive and (possibly) ineffective psychotherapeutic treatment in hospital.

Eysenck suggests that given the different options available that aversion therapy was the most appropriate and, indeed, the most effective form of treatment for all concerned. One could argue whether it is ethically right to *not* use an effective treatment simply because some people feel it degrades the individual to some extent. This argument was developed by Eysenck who argued that the patients themselves were the ones that underwent the therapy and they were not complaining (as we will see this is contentious). Eysenck claimed that many people went to great lengths to seek out behavioural therapy and they should not be denied their right to all treatment. Eysenck considered aversion therapy to be a safe and effective treatment for many conditions that are difficult to correct, and wrote that it was only fair to allow the ultimate decision to be made by the sufferer themselves. Indeed, from the patient's point of view one can argue whether it is right to actually prevent them from having a therapy that they themselves desire.

Of course, many people are still uneasy about using aversion therapy for conditions that do not cause any danger to society. An example of a behaviour that aversion therapy has been used to alter in the past is homosexuality. The homosexual who wants to change their sexuality is likely to be trying to do so because of social disapproval. Social disapproval and peer pressure can still be a powerful force in making a homosexual want aversion therapy. It may be the case that we should argue that such treatments should not be available for homosexuals and, rather, counsel them to accept their homosexuality and to understand that the problem in this case lies with society rather than individuals themselves.

The 'treatment' of homosexuality in the past, typically involved showing pictures or films of nude males (Smith et al., 2004). These films constituted the conditioned stimuli. In these experiments emetics and/or electric shocks were used as the unpleasant or unconditioned response. Electric shocks have a number of advantages over the use of emetics. First, the strength of the shock can be regulated much more accurately and the timing can be also much more accurate because nausea and vomiting after the injection of a drug is not timed as accurately as a shock. A shock can be predicted within a second, whereas the nausea sometimes takes effect over a number of minutes. According to conditioning principles the timing of the unconditioned response is particularly important for the learning process. That is, the shorter the time delay of the response, the more readily they are associated – this is called the law of contiguity.

With regard to homosexuality one of the questions that arises relates to the possibility of changing a person's sexual behaviour through the use of such therapy. One would have thought that having stopped sexual desire for members of the same sex the patient would be left without any sexual desire at all. Many critics of aversion therapy argue that this is exactly what happens. However, Eysenck claimed that in the majority of cases there was an increase in interest in members of the opposite sex concomitant with the decline in interest in members of the same sex. That is, a homosexual treated along these lines was not likely to remain asexual but would more often than not adjust to a heterosexual lifestyle. It has been reported that Eysenck did accept that in a minority of cases some homosexuals did become sexually dysfunctional as a result of aversion therapy (The Guardian, 1997).

Although Eysenck and other advocates of aversion therapy claimed 'cure' rates as high as 50 per cent, these claims were never satisfactorily supported. There are even claims that patients who were rendered asexual in response to the therapy were counted among the successful treatments. Many psychiatrists abandoned the use of aversion therapy not out of any ethical concern for their patients or because they thought such treatment was inhumane, but because they thought it simply didn't work. It has been documented that some homosexual men who underwent aversion therapy have suffered serious long-term psychological effects, including depression, despair and attempted suicide. A more recent study (Bartlett et al., 2009) has stated that there is no evidence to support treatments to 'cure' homosexuality despite 17 per cent of mental health professionals admitting that they had 'helped' lesbian, gay and bisexual clients to reduce their sexual feelings and that 'the best approach is to help people to adjust to their situation, to value them as people and show them that there is nothing pathological about their sexual orientation'(Kapp, 2010). Indeed, the American Psychological Association (2009) hold that healthcare professionals who attempt to change sexual orientation may be committing human rights violations. It is discrimination against homosexuality that is the problem not the sexual orientation itself.

As with so many contentious debates in psychology, one of the main players was a controversial figure. Hans Eysenck's combative style caused a biographer to call him the 'controversialist in the intellectual world' (Gibson, 1981). Eysenck was well aware of this and seemed to revel in it. He wrote

> From the days of opposition to Nazism in my early youth, through my stand against Freudianism and projective techniques, to my advocacy of

behaviour therapy and genetic studies, to more recent issues, I have usually been against the establishment and in favour of the rebels . . . I prefer to think that on these issues the majority were wrong, and I was right.

(Eysenck, 1997)

He certainly polarised views in both academic and non-academic audiences alike and entitled his autobiography *Rebel with a Cause* (1997). One prominent critic has been the gay rights activist, Peter Tatchell, who had a series of well-publicised confrontations with Eysenck in the 1970s and 1980s.[2]

Tatchell and others vehemently questioned the use and success of aversion therapy, particularly in the treatment of homosexuality. Tatchell reported cases in which patients had become chronic depressives as a direct result of undergoing the therapy. Indeed the case of Captain Billy Clegg of the Royal Tank Regiment is often cited as an example of the abuse of the therapy. Billy Clegg was arrested in Southampton in the days when homosexuality was illegal. He was sentenced to 6 months compulsory aversion therapy at a local military psychiatric hospital. He died undergoing treatment and despite his death certificate stating that he died of natural causes there were many at the time

Figure 14.3 Brilliant but controversial psychologist: Hans Eysenck
Source: Getty Images

(including medical experts) that argued that he died from a coma and convulsions as a direct result of the apomorphine injections. Unfortunately, there are many other testimonies from young men who underwent appallingly painful and unsuccessful treatments in the 1960s under the guise of aversion therapy.

A Clockwork Orange

Parallels have also frequently been made between the use of aversion therapy and it's portrayal in the book and subsequent film *A Clockwork Orange* (1962). Although many behaviourists deny the link, the treatment of the main protagonist in the book, Alex, has certain similarities with the current case. The author, Anthony Burgess did, indeed, intend the novel to explore issues of free will and behaviourism. In the book, Alex, a teenage hooligan, is jailed for his crimes and agrees to 'aversion therapy' in order to get a reduced sentence. Once cured, he is placed back in society and is rejected by his friends and relatives. At one point he breaks into a house where an author is writing a book called *A Clockwork Orange* in which he argues that aversion therapy should not be used since it turns people into clockwork oranges (*ourang* is Malay for 'man', and Anthony Burgess served in the armed forces in Malaysia). Burgess's view was that the therapy denies people the chance to choose to be good, they thus lose their free will. Burgess wrote that

> in Britain, about 1960, that respectable people began to murmur about the growth of juvenile delinquency and suggest [that the young criminals] were a somehow inhuman breed and required inhuman treatment . . . There were irresponsible people who spoke of aversion therapy . . . Society, as ever, was put first. The delinquents were, of course, not quite human beings: they were minors, and they had no vote; they were very much them as opposed to us, who represented society.[3]

Any reader will see that the case of the prams and handbags patient should not really be compared with the treatment of homosexuals. However, prior to the early 1970s, homosexuality was actually classifiable as a psychiatric disorder. At the time, many people questioned whether aversion therapy should have been given to people who were, of course, indulging in practices through which no public harm was done. Further, there was a question of whether this kind of treatment should have been given to individuals even if they themselves asked for the treatment. Sometimes treatments are given to people although the treatment itself is ethically questionable. For example, body dysmorphia refers to a mental disorder defined as a preoccupation with a perceived defect in one's appearance. The media, as is their want, often incorrectly refer to it as 'imagined ugliness syndrome', since the ugliness is very real to the person concerned. A form of body dysmorphia is apotemnophilia, which is the desire to have a disabled identity in which sufferers with healthy limbs request one or two limb amputations. In cases where this has been refused, some people have been driven to 'do-it-yourself amputation' where they have placed their limb on a railway line.

In terms of homosexuals, it is frequently argued that the problem here lies with society, rather than the individual themselves. Advocates for the therapy argued that patients only received aversion therapy after having had the nature of the treatment thoroughly explained to them. They had obviously given their informed consent for the treatment and signed a legal document to this effect. However, opponents argued that many individuals were virtually blackmailed into agreeing to such therapy and given little option but to sign the appropriate forms. Given the choice between prison or treatment, many would have 'volunteered' for the latter. It was also argued that many homosexuals may have become so ostracised by society's rejection and oppression of homosexuals that they would have also volunteered, albeit unwillingly.

Aversion therapy in the laboratory has a number of disadvantages. As previously mentioned, the first one is that conditioned responses are subject to extinction when they are not continuously reinforced. This is why the 'prams and handbags' patient had to return for 'booster' courses. A person's conditioned response, like all conditioned responses, changes in its strength from day to day and hour to hour in the degree of its strength. This is a well-known laboratory phenomenon and has been demonstrated in dogs trained to salivate to the sound of a bell (food is previously paired with the sound of a bell). The change in strength is dependent on a great number of factors; obviously, the hungrier the dog, the greater the number of drops of saliva. The same can also apply to homosexuality or the case of the man who had a fetish about prams and handbags. If desire is strong at a particular moment and opportunity beckons, then people may not be so easily able to resist temptation. If this occurs, then some extinction of the conditioning process will occur and the next time they find themselves in a similar situation the temptation may be resisted less strongly. The principle of extinction will work against the therapy and in favour of the spontaneous remission of the conditioned response, which they have tried to replace. In other words, the conditioned response that they learned in the first place and which was their disorder, may actually re-occur. In cases such as this it is suggested that the aversive conditioning should occur well beyond the point where it has begun to have effect. This is sometimes called over-conditioning and certainly occurred in the case of the patient with the fetish towards prams and handbags. The patient himself said that he was cured days before he was actually allowed to leave hospital.

In practice, over-conditioning does not occur for very long, and does not continue over years. There are a number of reasons for this. Of course the first one would be that it would actually be excessively time consuming for the patient. In the second place, experiments or therapy using vomiting are messy and expensive in terms of therapeutic time. Third, the process is strenuous and unpleasant for both the experimenter and for the patient and consequently it is thought to be best to try to keep the therapy to as shorter time period as possible.

Many of these points that have been made show that it is actually better, as we have said earlier, to use electric shocks. So in terms of the topic of over-conditioning this is, of course, the standard medical practice for a variety of disorders. Patients, for instance, who have been de-sensitised against certain allergies often have to receive booster doses once a year to ensure that the immunity lasts. Injection doses are also given from time to time against various illnesses. It is standard practice, therefore, in some clinics for individuals who have been treated in this manner to be called back on an annual basis to receive short booster treatments.

Another interesting aspect of aversion therapy is that reinforcement works best when it's not based on 100 per cent or total reinforcement. The best way to condition is to use partial reinforcement techniques. In other words, if we want to train a dog to salivate to the sound of a bell, we don't produce the meat (the unconditioned stimulus) every time a bell is sounded. A far better method is to reinforce the conditioned stimulus (the bell) on only 25 per cent or 50 per cent of the trials. Although, intuitively, one would expect this to be a less effective method of conditioning, it actually works much better than total reinforcement techniques. Partial reinforcement makes extinction less likely and extinction is much slower than 100 per cent reinforcement is. Although it is not exactly entirely clear what the reasons are for this, one suggestion is that if you have been trained on total or 100 per cent reinforcement, the very first occasion that you hear a bell and you don't receive the meat you immediately realise the conditioning no longer occurs. But if you have only been conditioned on 25 per cent of occasions, then hearing a bell and not receiving meat would not guarantee that you wouldn't receive meat next time you hear a bell and thus the salivation response continues to the sound of bells.

The power of conditioning

We have discussed aversion therapy for a rather strange case of a man's erotic interest in prams and handbags and also for a treatment for homosexuality. Perhaps the best example of aversion therapy, though, is in the treatment of alcoholism. It has been used for a number of years, and the treatment for alcoholism has certainly got the longest history in psychology. The method used here involves conditioning once again. This takes place in a quiet, darkened room, typically with a spotlight on a number of alcohol bottles on the table in front of the person. The patient is the only person present, apart from the doctor. The doctor injects a mixture of emetine, ephedrine (a stimulant to improve the conditioning process) and pilocarpine (which makes the patient sweat and salivate profusely and adds to the symptoms produced by the emetine). So in this way the patient is brought to the verge of nausea and vomiting, and at this point any small amount of alcohol produces nausea and vomiting immediately.

The problem with this is that it is quite difficult to maintain a patient on the verge of vomiting and considerable experience is required, as well as individual knowledge of the patient in order to achieve this. Of course, between sessions the patient must be given soft drinks and water, in order to avoid the development of aversion to say the handling of glasses in general or the act of drinking non-alcoholic drinks themselves. Thousands of patients have been treated in this way, perhaps the most famous person being George Best. Although in George Best's case it does not seem to have been entirely successful. In the majority of cases half of the patients have remained alcohol free for at least 2 to 5 years after treatment and 25 per cent for 10 to 13 years after treatment. Some require further help with subsequent treatment over a number of years.

If you include the subsequent treatments over the years, the overall abstinence rate is believed to be around 51 per cent for all patients. This is an amazingly high recovery figure compared to treatments used by any other methods.

Other aspects of conditioning

It would seem that the effect of conditioning in the field of sexual adjustment has quite remarkable effects. However, when you actually start thinking about it, perhaps it appears less remarkable. For example, we take it for granted in western society that making love involves kissing and fondling of breasts. This is not the case in all societies, indeed in some societies breasts are of only functional importance in weaning and childrearing. For example, the South Sea Islanders could not understand the great interest shown by the white sailors in the female natives' exposed breasts.

Even in our own society the cult of the bosom or breast is a cultural phenomenon. In the 1920s the bosom was flattened out as much as possible and almost completely denied by women. This gradually changed in the 1950s and 1960s when an hourglass figure found favour. Nowadays, perhaps the reverse is true. Would Marilyn Monroe, a size 16, have become such an iconic figure today given the current trend for 'thin' women?

Cultural anthropologists have given many other examples of the changes that have taken place in particular cultures. Such differences exemplify the remarkable power of conditioning over sexual reactions of this type. One particular example of different sexual reactions between cultures are cultural bounds syndromes. *Koro* is a sexual disorder found only in South East Asia whereby men believe that their penis is retracting into their body and women believe that their breasts are retracting into their body.

Homosexuality was removed from the list of psychiatric disorders in the 1970s but that did not mark the end of the use of aversion therapy to treat non-conforming sexual behaviour. Although it is no longer sanctioned by the American Psychiatric Association as an appropriate treatment for homosexuality, some therapists continue to use it, especially those involved in the reparative therapy movement. In addition, aversion therapy has been used to treat paedophiles and other sex offenders.

Covert sensitisation is a more humane and physically safer variation of aversion therapy that has also been used with such patients. It involves both the deviant and aversive stimuli being imagined and described to the patient, rather than *actually* being experienced. A similar procedure called shame aversion therapy, involves subjecting the patient to public shame or humiliation allied to their deviant behaviour.

Studies have investigated the effectiveness of aversion therapy with other behaviours such as paedophilia, exhibitionism, and transvestism. Most studies have used nausea or drug-induced sleep deprivation. Covert sensitisation has also been used for paedophilia. In general, very few controlled studies with multiple patients have been conducted and thus no firm conclusions can be drawn as to the effectiveness of these treatments (Council on Scientific Affairs, 1987).

Notes

1   Material in this chapter has been drawn from Eysenck (1965), unless otherwise indicated.
2   For details see http://petertatchellfoundation.org/health/alan-turing-medical-abuse-gay-men.
3   Burgess, A. (2004), available at: http://batr.org/flicks.html.

References

American Psychological Association (2009). *Report of the Task Force on Appropriate Therapeutic Responses to Sexual Orientation*. Washington, DC.

Bartlett, A., Smith, G. and King, M. (2009). 'The response of mental health professionals to clients seeking help to change or re-direct same sex sexual orientation'. *BMC Psychiatry*, 26 (March): 9–11.

Burgess, A. (1962). *A Clockwork Orange*. London: Penguin.

Council on Scientific Affairs of the American Medical Association (1987). 'Aversion therapy'. *Journal of the American Medical Association*, 258(18): 2562–5.

Eysenck, H. (1965). 'The case of the prams and handbags'. In H.J. Eysenck, *Fact and Fiction in Psychology*. London: Penguin.

Eysenck, H. (1997). *Rebel with a Cause*. London: Transaction Publishers.

Gibson, H.B. (1981). *Hans Eysenck: The Man and His Work*. London: Peter Owen.

The Guardian (1997). Prof H.J. Eysenck's obituary. 13 September.

Kapp, S. (2010). 'Treating homosexuality is unethical'. *The Psychologist*, 23(12): 952.

Smith, G., Bartlett, A. and King, M. (2004). 'Treatments of homosexuality in Britain since the 1950s – an oral history: The experience of patients'. *British Medical Journal*, 238: 427.

Wolpe, J. (1958). *Psychotherapy by Reciprocal Inhibition*. Stanford, CT: Stanford University Press.

Chapter 15

Freud's analysis of phobia in a young boy
The story of Little Hans

Sigmund Freud is the most recognised psychologist of all time. He produced a body of work covering a diverse range of topics from child and personality development, the meaning of dreams to the therapeutic treatments of mental disorders. Freud primarily used the case study method for his research. Although Freud mentions as many as 133 cases in his writings he only documents six detailed accounts of individuals. Such was Freud's influence that some of his patients subsequently became minor celebrities of their time. Despite his emphasis on the importance of childhood experiences on adult development, Freud only documented one case study of a child. Because of this, the case study of Little Hans is of crucial importance in Freudian theory. This landmark study of child analysis caused great excitement and controversy when first published and continues to do so to this day.[1]

Friendship with Freud

Max Graf (1873–1958) was, in his day, a well-known author, critic and acknowledged scholar on the history, theory and science of music. Nowadays, he is perhaps more famous as a good friend of Sigmund Freud (1856–1939). He holds a unique position in the history of psychoanalysis since he was also the father of 'Little Hans'.

Max Graf met Freud because his wife was one of Freud's early patients. Indeed, she was a patient of Freud's before she married Graf and it is reported that Freud encouraged their marriage. The couple used to attend a Wednesday night study group at Freud's home at 19 Berggasse, Vienna. Other notable members of the group included Alfred Adler and Carl Jung. These members might be regarded as Freud's early 'disciples' and the group later evolved into the Vienna Psychoanalytic Society. Freud hoped that psychoanalysis might break through the discipline boundaries, and so people like Max Graf, drawn from the artistic field, were particularly welcome. Graf was obviously a huge admirer of Freud and later described him as the most cultivated person he knew (Graf, 1942).

Freud encouraged his group members to collect developmental data on their own children and the Grafs proved to be particularly diligent at this. They started to keep detailed notes of their son's early years. Max Graf took this a stage further and under Freud's guidance attempted the first analysis of his own son. Throughout this period of analysis, Max Graf consulted Freud and Freud closely monitored and advised on the therapeutic process. This process was subsequently reported by Freud in 1909 in a paper entitled 'The Analysis of a Phobia in a Five Year Old Boy'. The 5 year old was given the pseudonym 'Hans'.

Freud had already written an account on the theory of childhood sexuality published in 1905 and he intended to use the Little Hans case study as a test of his theory. His theory of sexuality had not been well received in many quarters and had variously been described as abominably immoral work and obscene (Freud, 1905). In addition, Freud set out to detail the development and resolution of a phobia as a form of neurotic disorder.

Freud mentioned Hans briefly in earlier writings. For example, in a 1907 article on sexuality he referred to a 3-year-old boy who guessed the truth about birth having seen his mother pregnant (Abraham and Freud, 2002). In these articles, Hans is referred to by his real name Herbert. It is believed that Freud decided to rename Herbert after a famous horse of the time nicknamed 'Clever Hans' who was reported to have been capable of simple mathematic tasks such as counting (the horse used to tap his hoof to supply the correct number).[2] Freud must have felt that the name was appropriate given Herbert's phobia of horses and the fact that he was such an intelligent boy.

'Little Hans'

'Little Hans' was born in Vienna on 10 April 1903. He was described as a cheerful, straightforward child with a loving upbringing in a typical middle-class family. He was happy and talkative and loved both his mother and father. The Grafs were close friends of Freud. Close enough for Freud to give Hans a generous birthday present. Surprisingly, given their son's horse phobia, Freud chose as a gift a rocking horse. In 1942 Max Graf claimed this was given on Hans's third birthday (Graf, 1942), but 10 years later he referred to it as his

Figure 15.1 Sigmund Freud, the father of modern psychoanalysis

Source: Mondadori via Getty Images

son's fifth birthday. If it was a gift for his third birthday, it was a remarkable coincidence that he would later develop a horse phobia, so it seems more likely that Freud gave it to him on his fifth birthday as a convincing (and amusing) demonstration that his phobia had been cured. Incidentally, the giving of the present was only the second time that Freud met 'Hans'. Previously, they had met in a short therapeutic session. They did not meet again until many years later when Hans was an adult.

The close relationship his father had with Freud is demonstrated by the fact that Max Graf discussed with Freud the possibility of raising Herbert as a Catholic rather than a Jew. Graf had experienced at first-hand the hatred towards Jews in Vienna at the beginning of the twentieth century and sought advice from Freud as to the best course of action to protect his young son. Although no doubt recognising the dangers, Freud suggested that being brought up as a Jew subjected to discrimination would help foster an inner dynamism in Herbert that would be useful in later life and, thus, he remained Jewish.

So what techniques did Freud use in his study of Hans? Freud used the case study method and followed Hans (primarily using second-hand accounts from Max Graf) from the age of 3 to 5 years (1906–08). The data collected included biographical data and shorthand notes exclusively reported by Hans' parents. Max Graf also used to consult with Freud directly about his son. Freud only had one occasion to have a direct share in the treatment of Hans and that was a conversation that took place on 30 March 1908 when his analysis was coming to an end (Freud, 1909). The analytical techniques used included analyses of fantasies, his general behaviour and his phobias, as well as dream analysis. Freud believed that the interpretation of dreams was the 'royal road' to the understanding of the unconscious (Freud, 2001). For Freud, each dream has a manifest and latent content. The manifest part is that which can be recalled whereas the latent part is hidden. It is in the latent part that the real meaning of the dream might be uncovered.

The analysis of phobia of a young boy

The 'Little Hans' case study is detailed and complicated. Freud's writings about Little Hans when translated into English occupy about 150 pages. Apart from the original, there are numerous readable accounts of the details of the case (Gross, 2003). The psychoanalytic interpretation of events is often surprising and contentious. Freud's angle on the significant events of Hans's formative years can be summarised as follows.

Freud reports Hans showing 'a quite peculiarly lively interest in his "widdler"' (penis). Hans used to enjoy touching his own penis and to try to stop this one day his mother threatened to cut it off. Despite his castration anxiety, his pleasure in this sexual activity widened. For example, he observed that animals at the local zoo had 'widdlers' that were correspondingly much larger than his own and he also expressed regret that he had seen neither his father or mother's 'widdlers'. He assumed that since they were grown up their 'widdlers' would also be large 'like a horse'.

During one summer holiday, Hans's father was absent for long periods of time and Hans realised that he liked having his mother to himself. At first Hans wished his father would 'go away' but later he wished he would go away permanently, that is, die. The event that Freud supposed most influenced Hans's psychosexual development was the birth of his little sister, Hannah, when he was 3 ½ years old. The birth caused Hans great anxiety and he felt hostility towards his sister. Hans felt that his sister would occupy too much of his mother's time. Hans expressed his fear indirectly in a fear of having a bath. He thought that his mother might drop him in the bath but, in reality, he hoped that his mother might drop his sister. In analysis, Hans gave undisguised expression to his death wish against his sister, but didn't consider this as wicked as the one he had against his father.

One day while in the street, Hans had an anxiety attack. Although he could not say what he was afraid of, it appeared that his motive for being ill was the chance to stay at home and cuddle more with his mother. In time, his fear heightened to the extent that he was afraid even when his mother was with him. Hans also reported a quite specific fear that a white horse would bite him. Today this might sound rather an unusual fear but the Vienna that Hans knew would have had working horses everywhere transporting people and all manner of goods throughout the city.

There were two dimensions to Hans's phobia about horses. Hans had once heard a father warning his child when leaving on a horse drawn carriage 'Don't put your finger to the white horse or it'll bite you.' Freud guessed that the first half of this sentence echoed the wording his mother had used to warn Hans about touching his widdler. Hans was also informed by his father that women do not have penises. Hans made the connection with the castration threat from his mother earlier and reasoned that she must have had her penis cut off. Hans had made a connection between his castration anxiety and horses.

Hans next reported a fantasy about two giraffes. He reported a dream about taking away a crumpled giraffe (representing his mother) and a big giraffe protesting and crying out (representing his father). Freud informed Hans that the reason that he was afraid of his father was because of his hostile thoughts towards him. Freud also interpreted Hans's fear of horses as suggesting that the horse must represent his father. The black round the horse's mouth and the blinkers represented his father's moustache and glasses. After the meeting with Freud, Max recorded a conversation where Hans said 'Daddy don't trot away from me!'.

Hans gave further details of his phobia (which he referred to as his 'nonsense'). He reported being afraid of horses falling down, and frightened of heavily loaded carts, vans or buses. Hans also recalled an event where he saw a horse fall down in the street and kick about with its feet. He was terrified and thought that the horse was dead. Hans's father pointed out that when he saw the horse dead he must have thought of him. Hans displaced his fear of his father onto horses that reminded him of his father. For Hans, this realisation or explanation appears to have been a turning point. Freud reported that Hans appeared to accept this theory and from then on was unconstrained and fearless in his relationship with his father.

Hans also became gradually less fearful of horses. Two concluding fantasies suggested that he had resolved his feelings about his father. In the first, Hans reported that a plumber came and took away his 'widdler' and then gave him another larger one. In the second, Hans told his father that he imagined himself as the father of his imaginary children, not the mother as had usually been the case. According to Freud, both these fantasies showed that he had moved from wishing his father dead to identifying with him. With these two fantasies both Hans's illness and his analysis came to an end.

One of the key themes of Freud's work is the importance of the first few years of life in the subsequent development of personality. Freud believed that children experience emotional conflicts, and their future well-being depends on how well these conflicts are resolved. Freud believed that by communicating his fears Hans had successfully resolved all his conflicts and anxieties.

In contrast to the thinking of his day, Freud believed that children were not asexual until puberty. Freud believed that infantile sexuality shows up at different stages of development with the concentration at each stage on a different part of the body. Freud believed that the case study of Little Hans provided support for this concept. Freud argued that all children pass through five stages of development, namely the oral, anal, phallic, latent and genital stages. The first three stages occur during the child's first five years, and it was the phallic stage that Hans was passing through at the end of his analysis.

The phallic stage, from 3 to 5 years old was the stage where the child's sexual identification was established. During this stage Freud hypothesised that Hans, like all young boys, experienced what he called the Oedipus complex. The Oedipus complex is the desire of a child to sexually possess the opposite sex parent (in this case Hans's mother) and to exclude the parent of the same sex (Hans's desire to exclude his father Max Graf). Of course, Hans realised that this was impossible given the overwhelming power and strength of his father. According to Freud, Hans would have feared that his father might see him as a rival and castrate him. Such conflicts are disturbing to the child and one way to resolve them is to identify with the same-sex parent. According to Freud, Hans accomplished this by developing a mechanism called 'identification with the aggressor'. This can be seen in Hans's last fantasy in which he imagines himself as the father of his own brothers and sisters. In this way, all young boys learn to identify with their fathers. Freud proposed that girls experience an 'Electra complex' but his emphasis on male development has led to him being criticised for being sexist and 'phallocentric'.

Freud believed that the 'unconscious' is a part of the mind that we are not aware of and that it contained a number of unresolved conflicts such as the Oedipus complex. These conflicts affect our behaviour (Hans's phobia of horses) and are revealed in our fantasies and dreams (the giraffe and plumber fantasies). Due to their threatening or upsetting nature the conflicts appear in disguised form and need to be interpreted in order for their true significance to be revealed.

Sigmund Fraud?

So what has the Little Hans case study contributed to the field of psychology? Freudian supporters suggest that it demonstrates how some phobias develop in children – phobias are simply a means to cope with conflict and anxiety. Critics have put forward alternative explanations. Perhaps one of the most plausible of these is in terms of a conditioned fear response through classical conditioning (see also Chapter 10). The incident in which Hans witnessed the horse collapsing in the street was the actual cause of the disorder. The marked fear response to this initial event became generalised to all horses and a fear of going out in the street where Hans would undoubtedly have encountered horses.

Freud was the first to suggest that a so-called 'talking cure' would be applicable in the case of a child as young as Hans. Throughout the case study, Freud demonstrates his utmost respect for Hans's views. Indeed, at one point when Hans is castigated by his father for wishing his sister drowned Hans replies that it is good to think it because it is evidence that might be useful for 'the Professor' (Freud). Freud reported that he could have wished for 'no better understanding of psychoanalysis from any grown-up'. This incident might be viewed as an example of demand characteristics, where a participant (Hans) provides an answer that they think the researcher (Freud) would like to hear. As such it can also be viewed as a criticism of Freud's techniques. Despite this, it is not preposterous to suggest that Freud's innovative and pioneering work with Hans shaped the overall approach of much of the psychotherapeutic work conducted with children today. Furthermore, Freud's assertions that the unconscious plays an important part in determining much of our behaviour is widely accepted today.

Analysis of the Little Hans case study has concentrated on the subjective reporting of the case. All of the reports were either obtained from Max Graf (Hans's father) or from Freud. There was no independent collaboration of the case. Hans's father was already a strong supporter of Freud's theories and may have presented the evidence accordingly. The special relationship that Hans had to his analyst father may make the case unique and mean that the results cannot be generalised. Freud was aware of these possible criticisms but argued that the special relationship between Hans and his father was one of the reasons why the analysis was so successful. Freud argued that their relationship was a strength of the therapy not a weakness and that psychoanalysts should aim to foster strong relationships with their clients.

From its advent to the present day, psychoanalysis has remained controversial. Given the evidence and interpretations placed on the case by both Max Graf and Freud, it is no surprise that the Little Hans case study is regarded by some as the most farcical case history on record. Psychoanalyis has been claimed to be 'a scientific fairytale' and totally ineffective as a therapy beyond its placebo effect. Psychoanalysis has even been compared to a cult, with Sigmund Freud as the high priest. Articles have been written promising to 'bury Freud' (Tallis, 1996), and he has been denounced as a liar and a sexist. As the author of the 'seduction hypothesis' he has been held responsible for the misery of parents wrongly accused by their 'abused' children and in his subsequent renunciation of the hypothesis he has been held responsible for the abuse of children (Masson, 1985). People have wondered how such a flawed theory of the mind could have had such a marked influence on psychiatry for over 50 years. The way in which Freud's specious ideas, based on unconvincing evidence, have influenced psychiatry and society in general (for example, in the use of Freudian terminology), has been viewed as one of the most extraordinary events in the history of intellectual thinking in the twentieth century.

However, psychoanalysis has continued to develop since its Freudian beginnings. Freud was a product of his time and should surely be viewed as such. His approach into the inner workings of the human mind was revolutionary in his day. His approach may not pass muster in comparison to the scientific methods employed today but it compared well with contemporary methods. Freud was actually a trained scientist and regarded himself as an archaeologist of the mind, digging deeper and deeper into the unconscious. From his early days experimenting with cocaine, hypnosis and electrotherapy (all later abandoned) Freud had an intense, single-minded determination to succeed and make his mark in the world. He realised that some people viewed him as a monomaniac, but he was convinced with his theory of the unconscious mind that he had touched upon one of the great secrets of nature. His granddaughter Sophie Freud claimed that he always thought that he would become a great man. Few would dispute that he achieved this. Whether he exaggerated the evidence or not, one has to admire his will and determination to take the most complex structure in the universe, the human mind, and seek to explore it. Fraud or not, Freud provided much food for thought.

Perhaps it suits modern-day critics of psychoanalysis to overemphasis Freud's contemporary influence. The great mathematician, A.N. Whitehead (Whitehead, 1929) once claimed that 'a science that hesitates to forget its founders is lost', so perhaps it's time to move on from Freud. Contemporary psychoanalysis can still be seen to have, at the very least, three points in its favour. First, it emphasises the importance of child development on later adult personality; second, it emphasises the importance of human relationships for psychological well-being; and finally it provides a language for exploring and expressing all kinds of feelings.[3] For example, the Little Hans case study was the first time that Freud used the term 'transference' in his writings. Transference is the displacement of one's unresolved anxieties and conflicts onto a substitute object. Hans's anxieties towards his father were transferred onto a substitute object, in his case, horses. The phobic object became a useful vehicle for the expression of his feelings.

Herbert Graf: The adult 'Hans'

So what became of Little Hans? Some critics argued that Freud's intervention in Hans's life had robbed him of his innocence and foretold of an evil future for the poor little boy. Hans was even portrayed as a victim of psychoanalysis. Freud predicted this response in his original paper when he wrote 'I must enquire what harm was done to Hans by dragging to light in him complexes such as are not only repressed by children but dreaded by their parents?'. Freud suggested that doctors who misunderstood the nature of psychoanalysis would mistakenly think that wicked instincts were strengthened by being made conscious. Freud argues that the result of the analysis was that Hans recovered, he ceased to be afraid of horses and developed an even more friendly relationship with his father. Indeed, he reports Hans as saying to his father 'I thought you knew everything, as you knew about that horse.'

Freud lost contact with Hans in 1911 but there was to be one last meeting between the two of them. In the spring of 1922, Herbert Graf, now aged 19, strolled into Freud's consulting rooms. Freud reports a strapping youth who was perfectly well with no apparent troubles or inhibitions. He was emotionally stable despite experiencing his parents' divorce. Herbert had continued to live with his father (perhaps supporting Freud's view of Herbert's close relationship with his father) whereas his sister, of whom he was excessively fond, had gone to live with their mother. Herbert reported that when he had read the case history of Little Hans he did not realise that it was written about him! The analysis had not preserved the events from amnesia.

Herbert Graf, like his father, made a career in the musical arts. After working on various operas in Germany, Switzerland and Austria, Herbert moved to the United States in 1936 when he was 33 years old. Here, his career took off and he secured the prestigious position of the director of the Metropolitan Opera in New York. Following a successful period there, he moved back to his European roots and directed Maria Callas in Florence and was involved in acclaimed opera productions at Covent Garden and Salzburg. He was director of the Zurich Opera from 1960–62 and also became director of the Opera of Geneva. Herbert Graf was also a published author. In his 1951 book *Opera for the People* he wrote at length about all aspects of opera production. Herbert was described as a great man of the theatre, brilliantly creative and particularly welcoming to young artists.

Herbert entitled a four-part interview he gave to Opera News, 'Memoirs of an Invisible Man' (Graf, 1972) – the title a reference to his role as one who was always working behind the scenes, never on stage. The choice of a musical career shows a clear identification with his father, but it has been suggested that 'directing from behind the scenes' was also an identification with Freud's invisible role in his analysis (Holland, 1986).

Colleagues and acquaintances described Herbert as a man of great charm and intelligence. However, he was also portrayed with a few character flaws. It is reported that certain undesirable aspects of his personality were evident to all who worked with him, even if they had remained unnoticed by Freud all those years earlier! He was also described as a lover of both fine wines and pretty women (Holland, 1986). Herbert did not seem to have been particularly successful in love and did not have a family. Some have even suggested that such facts might be taken as (surely rather weak) evidence that his childhood analysis was not as successful as Freud might have hoped. Herbert became ill with cancer and died in Geneva in 1973. Despite his many noteworthy accomplishments in his adult life, Herbert Graf will perhaps forever remain more famous as Sigmund Freud's 'Little Hans'.

Notes

1   The majority of this chapter is drawn from Freud (1909).
2   It was subsequently found that the horse was merely responding to visual cues from its master and did not have any special mathematical abilities.
3   For an excellent extended essay on this topic see Jeremy Holmes (2005).

References

Abraham, K. and Freud, S. (2002). *The Complete Correspondence of Sigmund Freud and Karl Abraham 1907–1925*. London: Karnac Books.

Freud, S. (1905). *Three Essays on the Theory of Sexuality*. Pelican Freud Library, vol. 7. Harmondsworth: Penguin.

Freud, S. (1909). 'Two case histories: "Little Hans" and the "Rat Man"'. *The Standard Edition of the Complete Psychological Works of Sigmund Freud*. Vol. 10. London: Vintage, The Hogarth Press (reprinted 2000).

Freud, S. (2001). *Complete Psychological Works of Sigmund Freud. Vol. 5: The Interpretation of Dreams*. London: Vintage.

Graf, M. (1942). 'Reminisces of Professor Sigmund Freud'. *Psychoanalytic Quarterly*, 11: 465–76.

Graf, H. (1972). 'Memoirs of an invisible man: A dialogue with Francis Rizzo'. *Opera News*, 5 February: 25–8; 12 February: 26–9; 19 February: 26–9; 26 February: 26–9.

Gross, R. (2003). *Key Studies in Psychology* (4th edition). London: Hodder and Stoughton.

Holland, N. (1986). 'Not so Little Hans: Identity and ageing'. In K. Woodward and M. Schwartz (eds), *Memory and Desire*. Bloomington, IN: Indiana University Press.

Holmes, J. (2005). 'The assault on Freud'. Available at: http://human-nature.com/freud/holmes.html (accessed July 2014).

Masson, J. (1985). *The Assault on Truth: Freud's Suppression of the Seduction Theory*. London: Penguin.

Tallis, R. (1996). 'Burying Freud'. *The Lancet*, 347: 669–71.

Whitehead, A.N. (1929). *The Aims of Education and Other Essays*. New York: Macmillan, Free Press.

Chapter 16

The Three Faces of Eve
The story of Chris Sizemore

Multiple personality disorder (MPD), now called dissociative identity disorder,[1] was almost unknown until two American psychiatrists (Corbett Thigpen and Hervey Cleckley) published their case study in the 1950s. They described a patient they were treating who possessed three distinct personalities that they called 'Eve White', 'Eve Black' and 'Jane'. Each personality was separate and behaved in an entirely different way to the others. The subsequent award-winning film based on the case called *The Three Faces of Eve*, brought MPD to much wider public attention. Allied to further cases that caught the public imagination, most notably the 1970s book and film *Sybil*, MPD changed from being a largely unknown and seemingly rare condition to a widely recognised and much more commonly diagnosed disorder. In recent years, however, academics have begun to question whether MPD actually exists as a 'real' disorder or whether it is an iatrogenic disorder; a creation by therapists and 'placed' in the minds of their suggestible and vulnerable patients.[2]

What is MPD?

Multiple personality disorder (MPD) is one of the dissociative[3] psychiatric disorders, with its most noticeable symptom being that the person has at least one alternative or 'alter' personality that controls behaviour. The 'alters' occur spontaneously and involuntarily and, in the main, function completely independently of one another. In 1994 the American Psychiatric Association's DSM-IV (*Diagnostic Statistical Manual*) replaced the designation of MPD with DID: dissociative identity disorder. Although the diagnostic title has changed in the US, the old label (MPD) is still used in the UK and is favoured in this chapter since it remains the better known and arguably more descriptive label.

The change of name in the US has not altered the list of symptoms. The symptoms are diverse and vary from patient to patient and so it is difficult to describe a 'typical' case of MPD. Someone suffering from MPD can have any number of 'alter' personalities, typically up to 20 or 30. There is usually one 'core' personality that copes with ordinary everyday life. This personality is usually unaware of the presence of the other personalities or if they are aware it is in an indirect way. For example, evidence that they must have done something when they have no memory of doing so. The other 'alter' personalities may know about all the others and sometimes form friendships or alliances with each other to work against the others. Many of these 'alter' personalities are not fully developed and remain fragmentary. They can be of different ages, sexes or even nationalities. Each personality has a separate identity (which might involve different gestures, handwriting, speech and body image) from the others. A person with MPD could have hallucinations so marked that they actually perceive a different personality in the mirror (Sileo, 1993).

The history of MPD

Although certainly not well known prior to the Thigpen and Cleckley case study of Eve, MPD has a relatively long history. As long ago as 1784, there are reports of a country estate worker called Victor Race living in Soissons, France, who displayed symptoms of MPD. One day, Victor fell into an altered state of consciousness where his usual slowness of thought was replaced by a bright and quick-witted personality. When he recovered his usual state of consciousness he had no recollection of the events or the transformation in his personality (Crabtree, 1993).

Perhaps the first detailed account of MPD was published by Eberhard Gmelin in 1791 and involved a 21-year-old woman from Stuttgart who suddenly took on the personality and language of a Frenchwoman (Gmelin, 1791). In her altered state she believed that she had fled to Germany to escape the French Revolution. In this state of awareness, she could speak only rudimentary German with a French accent. The woman was unaware of the existence of this altered state (see note 2).

Although there were subsequent reports of multiple personalities in the literature, most notably Morton Prince's Miss Beauchamp study (Prince, 1906) (a study cited by Thigpen and Cleckley, 1954), its infrequent occurrence led to MPD being largely ignored in psychiatric circles. Indeed, Thigpen and

Cleckley wrote that 'multiple personality is a rarity in psychopathology'. They were to change all that with their case study of Eve published in 1954.

Eve

Corbett Thigpen was a psychiatrist who had been treating a 25-year-old married woman for 'severe and blinding headaches'. She also reported having 'blackouts' following the headaches. Thigpen and his colleague Hervey Cleckley named her 'Eve White' in their subsequent writings. After a series of infrequent therapeutic sessions they concluded that her symptoms were caused by a typical mixture of marital conflicts and personal frustrations. She had once forgotten details about a previous therapy session, but later recalled it under hypnosis. Nothing about her case stood out. But one day, out of the blue, Thigpen received a puzzling, unsigned letter that he realised had to have been written by Eve White. He noted, however, that the last paragraph had obviously been written by someone else. The immature content and handwriting style suggested it was the work of a child.

Questioned about the letter on her next visit, Eve denied any knowledge of it. She recalled starting the letter but believed she had destroyed it unfinished. Eve became quite agitated during the interview and suddenly asked whether hearing an imaginary voice was a sign of insanity. Thigpen was intrigued. Eve had never previously shown or mentioned any such symptoms. Before Thigpen had had a chance to answer Eve's question, she put both hands to her head as if overcome by a shooting pain. After a brief moment, she dropped her hands, gave a quick and reckless smile and in a bright voice said 'Hi there, Doc!'. The familiar retiring, conventional Eve White had been replaced by a newcomer with a devilish and carefree personality who talked at length about Eve White as a different person. On being asked who she was she replied 'Oh, I'm Eve Black.' To all intents and purposes, Thigpen had been joined by a completely different person.

Over the next 14 months, during a series of interviews totalling approximately 100 hours, extensive material was obtained about the behaviour and inner life of both Eve White and Eve Black. Thigpen and Cleckley reported that Eve Black had existed as an independent personality since Eve White's childhood and was a product of disruptive events in adulthood. Furthermore, while Eve White was unaware of Eve Black, Eve Black was aware of Eve White. When not 'out' Eve Black was aware of what Eve White was doing whereas the reverse was not true. Although Eve Black would often spontaneously 'pop out', it was found that initially she could be called forth only under hypnosis. After further therapeutic sessions, hypnosis was no longer necessary and Cleckley could simply call forth either of the personalities that he wanted to talk to. One unfortunate side effect of this was that Eve Black found herself more able to 'take over' Eve White than previously.

Thigpen and Cleckley suggested that the fragmentation of her personality had been a method to cope with experiences that she could not bear. This suggestion seemed to be supported by Chris Sizemore's (Eve's real name) biography where she outlined a number of traumatic incidents that she experienced growing up in North Carolina during the Depression (Sizemore and Pittillo, 1977).[4] The first involved her witnessing the dead body of a man being retrieved from a waterlogged ditch. It was surmised that he had fallen in and drowned when drunk the night before. Christine reports that she 'saw' on the bridge looking down on the scene a little girl whose red hair shone brightly in the morning sun and whose eyes were bright blue, calm and unafraid. Another incident of note involved her mother. Unaccountably while her mother was holding a glass milk bottle, it broke. Realising that Christine was directly beneath the broken bottle, her mother Zueline hugged the broken shards to her body in order to protect Christine. In doing this one of the shards of glass cut into her mother's left wrist. The sight of blood terrified Christine and despite being told to fetch help, she ran and collapsed in a heap in the corner of the room. The red-haired girl with the cold blue eyes appeared once again and stood watching the red blood mix with the white milk for some time before running for help.

Another traumatic incident was to follow shortly. Christine's father used to work at the local sawmill. A whistle used to sound for the start and finish of the day's work. One day at 10.25 a.m. the whistle sounded. At this time, the sound of the whistle could mean only one thing – there had been an accident at the mill. All the relatives of the workers immediately hurried to the mill to see what had happened. Christine was among them and arrived to see the grotesque sight of a man's body sliced in half above the waist. Each half lay either side of the saw a short distance apart. Christine also noticed that one of his arms had also been severed. Here was a body physically separated into three distinct parts.

Christine later wrote that a child should never have seen such horrible things and that she could not bear the sight of them (Sizemore, 1989). She suggests that perhaps the red-haired girl was someone who could watch what she herself could not face. Despite such incidents Christine lived in fairly favourable circumstances compared to many other children brought up during the Depression. For most of her childhood, she lived among her large extended family on a productive farm that they owned. The family had been fortunate to invest in land at just the right time and working the land meant that they avoided many of the dreadful hardships of the era. Nevertheless, Christine was always finding herself in trouble. She would do things she had been told not to and then deny having done them in the first place. These incidents and the subsequent 'lying' exasperated her parents and led to more severe punishments. As was commonplace at that time, punishments tended to be physical in nature. During these spankings, Christine often used to sob that 'She did it!' and continue to protest her innocence.

One particular feature of many subsequent MPD cases is the existence of child sexual abuse. Despite numerous therapy sessions often involving hypnosis, there was never any evidence that any such incidents had occurred to Eve. The catalyst to Eve's creation of 'alter' personalities seemed linked to traumatic incidents (not of a sexual nature) in her childhood.

Thigpen and Cleckley (1954) used contrasting techniques to explore Eve's personalities. Allied to the therapeutic sessions, they interviewed Eve's family (her parents and husband). More often than not, they substantiated various incidents reported by Eve Black. However, since Eve White had no access to Eve Black and Eve Black was shown to 'lie glibly and without compunction' the therapists were unable to verify all her stories. Eve White's husband and her parents had noticed many of the personality changes that the therapists had witnessed but without the knowledge of the existence of MPD had considered them more conceivably as 'fits of temper' or her 'strange little habits' as her mother innocently called them. They did note that her personality changes were in marked contrast to her more usual, gentle and considerate nature.

When confronted with her delinquency, Eve Black expressed amusement at 'popping out' to commit and enjoy some forbidden adventure only to disappear and leave Eve White to face the ensuing punishment. Eve White reported bewilderment at being punished for misdemeanours for which she had no memory. Eve Black followed a hedonistic lifestyle which involved, among other things, buying expensive and unnecessary clothes and flirting with strangers in cheap nightclubs. When confronted with her clothes purchases, Eve White denied all knowledge of them. Horrified to the same degree as her husband by being plunged into debt, she promptly took them all back to the shop for a refund. Unable to explain how the clothes had got into her cupboard, she suspected her husband of planting them there to make it appear that she was going 'insane'. Eve Black used to enjoy going out and getting drunk aware that it would be Eve White who would wake up with the hangover, unaware of the causes of it or what had happened the night before.

Eve White had a 4-year-old daughter who, because of Eve's psychiatric problems, was living with her grandparents. Having to work in a city 100 miles from the girl had caused Eve White a great deal of further unhappiness and despair. Eve Black was aware of the child but had no feelings towards her. She generally ignored the child or treated her with complete indifference. On one occasion, however, when the 'little brat got on my nerves' she admitted to trying to strangle her before Eve White's husband intervened. Aware of this incident, but unaware of her part in it, Eve White voluntarily committed herself to a psychiatric unit for some time afterwards. Eve Black totally denied marriage to Eve White's husband whom she despised. Thigpen and Cleckley stated that Eve White's marriage would probably have foundered given their incompatibility but the presence of Eve Black ensured that they eventually separated. Eve Black did not purposely set out to harm Eve White through maliciousness or cruelty, but felt no guilt or compassion if this turned out to be the case.

Psychological testing

Thigpen and Cleckley also conducted EEG (electroencephalogram) tests and a number of psychometric and projective tests including, intelligence tests, memory tests and Rorschach (ink blot tests) on both Eve White and Eve Black. A summary of the findings is shown in Table 16.1.

These psychological tests were conducted by an independent clinical psychologist called Dr Leopold Winter. His report supported the diagnosis of MPD and gave further details of the contrast in the personalities of the 'two' women. He argued that the projective tests showed that Eve Black's personality was the result of a regression to a time before the marriage. He argued that there were not two different personalities but one personality at different times of her life. Adopting a psychoanalytic approach, Winter suggested that Eve White experienced great anxiety over her role as a wife and mother. Only with a supreme amount of effort could she function in either or both of these roles. The effort required caused her further anxiety and ever-increasing hostility to her dual roles. This hostility was unacceptable to her and so she employed

Table 16.1 Summary of findings from diagnostic tests conducted on Eve White and Eve Black

Characteristic	Eve White	Eve Black
Personality	Demure, almost saintly	Egocentric, party girl
Face	Quiet sweetness, contained sadness	Eyes dancing with mischief, expression of wilfulness, will never know sadness
Clothes	Simple, neat, conservative	A little provocative
Posture	Slight stoop. Dignified careful movements	A touch of sexiness pervades every gesture
Voice	Soft, feminine restraint	Coarse, teasing, witty, constant use of vernacular
Character/attitude	Steadfast, industrious, contemplative, passive strength, lacking initiative; seldom animated, rarely jokes	Whim-like, momentary, spontaneous, unthinking, callous, prankster, ready wit, amusing and immediately likeable
Intelligence (IQ) test score	110 (score may have been affected by anxiety)	104 (score may have been affected by indifference)
Memory test performance	Superior to Eve Black and above that expected in comparison to IQ score; a surprising finding given her history of amnesia	Inferior to Eve White but consistent with intelligence score
Rorschach test results	Very anxious about her role as wife and mother; has obsessive-compulsive traits	Slight hysterical tendency but healthier than Eve White
Other projective test results	Repression	Regression
Physical health	No allergies present	Allergy to nylon

a defence mechanism, in this case, regression, to cope with these feelings of anxiety. She removed the conflicting situation from her conscious awareness. At the same time, she (unconsciously) played the role of Eve Black in order to direct her hostility towards Eve White, for whom she showed utter contempt. Contempt due to her lack of foresight over the situation she found herself in and contempt for her lack of courage to solve the situation. (The 'defence mechanism' explanation echoes the explanation of 'Little Hans' phobia.)

During their exploration of the case, Thigpen and Cleckley came across a distant relative who revealed that Eve White had been married before. Eve White denied any such union as did Eve Black. However, after further repeated questioning, Eve Black did admit she had been married previously but that only she had been the bride, not Eve White! Eve Black reported that one night when Eve White was working many miles from her parents' home she had 'popped out' and gone drinking and dancing. After a particularly wild night she had half jokingly agreed to marry a man she scarcely knew. Although there were no official records of the marriage that could be located, Eve Black reported that there was certainly some sort of informal marriage ceremony and she believed that she had married him. She lived with this man as his 'wife' for a number of months. During this time, Eve Black seemed to be dominant over Eve White. Eve White had no recollection of any such marriage. Eve Black claimed that this was because she was able to erase certain aspects of Eve White's memory.

Treatment of Eve

After about 8 months of psychiatric treatment Eve White seemed to be making encouraging progress. She had not been troubled by her headaches or 'blackouts'. She had been promoted at her work (a telephone operator) and had made some new friends. Eve Black was bored by Eve White's work and seldom appeared during work hours. She continued to appear infrequently in leisure hours to pick up unsuitable men.

At this point, Eve White's headaches and 'blackouts' returned. It had been noticed that the 'blackouts' often occurred when the two personalities were changing, but Eve Black denied all knowledge of them. Eve Black appeared curious as to the cause of the blackouts and was quoted as saying intriguingly, 'I don't know where we go, but go we do.' On more than one occasion, Eve White was found by a housemate lying on the floor unconscious. (By this time, Eve had left her husband because of her problems and they eventually divorced.) There appeared to be no doubt that Eve's condition was deteriorating. She was threatened with detention in a psychiatric institution in the hope that Eve Black would start to co-operate with the therapy for fear of being similarly confined. One day during a session where she was recounting an incident from her childhood, she closed her eyes and fell silent. About 2 minutes later she opened her eyes and looked around the room in a state of bewilderment before turning to Thigpen and asking in an unknown husky voice 'Who are you?'. A third personality had emerged, one who called herself Jane.

It was immediately obvious that Jane did not possess Eve Black's faults and was more mature, vivid, capable and possessing more initiative than Eve White. Jane was also aware of what both Eve White and Eve Black did. Jane was a mechanism through which the therapists could tell whether Eve Black was lying. Although Jane did not feel responsible for Eve White's role of wife and mother, she showed a great deal of compassion to Eve White's predicament. Jane started to take over some of Eve White's tasks at both home and work. Jane showed a ready willingness to take an active role in the upbringing of Eve White's child.

Soon after Jane appeared the three personalities were given electroencephalogram tests (EEG). It was possible to make a clear distinction between the readings of Eve Black and the other two personalities. Eve Black's relaxation rhythm was recorded at 12½ cycles per second, which showed her to be the most tense of the three personalities and on the borderline of abnormal. Eve White was next, with Jane the least tense – both the latter's recording were in the normal range.

Since MPD is a dissociation of one personality, earlier on in the therapy, Thigpen and Cleckley had attempted to re-integrate the original two personalities. They had tried this by calling out for both personalities at once. This had resulted in a violent headache and emotional stress so severe that Thigpen and Cleckley concluded it would have been unwise to proceed in this way. However with the more confident Jane now emerging, the possibility existed of getting Jane to integrate all the personalities and remain in full control.

Thigpen and Cleckley wrestled with the idea of trying to promote the personality of Jane at the expense of the other two personalities. However, they wrote that Jane shared their reluctance to participate in any act that would contribute to Eve White's extinction. Although the mother of Eve White's child would still physically exist, Jane did not feel she was the actual mother. Eve White herself recognised the possibility of Jane taking over and seemed to accept that her extinction might enable Jane to succeed in the maternal role in which she had so failed. In effect, Eve White seemed willing to lay down her life for that of her child.

Near the end of the case study, Jane wrote a letter to Thigpen recounting an incident whereby Eve White risked her life by jumping into the road to grab a small child from being hit by a car. She wrote that Eve White walked away hugging the relieved little boy. She tells how she (Jane) had to emerge and return the boy to a nearby policeman for fear of Eve White being arrested for kidnapping! Jane wrote that she couldn't face such a worthy person dying. Jane argued that Eve White should survive, not her. Furthermore she wrote that she could no longer feel Eve Black and wondered whether Eve Black had simply given up. This last event hinted that the personalities were becoming successfully resolved.

Questions to consider

This was not to be the end of the case. Thigpen and Cleckley wrote up the Eve case study into a book (1957) and this spawned a subsequent film of the same name (*The Three Faces of Eve*, 1957, starring Joanne Woodward). Both the book and the film were huge hits. The book was translated into 22 different languages and received a number of literary non-fiction awards. The actress, Joanne Woodward won both a Golden Globe award and an Oscar (best actress) for her portrayal of Eve in the film. Both the book and film also helped bring MPD to public prominence.

Figure 16.1 Joanne Woodward in *The Three Faces of Eve*, 1957
Source: Getty Images

Some questions were posed as to Thigpen and Cleckley's original reporting of the case. Some of these issues, including the question of whether Eve was a 'hoax', were even discussed in the case study report. Thigpen and Cleckley had spent a great deal of time with Eve and believed that not even a professional actor could have taken on the different roles portrayed so convincingly and consistently. Thigpen and Cleckley made efforts to substantiate the information reported and were able to corroborate much of it through relatives. They also asked Dr Winter, an independent expert, to take various physiological and psychological measures and these appeared to confirm the existence of distinct personalities.

However, as with any case study it is difficult to know whether the findings can be generalised beyond the specific case study in question. Was Eve a unique case or was she typical of other MPD cases? The emergence of different identities and the amnesic aspects of them are consistent with 'typical' (if such a thing exists) MPD, but the lack of evidence of any child abuse is unusual.[5] This case study relied on retrospective memory accounts of events and these may not have been particularly reliable. The events related by Eve Black, a consummate liar, are particularly open to this criticism. With over 100 hours of therapy over a 14-month period there is no doubt that the therapists forged a close relationship with Eve. Although this may be seen as an important part of the therapy, there is a danger that the therapists selectively reported the data in a biased way.

There were a number of ethical issues to consider in this case study. Thigpen and Cleckley recognised this when it came to the possible killing of one of the personalities, and they concluded that 'we have not judged ourselves as wise enough to make active decisions or exert personal influence in shaping what impends'. Some have argued that by publishing the study, Thigpen and Cleckley intruded into Eve's life in an unnecessary way and, given her problems, it remains unclear whether they got her *informed* consent prior to publication. In essence, their good fortune (increased status and financial gain) came about as a direct result of exploiting Eve's misfortune. However, they did not reveal Eve's real identity and they argued that they helped to raise the profile of an important psychiatric disorder. This may have helped other people suffering from MPD.

Eve's reappearance

Nothing much more was heard of the case until 1977 when Chris Sizemore revealed herself to be the real Eve (Sizemore and Pittillo, 1977). Some of the details of the case she disclosed were different to those reported by Thigpen and Cleckley. She revealed that she had approximately 22 personalities and that these were present both before and after the therapy. She further asserted that she had not been cured by Thigpen and Cleckley. In a talk in London in 2009, Sizemore stated that she was grateful to Thigpen and Cleckley for trying to help her and for having the strength of character to pursue an unusual diagnosis, but that their treatment had not been as successful as they had claimed. She had actually continued her therapy with another doctor called Tony Tsitos. In a more recent book (Sizemore, 1989) she stated that she was finally cured after having had MPD for 45 years and after undergoing 20 years of therapy. Sizemore believes that she became the integrated sum of all her personalities claiming that 'I'm not any one of them, I'm all of them.' After this integration, Sizemore reclaimed many of the memories that had only been accessible to the individual personalities. Sizemore further stated that 'Eve Black was my favourite personality – she sure did have fun and that's important.' Sizemore always resented the way that Thigpen made money out of her story by publicising it and promoting the Hollywood portrayal. Indeed in 1989 Sizemore

Figure 16.2 Chris Sizemore poses with one of her paintings, 1975

Source: The Washington Post/Getty Images

successfully sued Twentieth Century Fox for the rights to *The Three Faces of Eve* film. However, it must be stated that Thigpen never charged Sizemore for any of her treatment.

Sizemore has gone from strength to strength and has given much of her time to promoting the understanding of MPD. She has looked into the role of art as part of the therapeutic process, given numerous talks about MPD for the American Mental Health Association and received many awards for her efforts. She has also become an accomplished painter and has sold some of her work to prestigious art galleries.

The Sybil phenomenon?

Following on from the case study of Eve, the best known MPD case study surrounds the case of 'Sybil', a patient who developed as many as 16 separate personalities in order to deal with horrendous physical and sexual child abuse. The case was subsequently dramatised into a best-selling book by the journalist Flora Rheta Schrieber (1973). The book became one of the best-selling non-fiction books of the year. As with *The Three Faces of Eve*, the story was quickly made into a successful television film called *Sybil* (1976) with Joanne Woodward, who had played Eve in the earlier film, this time in the role of the therapist, Dr Cornelia Wilbur. Again echoing the earlier film, Sally Field won an Emmy for her portrayal of Sybil.

However, in contrast to the Eve case there are serious question marks as to the veracity of the case. Herbert Spiegel, a respected psychiatrist, knew both Wilbur and Sybil. In fact, he is briefly mentioned in the books' acknowledgements, but nowhere else in the book. This is a surprising omission given that he treated Sybil on occasions and she even participated in some of his hypnosis demonstrations at Columbia's University College. Spiegel categorised Sybil as highly suggestible, indicting that Wilbur may have induced the personalities later reported. Sybil may have been a classic example of an iatrogenic illness. This is one where the illness is induced in the patient by a physician's activity, manner or therapy. In essence, in Sybil's case the personalities may have been a by-product of Wilbur's suggestions during hypnosis. There are also other damaging claims about the processes involved in reporting the study (Borch Jacobson and Spiegel, 1997). For example, Wilbur promoted the idea of the book when she found she could not get the study printed in reputable journals. There are also claims that Schreiber insisted that Sybil be 'cured' before she would write the book.

Despite such criticisms the combined influence of the cases of Eve and Sybil led to the increased recognition of MPD among health professionals and the public alike.

What happened to Thigpen and Cleckley?

Cleckley and Thigpen were already respected academics prior to the publication of the Eve case study and continued with their careers. The book in particular led to their international recognition. In a subsequent follow-up paper (Thigpen and Cleckley, 1984) on the incidence of MPD, published 25 years after the Eve case study, Thigpen and Cleckley warned against the over-reporting of MPD. Due to their expertise, they had had hundreds of patients specifically referred to them by therapists believing them to have MPD. However, they argued that in over 30 years of combined practice in which they had seen thousands of patients, there was only one other case that they believed was a genuine multiple personality. They describe the procession of these patients to their practice in Georgia as some sort of 'pilgrimage'. They even report one woman introducing all her different 'personalities' over the phone to them using a different voice for each!

Thigpen and Cleckley discuss the worry that some patients and indeed some therapists seek to draw attention to themselves by a diagnosis of MPD. They cite patients who move from one therapist to another until they find one who confirms their own diagnosis of MPD. Although recognising the need for help in such patients they do not recognise the high incidence of reported MPD. They even suggest that there is an unhealthy competition among some patients and therapists to see who can reveal the most personalities. They suggest the reason for such behaviour is the attention they receive once the diagnosis is made and the secondary gain that these patients obtain, namely, the avoidance of responsibility for their actions. They state that this secondary gain is most noticeable in criminal cases where a patient can gain a great deal by a diagnosis of MPD. They cite the celebrated case of Billy Milligan who was initially diagnosed as having MPD (a diagnosis also made by Dr Cornelia Wilbur of 'Sybil' fame) (Keyes, 1995). After treatment, he was judged competent for trial and then suffered a relapse prior to the trial. Thigpen and Cleckley suggest that a desire to avoid responsibility for one's actions in such cases might motivate a person to further dissociate. Of course, Milligan claims to be a genuine case of MPD, but perhaps surprisingly (or cleverly?) agrees with Thigpen and

Cleckley's general argument that many cases of MPD are 'created' by the psychiatrists themselves.

Thigpen and Cleckley also question whether a diagnosis of MPD should actually relieve a person of complete responsibility for their actions. They argue that although the main personality may have no memory of the behaviour of their 'alter' personalities, the 'alter' personality is aware of their behavioural actions and as such never performs actions that might be dangerous to the survival of the total person. They conclude that the diagnosis of MPD should be reserved for those very few persons such as Chris Sizemore, who are fragmented in the most extreme manner.

Cleckley, a Rhodes scholar who attended Oxford University in 1926, was already a professor of psychiatry and neurology at the University of Georgia Medical School prior to the 1957 publication of *The Three Faces of Eve*. He died on the 28 January 1984 aged 79.

Following a similar career pattern, Hervey Thigpen practised medicine for over 50 years and had become a clinical professor of psychiatry at the Georgia Medical School by the time of his retirement in 1987. Thigpen died on 19 March 1999 aged 80.

MPD: Real or created?

To this day, the diagnosis of MPD remains very unreliable. Some of the symptoms of MPD such as auditory hallucinations, the creation of fantasy worlds and self-mutilation can also occur with schizophrenia. Because of this there is often a confusion between MPD and schizophrenia. MPD is not a form of schizophrenia. In contrast to MPD, schizophrenia is a type of psychosis where contact with reality and insight are impaired. In essence, schizophrenia involves a 'splitting of one mind' whereas MPD involves the construction of many whole personalities. Schizophrenic patients can usually report their hallucinations and delusions to the therapist whereas a patient with MPD cannot due to profound amnesia. A biological or chemical cause of schizophrenia has been found whereas no such biological cause for MPD has been yet determined. Perhaps reflecting differences in diagnostic practices, MPD is far more prevalent in some western countries (for example, the USA and the Netherlands) than others (for example, the UK and Germany). In the first half of the twentieth century there were a handful of cases reported in the literature. With its introduction in the psychiatric diagnosis manual in 1980, MPD cases suddenly sprung up everywhere. In a large-scale survey of the population in the city of Winnipeg, 1 per cent of the adult population were deemed to have MPD related to childhood abuse (Ross, 1991).

MPD also remains primarily a western invention and is rarely reported in other cultures. Do these facts and figures indicate a greater recognition and understanding of the disorder or do they suggest an iatrogenic cause to the disorder? MPD cases involve a higher proportion of women (85 per cent) than men. Is this because there is an established history of MPD in women and hence the tradition is more likely to be followed by patients and therapists alike or does it reflect the way that women are treated in our society? Does it reflect a sex or gender link or are women more likely to be the victims of child abuse and have a greater need to fragment their personality to protect themselves from these ordeals? Another problem involves childhood amnesia. It is estimated that in 90 per cent of cases of MPD the precipitating cause is childhood trauma (most commonly that involving sexual abuse). However, children generally remember virtually nothing of their childhood prior to the age of three and very little accurately before the age of five. Proponents of MPD argue that the 'alter' personality holds on to the painful childhood memories because they can't be faced by the victim. Richard Kluft (1985) could corroborate only 15 per cent of reported accounts of childhood abuse in MPD patients. This low figure, in itself, does not prove that they didn't occur. After all, it is in the abusers interests to hide, destroy and deny all such evidence. Elizabeth Loftus (1997), one of the world's leading experts in memory research discounts the idea that young children can recall particularly painful memories. Intriguingly, she poses the question that if this is so, why do children not recall having injections or being circumcised? A possible answer from a psychoanalyst might be because they repress them! (See also Chapter 5.)

In terms of the diagnosis of MPD today, there is an additional problem. Ironically, this problem could be said to have its origins with the case study of Eve. Thigpen and Cleckley's case study became so well-known and spawned such a fascination in the public with MPD that today 'no case has been found in which MPD, as now conceived, is proven to have emerged through unconscious processes without any shaping or preparation by external factors such as physicians or the media' (Merskey, 1992). In the case of Sybil, she even obligingly read *The Three Faces of Eve* and was fascinated by it. It was argued that she had been excessively influenced by mass media coverage of the disorder. In essence, she had been taught how to act the part.

In a series of well-known studies in the mid-1980s, Nicholas Spanos (1996) found that he could convince people that they possessed 'alter' personalities with very little suggestion on his part. In many cases, he did this without even the need to hypnotise them. He further argued that repressed memories of childhood abuse and multiple personality disorder are 'rule-governed social constructions established, legitimated, and maintained through social interaction'. In other words, the majority of MPD cases are created by therapists with the co-operation of their patients and the rest of society (see also Chapter 5). As can be seen, there is a chasm of opinion in psychiatric circles about the authenticity and diagnosis of MPD. Whether MPD is a real or iatrogenic disorder, patients who believe they have MPD should, on the whole, deserve help, not blame.

In 1987, Paul Chodoff wrote that 'there is a tendency in the history of psychiatry for certain conditions to be recognised, rise in popularity and then decline in accordance with largely cultural determinants'. Is this the fate that awaits MPD?

Notes

1　There remains considerable dispute about the most appropriate term to use. See the article entitled 'Dual personality, multiple personality, dissociative identity disorder – What's in a name?', available at: http://dissociation.com/index/ Definition/ for further details.
2　The majority of this chapter comes from Thigpen and Cleckley (1954).
3　Dissociation is a mechanism that allows the mind to separate or compartmentalise certain memories or thoughts from normal consciousness. The distinctive feature of dissociation is 'a disruption in the usually integrated functions of consciousness, memory, identity, or perception of the environment'. See *Diagnostic Statistical Manual* (1994).
4　In a subsequent book (*A Mind of My Own*, published in 1989), Sizemore argued that her personalities had been present at birth.
5　The existence of child abuse is a fairly consistent feature of *subsequent* cases of MPD, although this was not the case in 1954.

References

American Psychiatric Association (1994). *Diagnostic Statistical Manual of Mental Disorders: DSM IV* (4th edition). Washington, DC: American Psychiatric Association.

Borch Jacobson, M. and Spiegel, H. (1997). 'Sybil – The making of a disease: An interview with Dr Herbert Spiegel', *New York Review* (April).

Chodoff, P. (1987). 'Effects of the new economic climate on psychotherapeutic practice'. *American Journal of Psychiatry*, 144: 1293–7.

Crabtree, Adam. (1993). *From Mesmer to Freud: Magnetic Sleep and the Roots of Psychological Healing*. New Haven, CT: Yale University Press.

Gmelin, E. (1791). *Materialen Für Die Anthropologie*, vol. 1. Tübingen, Germany: Cotta.

Keyes, D. (1995 re-issue). *The Minds of Billy Milligan*. New York: Bantam Books.

Kluft, R.P. (1985). 'Childhood antecedents of multiple personality disorder' (Clinical Insights Monograph). *American Psychological Association*, Washington, DC.

Kluft, R.P. (1985). 'Childhood antecedents of multiple personality disorder' (Clinical Insights Monograph). *American Psychological Association*, Washington, DC.

Loftus, E.F. (1997). *The Myth of Repressed Memories*. New York: St. Martins Press.

Merskey, H. (1992). 'The manufacture of personalities – The production of multiple personality disorder'. *British Journal of Psychiatry*, 160: 327–40.

Prince, M. (1906). *The Dissociation of Personality*. New York: Longmans, Green.

Ross, C.A. (1991). 'Epidemiology of multiple personality disorder and dissociation'. *Journal of the Psychiatric Clinics of North America,* September, 14(3): 503–17.

Shreiber, F.R. (1973). *Sybil. The True Story of a Woman Possessed by Sixteen Separate Personalities*. London: Penguin.

Sileo, C.C. (1993). Multiple personalities: The experts are split. *Insight on the News*, October, 9(43): 18–22.

Sizemore, C. (1989). *A Mind of My Own*. New York: William Morrow and Company.

Sizemore, C. and Pittillo, E.S. (1977). *I'm Eve*. New York: Doubleday.

Spanos, N.P. (1996). 'Multiple identities and false memories: A sociocognitive perspective'. *American Psychological Association*, Washington, DC.

Sybil (1976). Directed by Daniel Petrie. CBS Fox.

The Three Faces of Eve (1957). Directed by Nunnally Johnson. Twentieth Century Fox.

Thigpen, C.H. and Cleckley, H. (1954). 'A case of multiple personality'. *Journal of Abnormal and Social Psychology*, 49: 135–51.

Thigpen, C.H. and Cleckley, H. (1957). *The Three Faces of Eve*. London: Secker and Warburg.

Thigpen, C.H. and Cleckley, H.M. (1984). 'On the incidence of multiple personality disorder: A brief communication'. *The International Journal of Clinical and Experimental Hypnosis*, 32(2): 63–6.

Chapter 17

The Boy Who Couldn't Stop Washing
A story of OCD

By the age of 14, Charles was spending at least 3 hours per day in the shower. He had been doing this for years. He couldn't help himself, he just had to do it.

This is the way Judith Rapoport introduced one particular case study in her 1989 book *The Boy Who Couldn't Stop Washing*. The book is now considered a psychology classic and was one of the first to raise the topic of obsessive-compulsive disorder or OCD.[1]

The essential feature of OCD is recurrent obsessional thoughts or compulsive acts. Obsessional thoughts are unwanted ideas, images or impulses that occur over and over again in an individual's head. They can include persistent fears that harm will come to them or loved ones, an unreasonable fear of disease or contamination or an excessive need to do things perfectly. Charles displayed such disturbing thoughts regarding the need to wash himself almost continuously. Compulsive acts are stereotyped behaviours that are repeated again and again. The most common of these are washing and checking. Indeed, sufferers can often be categorised into 'washers' or 'checkers'. Charles fell into the former group. These behaviours are not inherently enjoyable but may serve to relieve some of the anxiety associated with the OCD. Other common compulsive behaviours include counting and hoarding.

For many years, OCD was thought of as a rare disease because many people with OCD kept their thoughts and behaviours secret and failed to seek treatment for their condition. This led to under-estimates of the incidence of the disease. Rapoport's book helped to uncover the scale of the problem. The book showed that OCD was far more common than other better known disorders such as bipolar disorder (manic depression) or schizophrenia. It is now estimated that as many as 2 per cent of the population suffer from OCD and it afflicts males and females in equal numbers.

The boy who started it all

Charles was an ideal case study into OCD because he displayed many of the classic symptoms of OCD. OCD is one of the anxiety disorders and is a disabling condition that can last a lifetime. Typically, OCD symptoms emerge during the teenage years, however they can occur at younger ages. Suffering from OCD during the early stages of a child's development can have serious effects on later behaviour. If left untreated, OCD can destroy a person's capacity to lead a normal life. This was certainly the case for Charles.

At school Charles had been an enthusiastic student with particular ability in chemistry and biology. There had been talk of him pursuing a medical career. However, at about the age of 12, he had started to wash compulsively. There appeared to be no reason why this behaviour started but washing took up more and more of his time each day.

Most OCD sufferers struggle to stop their obsessive thoughts and prevent their compulsive actions. Charles was no different. For a while he was able to keep his obsessive-compulsive symptoms under control during the time he was at school. However, over the months, his resistance weakened and his OCD became so severe that his time-consuming rituals took over his life. Charles was forced to leave school because he was spending so much of the day washing. His washing ritual always followed the same deliberate pattern. He would hold the soap under the water spray for one minute in his right hand and then out of the water for one minute in his left hand. He would repeat this for at least one hour. After washing for about 3 hours, Charles would spend about 2 hours getting dressed.

As with many OCD sufferers, Charles' behaviour was affecting other people's lives as well as his own. His mother was at her wit's end. At first she discouraged his strange washing rituals, but later, not wanting to see his misery, 'helped' him by obsessively cleaning items in the house that might 'contaminate' him. She cleaned everything he might touch in the house with alcohol and stopped people from entering the house with their 'germs'. Charles's father could not understand these behaviours and spent more and more time at work.

Rapoport reports that Charles was a very easy going boy with a friendly and playful disposition. He willingly sought Rapoport's help since he was aware of his OCD and wished to overcome it. Rapoport proposed to study Charles's brain waves using an EEG. An EEG or electroencephalogram allows a graphical recording of the electrical activity of the brain. Unfortunately in order to do this, electrodes have to be stuck onto the scalp using a conducting paste. This paste is very sticky and was anathema to Charles. He could not bear the thought of putting something sticky on his body. He claimed: 'Stickiness is terrible. It is some kind of disease, it is like nothing you can understand'. Luckily, they managed to persuade him to undertake an EEG and Charles spent all night washing.

Why?

Rapoport spent hours talking to Charles trying to understand why he had developed his OCD. Charles felt that he was compelled to do so by something inside him. He did not hear voices telling him to do it but he did feel some internal and insistent sense of having to wash compulsively. He was aware that his behaviour appeared crazy to others but didn't feel crazy. Like many other OCD sufferers, Charles showed insight into his condition. He recognised that his obsessions and compulsions were ridiculous, but just couldn't help himself. He just felt this compulsion to wash. He really was the boy who couldn't stop washing.

Figure 17.1 Frequent handwashing: one of the classic signs of OCD
Source: © Shutterstock

Charles was asked what would happen if he didn't wash. He believed that he might become sick or that it would be bad luck to stop washing. Although a bright boy he couldn't adequately explain why his compulsion had started or, indeed, why it continued.

Charles had never met another person with OCD. He could not have learned his strange behaviours by directly observing others, since he was not aware of other people carrying out any such bizarre behaviours. So what had caused his OCD?

Causes

Current explanations for the cause of OCD concentrate on biological factors. OCD patients appear to benefit from drug treatments. Charles certainly did until he developed drug tolerance and the beneficial effects waned. This suggests that the disorder has a neurobiological basis. Nevertheless, there appear to be environmental influences that can predispose a person to develop the disorder and thus research concentrates on the interaction between neurobiological factors and environmental influences, as well as cognitive processes.

Brain scans of patients with OCD suggest that their patterns of brain activity are different from those with no reported mental illness. For example, OCD sufferers appear to have significantly less white matter, but significantly greater general total cerebral cortex than so-called 'normal' control participants. This finding also suggests a neurobiological cause of OCD (Jenike et al., 1996).

Treatment

Charles was treated with the drug Anafranil and his symptoms disappeared for about a year. Unfortunately, he developed a tolerance to the drug. This involves a decreasing response to constant doses of a drug or the need for increasing doses to maintain a constant response. Although some of his symptoms returned they were not as marked as before and he was able to control the amount of washing he did. Charles found that by conducting his washing rituals in the evenings they did not interfere so much with his day-to-day activities.

There are two main therapeutic approaches for OCD: drugs and behaviour therapy. These therapies can be used simultaneously and this is usually decided in a joint consultation between the patient and therapist.

Drugs that affect the neurotransmitter serotonin have been shown to be effective in decreasing the symptoms of OCD. Anafranil was one of the first of these and was the drug used with Charles. This group of drugs work by inhibiting the re-uptake of serotonin during synaptic transmission. Studies have shown that there is a correlation between reduced levels of serotonin and clinical effectiveness. Indeed, three-quarters of patients report some improvement with the use of such drugs.

Behaviour therapy is believed to be the most effective treatment for most types of OCD. It involves experiencing the fearful situations that trigger the obsession (exposure) and taking steps to prevent the compulsive behaviours or rituals (response prevention). Studies have shown that three-quarters of patients who complete about 15 treatment sessions will show significant and lasting reductions in their obsessive and compulsive symptoms. When compared to drug treatments, behaviour therapy most often produces stronger and more lasting improvement. However, up to one-third of people with OCD will refuse or drop out of behaviour therapy. Understandably, there is often a reluctance to endure the discomfort that is involved in exposure to fearful situations.

More recently, psychologists have been adding cognitive interventions to behaviour therapy treatments. Referred to as cognitive behaviour therapy (or CBT), this approach helps people change the thoughts and beliefs that may be reinforcing obsessive and compulsive symptoms. Together with traditional behaviour therapy, this approach has been shown to be effective in offering hope to individuals suffering from OCD.

Charles displayed many of the classic symptoms of OCD. By actively seeking help, he was put on an appropriate treatment programme that helped to reduce many of his symptoms. He was able to resume a more normal life. The publication of his case study also had the effect of bringing OCD to the attention of the public. Many other OCD sufferers suddenly recognised that they were not alone; they became less secretive, sought treatment and helped to contribute to our increasing knowledge of this area.

Note

1   The material in this chapter is drawn from Rapoport (1989) unless otherwise indicated.

References

Jenike, M.A., Breiter, H.C., Baer, L., Kennedy, D.N., Savage, C.R., Olivares, M.J., O'Sullivan, R.L., Shera, D.M., Rauch, S.L., Keuthen, N., Rosen, B.R., Caviness, V.S. and Filipek, P.A. (1996). 'Cerebral structural abnormalities in obsessive-compulsive disorder. A quantitative morphometric magnetic resonance imaging study'. *Archives of General Psychiatry*, 53(7): 625–32.

Rapoport, J. (1989). *The Boy Who Couldn't Stop Washing*. New York: Signet.

Part 5

Physiological psychology

Chapter 18

The men who didn't sleep
The story of Peter Tripp and Randy Gardner

Peter Tripp was a world famous New York disc jockey in the late 1950s. Randy Gardner was an ordinary schoolboy from San Diego. They both decided to do something extraordinary. They would each try to break the world record for the longest time without sleep. Psychologists who heard of the attempt warned them of the dangers involved but their minds were made up. They both achieved their goals but in very different ways. Their experiences helped psychologists to discover some of the mysteries of sleep. In the scientific literature, they would always be known as 'the men who didn't sleep'.[1]

Why do we sleep?

Psychologists still don't know the answer to questions such as 'Why do we sleep?', 'How much sleep do we need?', and the more fundamental inquiry, 'Do we really need sleep at all?'. One way of answering such questions would be to find an individual who never sleeps but is nevertheless perfectly healthy. Unfortunately, there aren't any documented cases like this and it's most unlikely that there ever will be. Perhaps that fact in itself does answer the fundamental question.

Another way of studying the function of sleep would be to deprive individuals of sleep and note any effects. A distinction needs to be made at the outset between total and partial sleep deprivation studies. Sleep may appear to be a single state of rest, but in reality, it is composed of a number of distinct stages. These stages can be detected using an electroencephalogram (EEG), which can record brain waves. There are four stages of slow wave sleep (SWS) and a fifth stage, which is known as REM (rapid eye movement) stage. In REM sleep, bursts of rapid eye movements are detectable and it is here that most dreaming takes place. A complete cycle of sleep typically lasts about 90 minutes and therefore during an average night a person will experience four to five complete cycles. Using a laboratory situation and an EEG it is possible to deprive sleepers of particular stages of sleep. This is called partial sleep deprivation. Depriving people or animals of all sleep is called total sleep deprivation.

Studies have investigated the effect of total and partial sleep deprivation in animals. The earliest were performed by Marie de Manaceine in 1894 when she deprived puppies of all sleep. She found that they all died within 4 to 6 days. Jouvet (1967) devised an ingenious, but cruel method to deprive cats of dream or REM sleep. The laboratory cats were placed on tiny islands (upturned flowerpots) surrounded by water. When a cat enters REM sleep their postural muscles relax. This meant that the cats lost balance and fell into the water. This woke them up and they climbed back on to the flowerpots and started the sleep stage process all over again. The cats could go through all the stages of sleep except REM sleep. Interestingly, the cats became conditioned, even while asleep, to wake up when they went into REM sleep and didn't have to fall into the water each time. The cats became disturbed very quickly and died after an average of about 35 days.

Of course, such findings may not be relevant to human behaviour. The ideal scenario would be to find a human who would try to stay awake as long as possible for days on end. The first human sleep deprivation study of this sort was conducted by Patrick and Gilbert in 1896 when they kept three men awake for 90 hours. The participants reported decreases in sensory acuity, reaction times and memory ability. One of them suffered from visual hallucinations.

The willingness to take part in competitions to stay awake has a chequered history. Perhaps the most interesting examples of this involve the so-called Dance Marathons (or 'Derbies'). These reached their height of popularity during the Depression years (1920–30) in the USA, but it is believed that the first recorded case of such a marathon took place in London in 1364. The rules of the competitions in 1920s America were very simple. Dancing couples had to stay awake for as long as possible and 'dance' to the music. The last couple standing won the cash prize. Prizes ranged from $500 to $3,000 – huge sums in the 1930s. Some contests allowed rest breaks and some allowed one partner to fall asleep while the other held them up and continued 'dancing'. The longest dance marathon lasted over 22 weeks! Eventually, such contests fell out of favour and were outlawed in many states in America. An academy award winning feature film called *They Shoot Horses, Don't They?*, starring Jane Fonda, portrays this issue.

Peter Tripp

One of the first scientifically observed studies of human sleep deprivation took place in 1959 and involved a very famous New York disc jockey called Peter Tripp (Dement and Vaughan, 2001). In a stunt that would later inspire Randy Gardner, Tripp decided to raise money for a charity by staying awake for 8 days and 8 hours. Although this was ostensibly a publicity stunt, some psychologists and medics were given the chance to study the effects that this might have on his behaviour. Tripp continued throughout the stunt to broadcast from a glass booth in Times Square, where people gathered to watch. Initially, the 32-year-old Tripp seemed to cope extremely well without sleep. His broadcasts remained entertaining and he laughed and joked his way through his daily 3-hour shows. However, by the third day, Tripp started to be abusive to colleagues and, not surprisingly, reported himself to be extremely tired. He started to suffer from visual hallucinations, for example, he reported finding cobwebs in his shoes. After 100 hours without sleep, the mental agility tests he was asked to perform became intolerable for him. He saw one of the suits of the scientists studying him as being composed of furry worms. After 120 hours, he went to the Hotel Astor to change his clothes and on opening a drawer, he 'saw' a fire ablaze and ran out into the street for help. When it was pointed out that there was actually no fire, Tripp accused his doctors of staging the event to 'test' him.

In the last few days of his stunt, Tripp's speech became slurred, he developed an even more acute paranoid psychosis and experienced further auditory and visual hallucinations. He began to accuse people of trying to poison him, he reported seeing kittens and mice and questioned whether he really was Peter Tripp. He could not perform simple tasks such as reciting the alphabet and became convinced that his doctors were conspiring to send him to prison. On the last morning, he mistook one of his doctors for an undertaker who had come to collect his body!

Throughout his test of endurance, scientists had attempted to test Tripp on a daily basis. Unfortunately, in the later stages, many of these tests were not completed since Tripp refused to co-operate with his 'conspiring' doctors. There is little doubt that in Tripp's case the lack of sleep resulted in the development of a mental disorder. The doctors described his mental state as 'nocturnal psychosis'. The evidence appeared to show that sleep is essential for normal functioning. Put simply, the body and brain require sleep. Indeed, although awake throughout his stunt, Tripp's brain patterns often resembled those seen in sleep. Tripp gained his world record by staying awake for 201 hours. Tripp's 'wake-athon' became a scientifically cited case study. According to his son Peter Jr, 'What started out as a stunt has become required reading in the behavioral sciences at colleges and universities from coast-to-coast.' However there were two unique factors concerning this sleep case study that question its relevance to sleep debt research. The first was that Tripp used large amounts of stimulants to stay awake during the last 66 hours of his marathon. The second was that Tripp's experience may have been adversely affected by the fact that it took place on a public stage. His ordeal, and, indeed, his symptoms may have been worsened by the use of drugs and the glare of publicity. Due to these factors, many scientists have questioned whether the results gained from such a study can be generalised to a wider population.

After his wake-athon, Tripp slept for 13 hours and 13 minutes and spent the majority of this time in REM sleep. Indeed, one episode of REM sleep was one of the longest ever recorded. The phenomenon where sleep deprived people spend a higher proportion of their sleep on subsequent nights in dream or REM sleep is called 'REM rebound'. It appeared that the loss of REM sleep had led to the psychotic symptoms evident with Tripp. William Dement, one of the sleep researchers involved in monitoring the attempt, concluded that if people were not allowed REM sleep they would become mentally unstable. Indeed, Dement originally suggested that the results gained from this study provided evidence to support Freud's theory that if taboo thoughts or desires were not expressed through dreams (REM sleep), the psychic pressure would build up and lead to psychotic hallucinatory episodes. In summary, he felt that dreams were the safety valve of the mind. Without this safety valve, Tripp became mentally unstable.

With the benefit of hindsight and years of subsequent research, (not least the case of Randy Gardner below), Dement questioned his original position. Dement never consistently found that REM deprivation caused mental illness. In fact, Dement believed it was far more likely that the amphetamine-like stimulant, Ritalin, given to Tripp in large doses to stay awake, accounted for his paranoia and hallucinations. At the time, little was known about the effects of such drugs but now amphetamine-induced psychoses, almost identical to Tripp's, are widely reported in the scientific literature. It appears that Peter Tripp literally went on a 'trip' and that his psychotic episodes were drug-induced rather than caused by a lack of sleep, or more specifically, REM sleep.

Tripp appeared to recover from his marathon and resumed his work. However, his career nose-dived and after a series of financial scandals he lost his job in 1967. It is often reported that the sleep marathon had a long-term effect on his personality. However, he was very successful in a number of subsequent, diverse jobs and it appears unlikely that the effects of his sleep deprivation stunt were permanent or long-lasting.

Randy Gardner

Six years later, Randy Gardner read about the sleep deprivation stunt conducted by Peter Tripp while he was wondering what he could possibly do to win the San Diego Science Fair. With the help of two friends, he decided to try to beat Tripp's world record by going 11 days without sleep. Gardner reckoned that he could do this and, in his own words, 'not go insane'. This case study was also observed by William Dement and it would change his mind about the psychological effects of long-term sleep deprivation.

Dement found out about the Randy Gardner world record attempt while reading a local newspaper. The newspaper reported that Randy had already successfully completed 80 hours of his planned 264 hour ordeal. Dement immediately contacted Randy and his parents and offered his assistance. Randy's parents in particular were grateful for the medical expertise that was offered. They had been extremely anxious about the consequences that might ensue from such an attempt.

Dement and a colleague, George Gulevich, agreed to supervise and authenti-cate the attempt. They found Randy to be a cheerful, happy, physically fit 17 year old who initially had little difficulty coping with his sleep deprivation. However, this state of affairs slowly changed. During the nights, the researchers found it increasingly difficult to keep him awake. Randy would ask to shut his eyes in order to 'rest' them but not to fall asleep. The hours between 3 a.m. and 7 a.m. were particularly testing. Occasionally, Dement would have to shout at Randy in order to keep him awake. Sometimes, Randy got extremely angry and occasionally he forgot why he wasn't allowed to sleep. In order to cope with this, a number of techniques were employed to prevent him falling asleep. Dement and Gulevich ensured that Randy was physically active whenever he felt particularly drowsy. They would make him go and play basketball in his backyard in the middle of the night or Dement would drive him around in his convertible with the radio blaring loudly. Randy had to be watched like a hawk at all times to prevent him nodding off. During his record attempt, Randy took no stimulant drugs, not even coffee.

Figure 18.1 William Dement and Randy Gardner
Source: Time & Life Pictures/Getty Images

One side effect of this regime was that the two researchers also became sleep deprived. Indeed, on one occasion, Dement was fined and cautioned for mistakenly driving down a one-way street. His protestations – that he was merely conducting a study into sleep deprivation got him nowhere with the police officers involved. Later, Dement recognised that driving while tired is an extremely reckless thing to do and he fully deserved his citation.

On the last night of the study, Dement took Randy to a games arcade and they played about 100 games on a mechanical baseball game. Randy won every game, which showed that either he had coped remarkably well without sleep or Dement was particularly poor at the game! Dement recalls that near the end of the ordeal Randy was helped by all the publicity that his feat was attracting. Newspaper and television reporters from all over the globe were descending on San Diego to see the world record being broken. Randy found this extremely exciting and it no doubt increased his motivation to keep going. Randy did not want to fail in front of a worldwide audience.

At 5 a.m. on his eleventh day without sleep, Randy gave a press conference to announce that he had broken the world record for sleep deprivation.[2] His performance during the conference was described as 'flawless'; he spoke eloquently and there was no obvious sign of sleep deprivation. Randy declared that sleep deprivation was simply a question of 'mind over matter'. He even declared that he thought he could cope with another day or two without sleep but was aware of the need to go back to school after his Christmas break! Dr John Ross of the local Naval Hospital had volunteered to monitor Randy's sleep on subsequent nights and at 6 a.m. Randy fell asleep. He had achieved his world record of 264 hours without sleep. It is reported that it took him a mere 3 seconds to fall asleep after his head hit the pillow. He slept for 14 hours and 40 minutes and felt well enough to go to school the next day. The following night he slept for 10½ hours before being woken to go to school. It was estimated that Randy had missed out on approximately 75 hours sleep over the 11-day period. He did not fully make up for this lost sleep in subsequent nights, although he did experience 'REM rebound' and recovered most of this sleep stage. In all, only 24 per cent of his total sleep loss was recovered. This evidence suggests that REM sleep is a particularly important type of sleep. In contrast to his earlier conclusions based on the Tripp study, the Randy Gardner case led Dement to conclude that sleep deprivation does *not* inevitably lead to psychosis. The loss of sleep did not make Randy crazy. Forty years later, no-one has broken Randy's record and it is unlikely that they will due to the possible dangers involved. Indeed, Dement questions whether any such proposed study would pass a university ethics committee today.

There have been other reports of human volunteers who have stayed awake for 8–10 days in carefully monitored laboratory situations. Like Randy, none of them have suffered serious physiological or psychological problems. Again, like Randy, all of them suffered a gradual decline in concentration, motivation and perception as their sleep debt increased. All of these volunteers fully recovered after a few nights sleep.

It is often reported that Randy suffered no ill effects of his marathon wake-athon. Indeed, Coren (1998) states that 'this conclusion is so widespread that it has now become a stock "fact" presented in virtually any psychology or psychiatry book that has a chapter on sleep'. However, Dement does mention some side effects experienced by Randy. Dement notes that Randy's analytical abilities, memory, perception, motivation and motor control were all affected in varying degrees. He had delayed reactions and sometimes couldn't perform simple mathematical calculations. Nevertheless, many of these deficits are often not given the prominence that might have been expected.

John Ross of the US Navy Medical Neuropsychiatric Research Unit reports Gardner's symptoms in greater detail (Ross, 1965). He reports that by Day 2, Randy had difficulty focussing his eyes and by Day 4 he was suffering from hallucinations (he saw a street sign as a real person) and delusions (he thought he was a famous black football player), which continued on and off throughout the period of study. He had episodes of disjointed thinking and his attention span was extremely short. When asked to subtract backwards from 100 in blocks of 7, he could only reach 65 before forgetting the task. Coren remains convinced of the opinion that 'prolonged sleep deprivation does lead to the appearance of serious mental symptoms'. Dement, however, retorts that 'I can say with absolute certainty that staying awake for 264 hours did not cause any psychiatric problems whatsoever'.

It is generally accepted that Randy showed some definite neurological changes. The dispute centres on the extent of his symptoms. Were his symptoms relatively minor or more serious? The former view suggests that sleep depriva-tion doesn't cause mental health problems; the latter view suggests the opposite. Dement proposed that Randy coped well with a lack of sleep because he was young and physically fit. It has subsequently been demonstrated in animal studies that such factors are vitally important to how rats can cope with sleep deprivation.

So did Randy provide us with the answer as to whether sleep is necessary for normal human functioning? As mentioned, researchers continue to dispute the Randy Gardner case. It is also worth pointing out that there are a number of problems with sleep deprivation studies. Perhaps the most important concerns the argument that an understanding of sleep deprivation does not logically imply the function of sleep. For example, other physiological mechanisms might compensate for any effects of the loss of sleep. This has been shown to occur in molecular biology, where the knockout of a particular gene does not always lead to a clear phenotype. Conversely, a behaviour that is adversely affected by sleep loss suggests that sleep plays a role in that behaviour but it does not prove that sleep alone is responsible for it. In addition, since the Gardner study, researchers have demonstrated the existence of momentary lapses into sleep called 'microsleeps'. These only last for a few seconds but Dement accepts that Randy probably experienced these. They are only evident with continuous physiological recording equipment, so any future study would need to employ such techniques to ensure that these 'microsleeps' don't add up to a significant amount of sleep over a long period.

William Dement is one of the world's leading experts on sleep. He was involved in both the Peter Tripp and Randy Gardner cases. He reports conflicting results from each and explains his conclusions from each. Despite arguing that Randy Gardner suffered few side effects from his sleep deprivation marathon, Dement believes that a lack of sleep *does* have severe consequences. He argues that major industrial disasters such as the grounding of the Exxon Valdez, the crash of the space shuttle Challenger and the nuclear disaster at Chernobyl can all be traced back to decisions made by people who were suffering from a lack of sleep. He estimates that 24,000 car fatalities in the USA each year are also attributable to tiredness. He suggests that the average adult needs about 8 hours of sleep per night and recommends that people do not build up a sleep debt.

Randy Gardner subsequently got a job with one of the sleep researchers after successfully completing his education. He suffered no long-term effects from his sleep deprivation exploits and is now retired and still living in San Diego. Randy Gardner will forever more be known in the scientific literature as 'the boy who didn't sleep'.

Notes

1 The material in this chapter is drawn from Dement and Vaughan (2001) unless otherwise indicated.
2 Randy's world record attempt was never verified to World Record standards. The record for time awake is attributed to Mrs Maureen Weston (p. 322) (449 hours or 18 days, 17 hours). The *Guinness Book of World Records* (1990) attributes the record to Robert McDonald who spent 453 hours, 40 minutes awake in a rocking chair.

References

Coren, S. (1998). 'Sleep deprivation, psychosis and mental efficiency'. *Psychiatric Times*, March, 15(3).

Dement, W. and Vaughan, C. (2001). *The Promise of Sleep*. London: Pan Books.

Jouvet, M. (1967). 'Mechanisms of the states of sleep. A neuropharmacological approach'. *Association for Research in Nervous and Mental Disease*, 45: 86–126.

Manaceine, M. de (1897). *Sleep: Its Physiology, Pathology, Hygiene and Psychology*. London: Walter Scott, 341.

Patrick, G.T. and Gilbert, J.A. (1896). 'On the effects of loss of sleep'. *Psychology Review*, 3: 469–83.

Pinel, J. (2000). *Biopsychology*. Boston, MA: Allyn and Bacon.

Ross, J.J. (1965). 'Neurological findings after prolonged sleep deprivation'. *Archives of Neurology*, 12: 399–403.

Chapter 19

The man who lived with a hole in his head

The story of Phineas Gage

Phineas Gage was a railway foreman working near Vermont in the 1840s. He was responsible for blasting rock in order to pave the way for the laying of railway tracks. One day, he made a vital mistake and his 1- metre tamping iron, used to pack down the explosive powder blasts, shot off and landed 30 yards away. Unfortunately, on its way, it entered Gage's chin and exited through the top of his head. Amazingly, Gage lived to tell the tale but with a changed personality as a result of his accident. He became a textbook case in brain science and one of the most famous case studies in psychology.

The luckiest man alive

On 13 September 1848 Phineas Gage went to work as usual, little knowing that by the end of the day he would be the luckiest man alive.[1] His job was to organise a gang of workers to clear a path through granite rock for the construction of a new railway line. He was an exceptionally good worker, very thorough and meticulous and also popular with his colleagues. He took charge of the laying of explosives personally. This was a dangerous job but one that suited Phineas's precise personality. The procedure used to lay explosives always remained the same. His assistant would place the powder in the hole drilled in the rock, Phineas would then carefully press down the powder before his assistant set the fuse and filled the hole with sand. Finally, Phineas would use his metre-long iron rod to 'tamp' down the sand to act as a plug so that the blast would channel down into the rock. Phineas was an acknowledged expert with the tamping rod. Indeed, he had had his own custom rod made by the local blacksmith. No-one is certain exactly whose fault it was but Phineas began tamping down the powder before his assistant had placed the sand. It is most probable that a spark from the iron rod hitting the granite set off the explosive and this sent the tamping iron firing through the air with Phineas still leaning over it.

The iron rod landed 20 to 25 metres away covered with blood and bits of Phineas' brain. The rod had entered under his left cheekbone and exited a fraction of a second later through the middle of his forehead just above his hairline. His workmates ran up to him assuming him dead. Unbelievably, Phineas sat up with blood pouring from the exit wound. He was conscious and coherent and immediately started talking about the incident. He was placed on an oxcart and taken to the nearest town 1 km away for treatment by the local doctor. When the doctor arrived half an hour later, Phineas even joked about the extent of his injuries while sitting on the hotel porch. Although in considerable pain, Phineas was helped by the fact that there are no pain receptors inside the brain, only on the surface of the scalp.

His injuries and a conflict of views

Dr Harlow couldn't believe the extent of the injuries. There was little his medical expertise could do to help in such a situation so he simply shaved Phineas' head, removed some bone and brain fragments and pressed the larger still attached pieces of skull back into place. He cleaned the skin and bandaged the wound. Dr Harlow left the hole in Phineas' mouth untreated so that the wound could drain. There was little doubt in the Doctor's opinion that Phineas would be dead in a few hours. The town cabinet maker came to measure Phineas in order to make a coffin ready for him. Over the first few days, Phineas did remarkably well, managing to stay alert and talkative. However, the wound soon began to smell terribly and there was no doubt that it had become infected. A fungus began to grow from his brain. In those days, there were disputes between doctors as to what should be done in such cases. Some believed that the fungus might be part of the regenerating brain and should be pushed back inside the cranium, others believed it should be removed. Dr Harlow left the fungus growing for a while before a friend pointed out that recovery must be hampered by a fungus growing out of your head! Frustrated by his lack of knowledge and appreciating the simple, but likely, truth of this he immediately cut off the growth.

Phineas developed a fever and became quite delirious. Huge pockets of pus were drained from beneath his eyes. In those days, doctors knew nothing about bacterial infection, but the prognosis could not have been worse. Dr Harlow used the technique of 'bleeding' to draw off some of Phineas's blood. At the time, doctors believed (incorrectly) that patients suffered from having too much blood. Luckily for Phineas this technique may have actually helped considerably since it may have reduced the blood pressure and thus helped to reduce the pressure on his swollen brain. The fact that his skull was holed ensured that his swollen brain had room to expand within his cranium. However, 22 days after the accident, Phineas started to make a recovery and within 10 weeks was pronounced fully recovered from his injuries. Admittedly, he had lost his sight in his left eye but beyond this he was physically restored to normal. He was recovered physically but perhaps not psychologically.

'No longer Gage'

Dr Harlow reported that Phineas could perform all the tasks that he could do prior to the accident, but that somehow there was something strangely different about him. Dr Harlow worried about his mental state. Six months after the accident, Phineas returned to his former employers in order to reclaim his job. His physical capacities seemed restored, his speech was fine and his memory was intact. However, after a trial period his employers had to terminate his contract. Although many reports suggest that Phineas had recovered all of his physical powers there are conflicting reports that suggest that there was evidence of continuing physical weakness. However, far more marked was the change evident in Phineas's personality. Phineas was now unreliable, impatient, hostile, rude and abrupt. He used vulgar, coarse language and changed his plans from one moment to the next. He had become disinhibited and a risk taker. He could not be trusted in such a state and was described by his doctor and his friends as 'no longer Gage'. No amount of persuasion or reasoning could make Phineas change his ways, he seemed incapable of curtailing his offensive and unpredictable behaviour, even when it was obvious what a detrimental effect it was having on his life.

Meanwhile his case had started to attract the attention of other medical practitioners, particularly Dr Bigelow from Harvard University in Boston, Massachussetts. Bigelow arranged for Phineas to visit Harvard for a thorough examination of his case. In those days, there was no easy method for examining the brain. Doctors were trying to determine how the brain worked. One way to do this is to examine unique cases such as that presented by Phineas, where a freak accident had led to specific damage to one area of the brain. At the time there were broadly two schools of thought regarding the workings of the brain. There were those such as Dr Bigelow who believed that the entire brain is involved in all thinking and behaviour. They believed that damage to one area of the brain would mean that other areas of the brain would compensate for this deficit.

In the nineteenth century, phrenology was a widely followed paradigm used to explain brain functioning. The functions of each region were determined by examining the external features of skulls. Bumps and indentations on the skull were related to the character of that person and in such a way a 'mental map' of the brain was drawn up. Women particularly liked the idea of phrenology since no differences could be found between male and female skulls and thus it helped in their struggle for equality with men.

The other competing school of thought involved the belief in the so-called localisation of function of the brain (a view favoured by Dr Harlow). This suggests that specific areas of the brain have a specific function and that damage to one area would lead to a specific deficit in thinking or behaviour. The emerging 'science' of phrenology echoed this view and can often still be seen demonstrated on replicated Phrenological Model Heads.

Followers of both these schools of thought were particularly interested in cases such as Phineas Gage. It was rare indeed for doctors to be able to study the after effects of such profound damage to a person's frontal lobes. In virtually all such cases, a person would undoubtedly have died from their injuries. As is often the case in such disputes, Gage's case was cited as evidence by both groups to support their views. On the one hand, it was argued that other areas of Phineas's brain must have taken over the function of the damaged areas otherwise he would either be dead or much more profoundly affected and probably not be able to think properly, control his movements, talk and so forth. The Gage case was cited as supporting the idea that the brain is a complex, integrated organism working as one unit and that there is flexibility inbuilt to allow for other areas to take over destroyed areas. Dr Bigelow believed this view to be correct and may have deliberately under-emphasised the character changes exhibited by Gage after the accident in order to strengthen his position.

On the other hand, Dr Harlow, although trying to maintain patient confidentiality, reported to trusted colleagues that Gage was not his old self. This was taken as evidence that the areas of the brain destroyed were responsible for the specific thoughts and behaviours that Gage now appeared to lack. These were primarily concerned with a lack of planning, reasoning and a general disinhibition towards others shown by his lack of respect and gross profanities. Purely by chance, the phrenological model included the regions of benevolence

Figure 19.1 Phineas Gage

Source: From the collection of Jack and Beverly Wilgus, wikimedia.org

(kindness) and agreeableness in almost precisely the area that the rod passed through. Phrenologists and adherents of the belief in the localisation of function of the brain also cited the Gage case as supporting their view. However, Harlow did not come forward to publicly report the character changes of Gage until many years after his patient's death so Dr Bigelow's reporting of the case held sway; namely, that Gage was virtually unaffected by the accident.

It is a fascinating aspect of the case that the same information can be used to provide evidence for competing schools of thought. However, looking back on the evidence with the benefit of today's increased knowledge, it is unsurprising that both these groups used Gage to support their ideas, since both groups were correct to some degree. We now know that the brain is an amazingly complex inter-connected organism comprising 100 billion neurons, but that the brain does not work as a complete whole. It is perhaps more accurate to see individual circuits in the brain working together and that these specific circuits do operate specific functions. Even functions such as face recognition or name recall, which do appear to be fairly localised to specific parts of the brain, are inter-connected to other areas. In essence, the brain can be viewed as *both* localised and inter-connected. The one thing we can be certain of is that the 'science' of phrenology was incorrect.

'The only living man with a hole in his head'

Dr Bigelow declared the Gage case to be 'the most remarkable history of injury to the brain that has been recorded'. A plaster mask was made of his skull and this still resides in Harvard Medical School today. After a number of weeks exciting the interest of the medical school at Harvard, Phineas took to the road. There is some dispute as to what happened next in his life. It is possible that he travelled around the major towns in New England telling his story to paying customers who came to examine his skull and inspect his tamping iron. However, there are few records that can substantiate this. It has long been suggested that Phineas then took his tamping iron and trod the boards as a freak exhibit at P.T. Barnum's American Museum at Broadway. He is reported to have had a hole drilled in another skull to show people the damage that occurred to his own. He was billed as 'The only living man with a hole in the top of his head' and posters report to show him with the iron bar still sticking out of his head! Although this is a great story there is no corroborating evidence to support this and it seems likely that, if true, there would have been recorded evidence of his appearances from other sources. Indeed, it is unlikely that Phineas would have been much of a star attraction given that orang-utans, 'bearded' ladies and 'mermaids' were also on display.

It appears that Phineas spent the next 9 years in a series of jobs mainly concerned with horses. He worked at a livery and it's most likely that he spent many years as a stagecoach driver working in Chile. In 1859, Phineas returned to live with his mother in San Francisco and took a variety of farm jobs. Each job turned out to be temporary because he found it difficult to fit in and work with other people. Phineas started to have regular epileptic fits of increasing frequency and magnitude. The doctors did not know the cause of these seizures, but it is likely that the head injuries he suffered in his accident played a part in them. Eventually, on 21 May 1860, Phineas Gage died.

Phineas was buried without fuss in a small cemetery in San Francisco and that would have been the last we heard of him if Dr Harlow had not decided, in 1866, to try to find out what had happened to his most famous patient. Dr Harlow managed to track down Phineas's mother and eventually she gave her permission for Harlow to exhume Phineas's body and donate his skull to Harvard University Medical School. One other item was taken from the coffin of her son: the tamping rod that blew the hole in his brain and had been Phineas's constant companion throughout his life. Indeed, Phineas had become skilled at telling the extraordinary tale of his injury to anyone who was prepared to listen and had used the tamping rod in his demonstrations to accompany his tale.

Armed with Phineas's skull and the tamping rod and no longer worried about patient confidentiality, Dr Harlow publicised the case of Phineas Gage. He argued that his injuries had changed his personality and that he had suffered a great deal from the diminishment of his social skills. He could demonstrate that in the 11 years since his injury, Phineas's skull had not completely healed over and he had lived literally with a hole in his head for all that time. Harlow can be credited with bringing the Gage case back to prominence and preventing him from being largely forgotten in the annals of medical history.

Further research

Similar skulls of people who have suffered injuries from arrows or from the effects of trepanning can be seen today in the Science Museum in London. Trepanning (or trephining) is the most ancient form of brain surgery known. It involved boring a hole in the skull of patients with the belief that this would help liberate bad spirits or demons. These can be considered some of the earliest

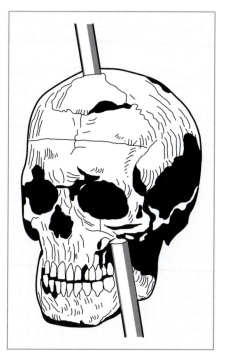

Figure 19.2 The rod entered under Phineas Gage's left cheekbone and exited a fraction of a second later from the middle of his forehead

forms of psychosurgery. They may have been used for the alleviation of severe headaches due to intracranial pressure and in cases such as these, may well have been a helpful therapy.

One year after Gage's death, a scientist called Paul Broca made a further breakthrough in our understanding of brain function through his study of a patient called Leborgne, who had suffered a stroke (Broca, 1861). Leborgne could understand speech but was unable to produce it, with the exception of one word 'tan' (the patient is often referred to as 'Tan' because of this). On Leborgne's death it was discovered that he had particular damage to a small area of the brain in the lower part of the left frontal lobe. Confirming this with other patient case studies, this area is now known as 'Broca's area'. In 1874 Carl Wernicke found another area that is crucial for language comprehension (Lanczik and Keil, 1991). People who suffer from neurophysiological damage to this area (called 'Wernicke's area') are unable to understand the 'content' words while listening, and unable to produce meaningful sentences; their speech has grammatical structure but no meaning. With these later insights, it seems amazing that Phineas did not suffer any speech or language deficits despite the nature of his injury.

Of course, given our understanding of brain science at the time, it is impossible to be certain exactly what damage Phineas incurred. However, since his accident there have been as many as 12 studies that have attempted to identify the exact journey of the tamping iron through his head. Perhaps the most recent provides us with the most accurate information. This was conducted in 1994 by Hanna Damasio and her team using Gage's skull and three dimensional computer modelling techniques. They produced possible trajectories and concluded that there was one trajectory that appeared to be the most likely path, given the entry and exit points identified on the skull. They even tried to account for the subtle anatomical differences that occur in each individual's brain. Even when the trajectory is accounted for accurately, one cannot be certain which areas have been damaged due to such differences. Damasio et al. (1994) compared Gage's skull with 27 normal brains and identified seven brains that had virtually identical anatomical measures to Gage. They simulated the tamping iron's trajectory through each of these brains and found that the areas of the brain damaged were identical in all seven cases. Hence, they were confident that they had located both the likely trajectory and the brain damage involved in the accident. To be precise, they identified the damaged parts as 'the anterior half of the orbital frontal cortex . . . the polar and anterior mesial frontal cortices . . . and the anterior-most sector of the anterior cingulated gyrus'. However, even here there are problems, since we cannot be sure what damage was caused by concussion at the time of the accident and damage caused by the subsequent brain infections, neither of which could be distinguished from the study of his skull. Furthermore, even if we do accept that we know the precise details of the damage to his brain, we cannot be certain what effect that damage had on Gage's personality or behaviour because he was never studied in a systematic way. There were no systematic neuropsychological assessments in those days.

Bringing Gage back to life . . .

Gage's contribution went beyond that of a medical freak. His injury changed our understanding of the localisation of brain function, particularly in the frontal cortex. Gage's case also made an important contribution to brain surgery in that it opened up the possibility that major brain surgery might be performed without fatal results. The importance of the Phineas Gage case is emphasised by the fact that the case is still mentioned in approximately 60 per cent of introductory textbooks in psychology.

In 2008 two collectors of old photographs called Jack and Beverly Wilgus posted an old daguerreotype picture on the Internet of what they thought was a whaler and his harpoon. Experts commented that the whaler was not holding a harpoon and then one eagle-eyed viewer, called Michael Spurlock, put forward the suggestion that it might have been Phineas Gage. Jack and Beverly Wilgus then checked the injuries evident on the picture and found that they exactly matched those on an image of Phineas Gage's life mask. Given that the writing on the tamping iron in the picture also matched that on the tamping iron displayed at Harvard experts are 99 per cent certain that this was indeed a picture of Phineas Gage (Wilgus and Wilgus, 2009). At last people were able to see what the legendary Phineas Gage looked like.

Although there have been cases that have come close to rivalling Phineas and his injury, he remains the best known example of a person who suffered gross brain injury and survived. To that extent, on that fateful September day in 1848, it's no exaggeration to say that he was, indeed, the luckiest man alive. For the remaining 11 years of his life, as he used to frequently tell, and forever more in the scientific literature, he was known 'as the man who lived with a hole in the head'.

Note

1   The most comprehensive book about Phineas Gage is without doubt the exceptionally thorough work by Macmillan (2002), from which the majority of the material in this chapter comes, unless otherwise stated. A less thorough but equally fascinating account of this case is Fleischman (2002).

References

Broca, P. (1861). 'Perte de la parole: Ramollissement chronique et destruction partielle du lobe anterieur gauche du cerveau'. *Bulletins de la Societe D'anthropologie*, 1st series, 2: 235–8.

Damasio, H., Grabowski, T., Frank, R., Galaburda, A. and Damasio, A. (1994). 'The return of Phineas Gage: Clues about the brain from the skull of a famous patient'. *Science*, 264: 1102–05.

Fleischman, J. (2002). *Phineas Gage*. Boston, MA: Houghton Mifflin.

Lanczik, M. and Keil, G. (1991). 'Carl Wernicke's localization theory and its significance for the development of scientific psychiatry'. *History of Psychiatry*, 2: 171–80.

Macmillan, M. (2002). *An Odd Kind of Fame: Stories of Phineas Gage*. Cambridge, MA: MIT Press.

Wilgus, J. and Wilgus, B. (2009). 'Face to face with Phineas Gage'. *Journal of the History of Neuroscience*, 18: 340–45.

Chapter 20

The man with no brain?

Prof John Lorber looked at the brain scan of the student in front of him. The student was studying for a Maths degree and had a recorded IQ of 126 (100 is the average). The student had been referred to Lorber by the university campus doctor who noticed that his head was slightly larger than normal. Knowing Lorber's research interests into hydrocephalus he thought that the student might be worthy of further investigation.[1] The brain scan showed that the student had practically no brain at all. It was estimated that his brain would have weighed no more than 150 grams, the normal size for a man of his age would be 10 times this at 1.5 kilograms. This, combined with further very rare cases, led Lorber and others to pose the question 'Is your brain really necessary?' (1981). Such evidence has questioned our understanding of the workings of the human brain and been cited as evidence to perpetuate the widely held belief that we only use 10 per cent of our brains.

Background

The human brain is the most complex organ known to man. The human brain has about 100,000,000,000 (100 billion) neurons and there are 1,000 to 10,000 synapses (connections) for *each* of these neurons. These synapses can transmit about 10 impulses per second, which works out at a maximum limit of 10 quadrillion synapse operations per second! The numbers are hard to appreciate but somebody has worked out that a pile of 100 billion pieces of paper would be about 5,000 miles high, the distance from San Francisco to London.[2] The average human brain weighs about 2 per cent of your body weight but greedily consumes about 25 per cent of the body's energy.

Given such facts and figures it is unsurprising that much is still unknown about the human brain. Physiologists and psychologists have spent years trying to locate areas of the brain responsible for different functions. The early science of phrenology, which originated in the theories of a Viennese physician called Franz Joseph Gall, tried to address this (Simpson, 2005). Gall believed that the shape of the brain was determined by the development of its constituent organs and, since the skull takes its shape from the brain, the surface of the skull should give clues to a person's psychological abilities and personality. For example, a bump on the forehead might indicate a person's kindness. After gaining great popularity in the Victorian era (in the 1830s, some employers even used to demand a character reference from a phrenologist to vet prospective job applicants) phrenology was almost completely discredited by the mid-nineteenth century.[3]

However, one of the assumptions behind phrenology, namely brain localisation of function, has survived to this day. Localisation of function simply means that different parts of the brain carry out different functions (e.g. vision, voluntary movement, language, and so on). Although this may seem obvious, some other internal organs, such as the liver, do not function in this way. That is, all parts of the liver do essentially the same task. It took years of further clinical research evidence to discover that the phrenologists' assumptions regarding the localisation of function in the brain, if not the precise details surrounding it, had been right all along.

Early research

One of the early pioneers to turn to these more scientific ways of studying the brain was Karl Lashley (1890–1958). Lashley hoped to find the location of memory traces or engrams in the brain. Working with rats, Lashley trained them to learn to run through mazes. Then he systematically removed (lesioned) portions (up to 50 per cent) of their cerebral cortex to see the effects. Lashley found that large portions of the cortex could be removed without apparently affecting the rat's memories (Lashley, 1950). Lashley used to joke that it wasn't a problem locating the engram, but finding where it wasn't! As a direct result of such work, Lashley formulated two principles. First, that all areas of the cerebral cortex are important in learning and memory and that one cortical area can substitute for another (this he called the 'equipotentiality principle'); and second, that memories for complex tasks are stored throughout the cerebral cortex (the principle of mass action) and are not isolated to any particular area. In essence, the strength of the memory depends on the amount of tissue available. The location of the lesion was not as vital as the amount of tissue destroyed.

The idea of rats with very little cerebral cortex still being able to recall their way through mazes led some people to question whether the cortex was a vital component in learning at all. Findings from studies including Lashley's were misinterpreted and soon it became a widespread belief that humans only use 10 per cent of their brain.

Other research involving experiments and case studies had found that there were, indeed, very specific areas of the brain responsible for different functions (e.g. 'Broca's area' controls speech production). Lashley's testing methods were simply not sophisticated enough to discover the source of memory. Nevertheless, Lashley was correct to hint that much learning involves wide parallel interconnections of neurons distributed throughout the brain. Such a process gives the appearance of 'mass action' (the brain operating as a single organism), but has been more accurately compared to a symphony orchestra with many separate sections (violins, percussion, and so on) contributing to the finished, coherent piece.

Despite increasing research evidence to the contrary, the public debate regarding the role of the cerebral cortex continued. For instance, although not documented, it is widely reported that Einstein once joked that his intelligence was the result of tapping into the unused areas of his brain (Gazzaniga, 1998).

The man with no brain

John Lorber, a paediatrician and acknowledged expert on Spina Bifida was thrust into this debate after examining a patient referred to him by a GP working on the campus of Sheffield University. Lorber was a surgeon who specialised in the treatment of hydrocephalus. Hydrocephalus comes from the Greek *hydro*, meaning 'water', and 'cephalus', which means 'head'. Hydrocephalus involves an abnormally large accumulation of cerebrospinal fluid (CSF) within the cavities (ventricles) inside the brain. If the CSF is not absorbed quickly enough, it builds up pressure in the ventricles and this causes the cerebral cortex to be crushed outwards against the skull. Lorber was performing surgery on people with hydrocephalus by inserting valves called 'shunts' in order to relieve the pressure caused by the build-up of CSF (Lorber, 1981). Lorber was surprised by a few patients who seemed to have little or no mental deficits but whose brain scans showed extremely enlarged ventricles, such that there was virtually no discernible cerebral cortex at all. His best known case involved a maths undergraduate with an IQ of 126 and who subsequently went on to gain a first class honours degree. Lorber claimed that his cerebral cortex on the scan was a mere millimetre or so thick (crushed by the effects of hydrocephalus) compared to the usual four or five centimetres. Lorber reckoned that his whole brain weighed a mere 150 grams compared to the typical 1.5 kilograms. Lorber subsequently published a paper with the provocative title of 'Is your brain really necessary?' questioning the need for areas of the cerebral cortex. On a subsequent television documentary he stated: 'My hunch is that we all have a substantial reserve of neurons and brain cells . . . that we don't need and don't use' (Beyerstein, 1998).[4] Lorber claimed to have documented about 600 such cases and categorised them into four groups. There were:

(1) those cases with near normal brains;
(2) those with 50–70 per cent normal function;

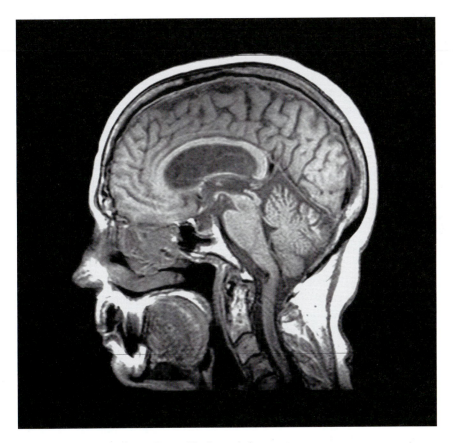

Figure 20.1 Brain showing effects of hydrocephalus

Source: Living Art Enterprises, LLC/Science Photo Library

(3) those with 70–90 per cent normal function; and

(4) those with 95 per cent of the cranium filled with CSF.

There were only about 60 cases of this last group and approximately half of these were profoundly retarded. The other half, which included the aforementioned maths graduate, had IQs above 100. In the past, in children where the skull had not yet calcified, the cranium would often balloon outwards due to the internal pressure. Before the modern technique of a shunt was used, such an affliction was likely to lead to death. So do such case studies suggest that much of the cerebral cortex is redundant or are there alternative explanations?

Conflicting evidence

The first point to be made is that in many of these cases there may have been some exaggeration of the extent of brain loss. Lorber used a CAT (computerized axial tomography) scan technique to view the internal structure of the brain. This is an x-ray procedure that, when combined with a computer, can generate cross-sectional views of the internal organs and structures of the body. It is suggested that a cerebral cortex of only a millimetre or so thick would probably not have shown up clearly on such a scan, suggesting that, in reality, the cortex might have been somewhat larger. Lorber conceded that the reading of CAT scans is difficult but remained convinced that his interpretation of the evidence was correct. More advanced brain scanning techniques have shown that the cerebral cortex is not 'lost' or destroyed but compacted into the smaller space available. If anything, this demonstrates the remarkable ability of the brain to adapt to circumstances. This is also supported by studies of neural damage in infants. It is well documented that children can more readily adapt to serious head injuries than adults because of the plasticity and adaptability of the human brain. There are cases of children who have one brain hemisphere surgically removed who have regained, after a period of some adjustment, most of their former abilities including language. This suggests that the remaining areas of the brain have taken over the functions of the removed hemisphere. This 'crowding' procedure may have also occurred with the maths graduate case study reported by Lorber.

There have also been question marks over the lack of deficit reported in some of Lorber's patients, most notably, the maths graduate. Some of the effects of hydrocephalus are quite subtle and are not readily detectable on standard cognition tests such as IQ.

How necessary is our brain?

Despite the Lorber case study, it appears that the cerebral cortex is essential. There are well-documented cases of people suffering extreme cognitive deficits after fairly minor neurological damage. If much of our grey matter was redundant then it would be expected that people could cope quite easily after such brain trauma. In addition, it seems unlikely that natural selection would have resulted in an organ that consumes so much energy for so little return. Other costs of having a large brain (and subsequent large head) concern the greater likelihood of dangerous complications during childbirth. A smaller, more efficient brain that could cope with the same cognitive functions would surely have been advantageous and therefore naturally selected. The fact that we do have a large brain suggests some sort of selective advantage. Redundancy is fine if there are no costs but here the costs of a large brain seem to outweigh the benefits of a small, but more efficient brain.

Modern brain scanning techniques have also shown how much of the brain is used in different activities. They demonstrate that large areas of the brain are used in almost all activities. Even during sleep, that seemingly most passive of activities, the brain is surprisingly active particularly when dreaming. So much so that dream sleep is often referred to as 'active sleep'.

Before his death in 1996, Lorber, who had a reputation for being deliberately controversial, conceded that he had perhaps over dramatised his evidence, arguing that this needed to be done in order to get people to listen. He believed that far too often results that don't fit existing explanations are marginalised as 'anomalous' results (Lewin, 1980). Lorber continued to argue that there must be some redundancy or spare capacity in the brain in much the same way that there is in the kidney or liver. There is some further experimental evidence from trials on rats to support Lorber's claims. Rats who have large areas of the cerebral cortex removed in one go seem to suffer from gross dysfunction, but rats who have the same amount of cortex removed in a series of stages can cope remarkably well and show little sign of impairment. This appears to mirror the gradual step-by-step effects of hydrocephalus seen in some of Lorber's patients. To this day, the idea of spare capacity in the brain remains a controversial and contentious argument, but it seems most likely that re-allocation of function is possible, particularly in the developing child's brain.

Given the evidence, it is certain that the cerebral cortex is necessary and that the claim that we only use 10 per cent of our brain is nothing more than a myth or 'urban legend'. We can be fairly certain that we use our entire brain all the time. The Lorber case study provides a fascinating peek into the workings of the brain, but rather than providing evidence of its redundancy it provides further evidence of its amazing adaptability and complexity. A complexity that we are only just beginning to comprehend.

Notes

1   Hydrocephalus: a condition, often congenital, in which an abnormal accumulation of fluid in the cerebral ventricles causes enlargement of the skull and compression of the brain destroying neurons in the process.
2   Source: www.brainconnection.com
3   Source: http://pages.britishlibrary.net/phrenology/overview.htm#whatwasit
4   A later version of this article was published in Della Sala (1999).

References

Beyerstein, B. (1998). 'Whence cometh the myth that we only use ten per cent of our brains?' In S. Della Sala (ed.), *Mind Myths: Exploring Popular Assumptions about the Mind and Brain*. Chichester: John Wiley and Sons.

Della Sala, S. (1999). *Mind-Myths*. Chichester: John Wiley and Sons.

Lashley, K . (1950). 'In search of the engram'. In J.F. Danielli and R. Brown (eds), *Physiological Mechanisms in Animal Behaviour*. New York: Academic Press, 454–82.

Lorber, J. (1981). 'Is your brain really necessary?'. *Nursing Mirror*, 152: 29–30.

Chapter 21

Charles Decker: Natural born killer?

The case of the 'crocodile man'

On 17 July 1974, 15-year-old Gail Sussman and her friend Deborah Sharp decided to hitch-hike to a friend's house in Pawtucket, Rhode Island, USA. They were picked up by Charles Decker (pseudonym) aged 23. At the outset seemingly calm and rational, Decker proceeded to undertake an unprovoked and horrifically violent hammer attack on the two girls before abandoning them in a local car park. The girls were bleeding so profusely that Decker thought that he might have killed them. He immediately called his father Nicholas Decker who happened to be a research scientist with a doctorate in endocrinology. With his son charged with attempted murder, Nicholas Decker set out to prove his son innocent; he argued that his son suffered from a lesion in his brain, specifically, in the limbic system, which meant that he was not responsible for his actions. At the trial, it was argued that, much like a crocodile's usual behaviour is determined primarily by the primitive urges of the limbic system, Charles Decker's actions that night were beyond his voluntary control. The Decker case opens up the whole notion of criminal responsibility and the free will/ determinism debate in psychology concerning the possible causes of behaviour. Are there other cases of human aggression in which biological causality can be demonstrated and, as such, should these people deserve our sympathy for their actions rather than our contempt ? Furthermore, what are the implications for society if biological causes for aggression are found?

Background

What is it that makes ordinary people commit extraordinary crimes? Violent crime committed by people with a history of violence is somehow less shocking and less surprising than that committed by people without a history of violence. Where a person's behaviour is said to be 'out of character', we find it difficult to explain their seemingly inexplicable behaviour. How can they have committed such aggression? What are the reasons and are they truly responsible for their actions?

There are numerous cases of people who have committed horrendous violent crimes and then insanity defences have been proposed to try to explain their actions. They have committed these acts because they have a mental incapacity and have been judged to be not responsible for their actions. Infamous cases such as Mark David Chapman, who shot John Lennon, cited messages in the book *Catcher in the Rye* (written by J.D. Salinger) and psychiatrists claimed at his trial that he suffered from psychotic and delusional episodes (although Chapman himself later pleaded guilty and did not pursue the insanity line). In a similar vein, John Hinckley Jr who attempted to assassinate President Ronald Reagan was later diagnosed as having a specific form of schizophrenia. What many of these cases have in common is that there have been long and detailed arguments as to the person's true mental state. Expert witnesses present evidence for and against, and the judge and jury typically have to weigh up this evidence. The decisions are often contentious and controversial since there are so many competing explanations as to the true cause of mental illness.

More often than not in such cases there is substantial earlier background evidence that points to or provides clues as to a person's subsequent violent behaviour. These might be biological, social or environmental factors. The Charles Decker defence case was one of the first to concentrate primarily on a chemical dysfunction of the brain to explain behaviour and, in addition, it was argued that while Decker was not fully responsible for his actions at that specific moment in time he was mentally competent at all other times.

The violence

The *Commonwealth v Decker* trial started on 5 April 1976 – over 2 years after the actual crime had been committed. The district attorney Frank O'Boy knew that the defence lawyer David Roseman had constructed a unique argument involving the issue of criminal responsibility and brain chemistry to get his client acquitted and that he was ready to argue his case. Gail Sussman started proceedings by describing the violence that occurred on that fateful evening of 17 July 1974.[1] Sussman and her friend Deborah Sharp had hitch-hiked to a friend's house but, on finding their friend out, had decided instead to go to Slater's Park in Pawtucket, Rhode Island. Around 7 p.m. a car passed them, stopped and came back to offer them a lift. The driver was Charles Decker, a 23-year-old tall, well-built man with blond hair and moustache. Getting into the car, the girls were offered a bottle of beer. All three occupants seemed to get on so well that they all agreed to go to get some cigarettes and beer from a nearby shop.

Sussman gave evidence that Decker was not drunk and appeared 'a nice guy' not 'upset about anything'. Decker told the girls that he was married and needed to go home to check on his wife and that he would return as soon as possible and they could continue driving around. The girls agreed and 20 minutes after dropping them off at a local restaurant parking lot Decker re-appeared with more beer and some marijuana. The three of them continued to drive, taking it in turns, and at one point during the evening they were stopped by a highway patrolman who questioned them because one of the rear tail lights was not working. Decker told the police officer that he was teaching his girlfriend to drive and convinced the officer that everything was fine. However, soon after this, events took a decided turn for the worse. During some gentle teasing from the girls, and with Gail Sussman driving, Decker grabbed a stonemason's hammer from under the seat and smashed it into her skull rendering her temporarily unconscious. When Sussman came round she saw Decker hitting Sharp while she tried to escape from the vehicle. Decker then proceeded to throw Deborah Sharp's now lifeless body into the back of the car before proceeding to try to choke the now awake Sussman. Almost as suddenly as the attack began it stopped. Decker started the car and drove on without saying anything.

Soon after on a deserted dirt track, Decker stopped the car and told Sussman to get out – he walked round and dragged Sharp out of the car. Decker threw a rock at Sussman and told her to take off her shirt. She refused and then Decker told Sussman to get back in the car and to help Deborah. Sussman assured Decker that she wouldn't tell anyone he had committed the attacks if he let them go. Decker said that he would drive them to a place where somebody could help them. Both girls were extremely bloodied and afraid but Sussman and Sharp did end up back in the car and Decker drove them to a marketplace where there was a light on in the local store. Sussman jumped out, helped the still unconscious Deborah out and she went to the store to call the police and ambulance as Decker drove off into the night.

A little after 10 p.m., Charles rang his father Nicholas Decker and said that he was afraid that he might have killed two girls. After further questioning he said that he didn't actually know what had happened. Charles said 'I went ape. They were teasing me and that's all I know.' Charles drove over to his father's house. Nicholas Decker heard Charles's account and believed that since both girls were conscious by the time Charles left them the attack couldn't have been as serious as relayed by Charles. He decided to leave it until the morning before calling his lawyer. In the morning his lawyer told Nicholas that he had already heard that two girls were seriously injured in hospital and that there was a chance that they might die. Furthermore, the local police were searching for the assailant. There was only one thing Nicholas Decker could do – hand his son over to the police.

Charles Decker was arrested and charged with two counts of attempted murder.

The psychology of mental illness

There are many biological and psychological explanations of human behaviour: both normal and abnormal. In terms of abnormal behaviour the most widely used approach to the causes and treatment of mental illness in the West is the medical model that was developed largely by the medical profession, hence its name.

The medical model has a number of key assumptions. First, that abnormal behaviour may be compared to a physical disease. It is assumed that all mental illnesses have a physiological cause related to the physical structure and/or functioning of the brain. A distinction is made between 'organic' and 'functional' disorders. Organic disorders involve obvious physical brain damage and/or disease (say, a brain tumour or chemical imbalance in the brain), whereas functional disorders do not have an obvious physiological cause (e.g. depression). Second, it is assumed that just as with physical illnesses, mental health illnesses have clear-cut symptoms that can be objectively diagnosed using well-established criteria. Psychiatrists also use diagnostic manuals for mental illness and compare symptoms with set classifications of illnesses. Brain scans can sometimes be used to help with the diagnosis, particularly with organic disorders. It is also assumed that genes have a major effect on the likelihood of developing a mental illness. People have a genetic predisposition to certain psychological disorders. Twin and family resemblance studies have shown that some mental illnesses 'run in the family'. For example, Kendler et al. (1985) found that relatives of schizophrenics were 18 times more likely to develop the illness than a matched control group. It is also assumed that chemical imbalances in the brain may be involved in certain mental illnesses. Neurotransmitters (chemicals in the brain) play an important part in behaviour, and an excess of dopamine has been detected in the brains of schizophrenics. However, such findings involve correlations and don't prove cause and effect. For example, it might be that it is the schizophrenia itself that is causing the dopamine excess, rather than the other way round.

Applying the medical model to abnormal behaviour exhibited by Charles Decker might have made it possible to diagnose Decker's aggression as having an 'organic' cause, assuming that there was an obvious brain dysfunction. Nicholas Decker set out to search for this.

Mad or bad?

It was extremely lucky for Charles Decker that his father was an endocrinologist and that he also had a good friend called Dr Mark Altschule. Dr Altschule was a specialist in the 'biochemistry of mental disease', and as a former chief medical officer of the Boston McLean Hospital, had been 'fighting for decades for recognition of the physical causes for mental illnesses' (Mayer and Wheeler, 1982: 29). Altschule was already familiar with some background behavioural problems in Charles and, suspecting a problem in the primitive limbic system of the brain, he was the ideal person to find evidence to defend Charles. Nicholas Decker and Mark Altschule set out to test Charles to see if there was any evidence to show that he had been acting with an unsound mind.

In a court of law psychiatrists are often asked to assess defendants with regard to their level of criminal responsibility. Often this is a matter of opinion and there may be conflicting viewpoints presented to the court. Frequently it is clear that the defendant has committed the act in question but it has to be judged whether they are also accountable for the act. The history of criminal responsibility dates back to the influential M'Naghten Rules (1843) that were formulated as a test for criminal liability in relation to mentally disordered defendants. The Rules were set up as a reaction to the acquittal of Daniel M'Naghten who mistakenly murdered Edward Drummond, the parliamentary secretary of his intended target, namely the British prime minister, Robert Peel. Defendants who satisfy these rules can be judged either 'not guilty by reasons of insanity' or 'guilty but insane' and may be sentenced to treatment in a hospital rather than detention in a prison. There are particular mental health issues that are more likely to be given credence for an insanity defence. These include so-called psychotic disorders, such as schizophrenia, because they are determined to have a greater influence on all behaviour.

Despite what the public may think, the traditional insanity defence is the plea of the last resort rather than the first. After all, if you think you may be found guilty it is not a good option to start claiming mental insanity since you are likely to face an indeterminate confinement in a mental institution rather than the other option of freedom (if found not guilty) or a pre-determined period in jail, which may be reduced through parole. Furthermore, even after release from a hospital a person has the double stigma of being judged both a criminal *and* a person with a history of mental illness. One only has to think of McMurphy in the book *One Flew Over the Cuckoo's Nest*, to realise that the insanity defence is not always a preferred option. Once institutionalised through reason of insanity in a hospital a person can be held until judged as no longer dangerous and, therefore, this could be a lifetime sentence. In the majority of minor crimes, defendants would rather serve the time in prison rather than risk an insanity defence. In more serious cases, such as murder, the option may be regarded as more attractive since the likely prison sentence would be lengthy, hence the greater preponderance of insanity pleas in such serious cases.

After intensive and numerous medical examination tests administered by Altschule it was concluded that Charles Decker suffered from Korsakoff's syndrome. This disorder was first described by Sergei Korsakoff in 1889 as 'an extraordinary amnesia, in which the memory of recent events, those which just happened, is chiefly disturbed'. This diagnosis helped to explain why Charles had little recollection of the details of the attack but this syndrome is most often found among chronic alcoholics and Charles' drinking problem was not that great. Notwithstanding this, it was determined that Charles was suffering from this incurable condition due to the advanced stages of chronic alcoholism (there is evidence that Korsakoff's syndrome does not always have to be linked to alcoholism). Vital for Charles's defence, Korsakoff himself had documented that victims of the disorder do exhibit irrational violent behaviour and that in some cases 'attacks of violence with confusion' had occurred without anxiety or irritability on behalf of the assailant. This seemed to fit with Charles Decker's crime perfectly. He had a neurological deficit linked to violent behaviour. However, a key problem remained. Under Massachusetts law the voluntary use of alcohol as a cause of criminal irresponsibility is not allowable since the mental condition was caused by the defendant's own choice to drink (or not). Luckily the defence managed to convince the judge that Charles Decker did not know of his problem related to alcohol consumption and previous minor isolated instances detailing earlier behaviour problems were kept out of the courtroom.

Altschule did a series of experimental tests on Charles that involved administering alcohol. It seemed to show that Charles had a remarkably high tolerance to the drug. However, with further testing they found that Charles's metabolic reaction to alcohol was extremely unusual. When Charles drank, an unknown substance, probably toxic, was released into his bloodstream, damaging his brain and sometimes causing violence. The defence argued that although the drinking by Charles was voluntary, the unexpected and abnormal consequences had been involuntary. It was up to the judge Thomas E. Dwyer to make the decision.

The crocodile brain

The limbic system is a series of structures concerned with emotion and survival. It is often portrayed as dealing with the four Fs: feeding, fighting, fleeing and fornication. It deals with primitive instincts but humans have developed the capacity for their cerebral cortex to overrule basic instinctual desires. Humans can stop and think about their behaviour in a way that some animals, such as crocodiles, cannot. Charles Decker's behaviour that July evening was compared to the instinctive behaviour of a crocodile who reacts to prey that presents itself without conscious thought.

A key component of the limbic system is an almond shaped structure called the amygdala, which plays a vital role in aggression. The part this plays was first explained by two physicians called Vernon Mark and Frank Ervin in their book *Violence and the Brain* (1970), and that was to influence the Decker court case. Mark and Ervin tried to demonstrate experimentally how abnormal brain tissue can cause aggressive behaviour specifically for a syndrome they termed 'behavioural dyscontrol syndrome'. They worked with patients for whom the most likely cause of episodes of violent behaviour was a malfunction in the limbic part of the brain. They cited the case of Charles Whitman who shot 41 people, killing 17 after climbing to the top of the Texas University campus tower and who weeks before had reported that he had 'forced thoughts' about killing and irresistible impulses to violence. His diary confession led to a post mortem analysis of his brain during which a tumour in the region of the amygdala was found. However, the problem with many such cases is that a tumour in the amygdala cannot lead us to conclude that this caused Whitman's violence – there is no proof of cause and effect. Did the brain tumour near his amygdala directly influence his violence or would he have done this atrocious act in any case? Researchers wanted to find experimental evidence that brain

Figure 21.1 Charles Whitman, the 'Texas sniper', shot 41 people
Source: Living Art Enterprises, LLC/Science Photo Library

deficits actually *cause* violence. However, it seemed unlikely that experiments would ever be allowed or devised to test this proposition in humans until Vernon and Mark reported on one very unusual case.

Vernon and Mark carried out one of the first experimental studies with humans and clearly showed how brain activity can cause violent behaviour. Their participant was an epileptic girl, Julia, who had fits of very violent behaviour. Indeed, in one incident after asking for help because she 'felt another spell coming on' Julia grabbed a pair of scissors from a nurse and stuck them into the nurses' lung. Luckily the nurse subsequently recovered. Suspecting a problem with her amygdala, Mark and Ervin borrowed a radio-controlled brain-stimulating device from Jose Delgado and implanted electrodes deep into Julia's right and left amygdala in order that they might stimulate this area of the brain. Although warned that this would happen Julia did not know *when* it would occur. During one such stimulation she was playing a guitar. When Mark and Ervin activated the electrode in her amygdala, she suddenly smashed the guitar against the wall. Other examples such as this led Mark and Ervin to conclude that this was the first human experimental demonstration of how brain stimulation can *cause* aggression without the cerebral cortex mediating the effect. Using this procedure for diagnostic purposes, Mark and Ervin claimed that they successfully treated Julia by making a destructive lesion in Julia's right amygdala, although these success claims have subsequently been questioned by a number of other psychologists such as Peter Breggin (Breggin and Breggin, 1994).

Mark and Ervin hoped that there might be a new form of psychosurgery that resulted from their experimental demonstrations. However, the prevailing public mood at the time was resolutely against any form of invasive brain surgery, primarily due to the overuse of lobotomies in the decades before (see Chapter 2), and it remains almost inconceivable that any ethical committee would approve such a procedure today.

Biology is destiny?

There are numerous other research studies that appear to show a link between biological traits and aggressive behaviour. Adrian Raine, a British born academic who is currently professor at the University of Pennsylvania, Philedelphia, in the departments of Criminology, Psychiatry and Psychology, conducted one of the best-known studies when he examined the brains of 41 psychopaths who had been convicted of murder.

In a classic study in 1997, Raine aimed to discover if murderers who had pleaded not guilty by reason of insanity showed any evidence of brain abnormalities (Raine et al., 1997). The study used Positron Emission Tomography (PET) brain scans to examine the brains of 41 people (39 males and 2 females) who were charged with murder and were pleading not guilty for reasons of insanity and compared them with 41 controls. The participants were matched by age and sex to a control group of participants who had no criminal history. All participants were injected with a glucose tracer and were required to work at a continuous performance task that was based around target recognition for 32 minutes, and then given the PET scan. Results showed that the murderers were found to have cerebral cortex differences to the controls, namely less activity in their pre-frontal and parietal areas, more activity in their occipital areas, and no difference in their temporal areas.

Raine et al. also found less activity in the corpus callosum and an imbalance of activity between the two hemispheres in three other subcortical structures, the amygdala, the hippocampus and the thalamus. They argue that the difference in activity in the amygdala (which is part of the limbic system) can be seen to support theories of violence that suggest that the violence is due to unusual emotional responses such as lack of fear. Indeed, there is evidence that people with a severed corpus callosum show inappropriate emotional expression and an inability to grasp long-term implications of a situation. It is important to note that Raine et al. are cautious about the implications of their findings. They conclude that there is data to suggest that murderers pleading not guilty by reasons of insanity have significantly different levels of activity in the brain and that these differences may predispose such individuals towards violence, but that this does not mean that violence is determined by biology alone. As with the Whitman case, there is no definite evidence of cause and effect. Indeed, by the time of the scans, many of the murderers had been in prison for months or years and so brain differences might have been due to the period of incarceration rather than a contributory factor to the incarceration in the first place. Nevertheless, studies such as Mark and Ervin and Raine et al. do open the possibility that violent individuals might be considered to be less responsible for their actions than those without such biological characteristics.

A more recent case involved that of Davis Bradley Waldroup Jr (Denno, 2011). On 16 October 2006 Waldroup killed his wife's best friend, Leslie Bradshaw by shooting her eight times and chased after his wife with a machete, chopping off her finger and cutting her numerous times. The case was particularly bloody and the crimes seemed intentional and premeditated. The case was certainly not a 'whodunit' but rather a 'why done it?'. The defence team concentrated on biological factors that might have contributed to the attack. Forensic psychiatrist William Bernet of Vanderbilt University took a blood sample and analysed the DNA of Waldroup. They found that Waldroup suffered from a defect in a particular gene that controls production of Monoamine Oxidase (MAOA) – this MAOA gene is more commonly known as the warrior gene because it is associated with violence. This meant that Waldroup had the high risk version of the gene, that is, low levels of MAOA contributes to an increased likelihood of aggression. Much research (Caspi et al., 2002) has shown that this may have an effect on subsequent behaviour particularly if the individual suffered from abuse or maltreatment as a child. Interestingly, evidence suggested that Waldroup was abused as a child. The defence team argued that these factors may have contributed to Waldroup's violence and that the jury should take this into account in their deliberations. In the state of Tennessee, Waldroup was facing a possible verdict of the death penalty. However, the jury seemed sufficiently swayed by the scientific genetic evidence for jurors to report that Waldroup may not have been entirely in control of his own actions. Judge Carroll Ross sentenced Waldroup to 32 years in prison warning him not to appeal the verdict in case another jury were not so swayed by the genetic arguments and the prosecution might once again press for the death penalty. Despite this, on 2 April 2012, Waldroup requested an appeal to his sentence. The voluntary manslaughter and attempted murder charges were affirmed.

Biological determinism

A major worry about the issue of biological determinism and criminality relates back to an earlier era when theories of inherited characteristics, including criminality, led a number of countries to introduce state-sponsored sterilisation programmes. These were seen as part of eugenics programmes designed to prevent the reproduction of those people in the population who were considered to be carriers of defective genetic traits. The USA was one of the first countries to adopt such programmes, when Indiana introduced sterilisation legislation in 1907 and Washington and California followed in 1909. The principal targets were the mentally ill and retarded, although some states included the deaf and blind and physically deformed (Stern, 2005). Many people link Nazi Germany with the Eugenic Movement and they would be correct to do so, since Hitler passed the Law for the Prevention of Hereditary Diseased Offspring in 1933. This ensured that doctors had to report patients who were judged either mentally retarded or mentally ill (including schizophrenia), blind, deaf or physically deformed. Identified individuals had their cases reviewed and could subsequently be forcibly sterilised (Proctor, 1988; Bock, 2004). It is estimated that by the end of the second world war as many as 400,000 individuals had been sterilised under German law. It is interesting to note, however, that during the Nuremberg trials, many Nazis justified their policy decision, claiming that they had been influenced by earlier, and ongoing, American practices (Kershaw, 2000).

The continuing worry is that *if* biological causes can be determined then biological interventions might be adopted instead of looking for wider factors. Such solutions might then be used against particular ethnic or social groups, for example, those that are disproportionately represented in crime statistics. Where is the emphasis – biological, social or environmental? For example, imagine you live in a town with a lot of air pollution and some people suffer from breathing problems. Should our emphasis be on these individuals and their predisposition to breathing problems and simply give them biological interventions such as drugs to help them or should we change the air quality (i.e. the environment) from which all individuals will benefit?

Perhaps the least controversial approach does not suggest that biological factors alone cause violence but that certain biological factors might make people more susceptible to 'bad' environments. Whether we (society) should concentrate our resources on investigating biological or social factors (or both) remains a matter of ongoing controversy and to some extent the answer depends on one's philosophical viewpoint.

Furthermore, one very controversial suggestion is that measurable biological deficits can be detected, identified and maybe even fixed in the near future as medicine and psychology advance. The argument for an innate predisposition to violence, which might be identified before the violence (if any) takes place, can be seen as misguided and something akin to the sci-fi film *Minority Report* (directed by Spielberg). Nevertheless, academics and politicians have spent time trying to identify and manipulate social environments to change behaviour for the better, leading some to argue that identification and manipulation of biological factors is an inevitable consequence of scientific gains. Perhaps society needs to contemplate a future in which we deal with the biological underpinnings of aggression in the same way that we have tried to address social causes.

The issue of free will

The Decker case and others like it can be used to examine a key debate in psychology – namely that of free will versus determinism. To what extent are we free to choose to act in whatever way we want to?

There are several elements to free will. The first is that in order to act freely or not, one must have alternative possibilities available. If people are compelled to act in a specific way (in Decker's case, perhaps because of brain chemistry) they cannot be said to be acting freely. Furthermore, behaviour that is not taking place for an intelligible reason is also not considered free willed (Kane, 1998). For instance, a person who attacks their partner during a sleep–walking episode would not be said to be responsible for their action and is therefore not an example of free will.

Mental disorders frequently feature in free will debates. There are cases where people's behaviour and thinking have been considered to be so disordered that they have not been held responsible for their actions (Meynen, 2010). However Frankfurt (1971) considers the case of the drug addict. According to Frankfurt

(1971) acting of one's own free will implies that one wills the action and also wants to have the will to perform the action. For instance, did an addict's original decision to use heroin cause the heroin addiction and thus also cause any negative actions that subsequently resulted from the heroin addiction? In brief, a central issue is, how does the person's behaviour and the disorder relate and how can they be distinguished when it comes to the initiation of actions? Charles Decker's case and his reaction to alcohol can also be seen in this light.

There is also the question of degree of responsibility or 'reduced' free will. A child will be viewed as less responsible for their actions than an adult. Are there certain disorders that have more pronounced effects on free will, such as psychotic disorders and are there other biological factors that may undermine the notion of free will?

According to determinism, an individual's behaviour is governed by internal or external forces: that is, all behaviour has a cause. If behaviour is the result of external forces it is called environmental determinism, while if it is the result of internal forces it is called biological determinism. Determinism implies that behaviour occurs in a regular, orderly manner that is totally predictable, and this makes this viewpoint compatible with the scientific method. It also

Figure 21.2 Charles Decker's behaviour was compared to the instinctive behaviour of a crocodile

Source: © Shutterstock

implies that an individual's behaviour is beyond his/her control, and therefore individuals cannot be held responsible for their behaviour. It also assumes that people are passive respondents and are not free to behave as they choose. Was Charles Decker free to act the way he did or was he suffering from biological determinism and, if so, to what extent (if at all) did this excuse his violent actions?

Judgement day

Judge Thomas E. Dwyer had to decide whether Decker was responsible for the crime and be sentenced to jail or whether there were sufficient mitigating circumstances. Was Decker not acting freely when he attacked the girls? Was he suffering from biological determinism? Should Charles have known through previous experiences about the 'unexpected consequences' of his drinking?

After weighing up the evidence, the judge decided that Decker was guilty of the attempted murder of both girls and the prosecution recommended that Decker be sent to a medium security jail for 18 years, but to be eligible to apply for parole after only 2 years. After a 30-day delay, the judge did indeed sentence to Charles Decker to 18 years but the execution of the sentence was suspended and he was placed on probation for 6 years. Decker escaped incarceration providing he met the probation conditions, namely, abstinence from drugs and alcohol, full-time employment and counselling.

Would Charles Decker have won his case without such a committed and brilliantly informed father? Might Charles Decker have served a number of years in jail for a crime beyond his control or did he actually deserve to be sent to prison as a punishment for his crime? Might he have found a sympathetic judge and jury who could have sent him to a psychiatric institution where he may have found early release when they found that he was no longer a danger to himself or society? Who knows? There must be thousands of cases similar to the Charles Decker case where defendants have not had the dogged determination and expertise of a father convinced of their son's innocence. In years to come, perhaps science will develop better diagnostic tests to determine mental competence but there may always be questions that arise about exactly how responsible we are for our own actions and behaviour and, in the end, this may often remain a judgement call for a judge and jury.

Was Charles suffering from reduced free will? Should we feel sorrow for him or should we feel that he should be punished for his actions? Psychologists and psychiatrists find it difficult to determine a person's current mental functioning. Trying to determine the causes of behaviour months earlier (or in Charles Decker's case 2 years earlier) can be even more problematic. Given this situation, it does not mean that we shouldn't continue to try in order to improve our identification of those defendants who need our sympathy or contempt. Perhaps future research should also include people such as Charles Decker who have been involved in these issues first hand. After all, people like Charles Decker may well have a good deal of experience and knowledge to bring to the debate on criminal responsibility and free will.

Note

1   Material in this chapter has been drawn from Mayer and Wheeler (1982) unless otherwise indicated.

References

Bock, G. (2004). 'Nazi sterilization and reproductive policies'. In D. Kuntz (ed.), *Deadly Medicine: Creating the Master Race*. Washington, DC: United States Holocaust Memorial Museum.

Breggin, P.R. and Breggin, G.R. (1994). *The War Against Children: How the Drugs, Programs, and Theories of the Psychiatric Establishment are Threatening America's Children with a Medical 'Cure' for Violence*. New York: St. Martin's Press.

Caspi, A., McClay, J., Moffitt, T.E., Mill, J., Martin, J., Craig, I.W., Taylor, A. and Poulton, R. (2002). 'Role of genotype in the cycle of violence in maltreated children'. *Science*, 297(5582): 851–4.

Denno, D. (2011). 'Courts' increasing consideration of behavioral genetics evidence in criminal cases: Results of a longitudinal study'. *Michigan State Law Review*, 967–1047.

Frankfurt, H. (1971). 'Freedom of the will and the concept of a person'. *Journal of Philosophy*, 68(1): 5–20.

Hare, R. (1993). *Without Conscience: The Disturbing World of the Psychopaths Among Us*. New York: Simon & Schuster.

Kane, R. (1998). *The Significance of Free Will*. New York: Oxford University Press.

Kendler, K.S., Gruenberg, A.M. and Tsuang, M.T. (1985). 'Psychiatric illness in first-degree relatives of schizo-phrenic and surgical control patients: A family study using DSM-III criteria'. *Archives of General Psychiatry*, 42: 770–9.

Kershaw, I. (2000). *The Nazi Dictatorship. Problems and Perspectives of Interpretation* (4th edition). London: Hodder Arnold.

Korsakoff, S.S. (1889). 'Psychic disorder in conjunction with multiple neuritis' (English translation with commentary). *Neurology* (1955), 5: 394–406.

Mark, V. and Ervin, F. (1970). *Violence and the Brain*. New York: Harper and Row.

Mayer A. and Wheeler, M. (1982). *The Crocodile Man: A Case of Brain Chemistry and Criminal Violence*. Boston, MA: Houghton Mifflin.

Meynen, G. (2010). 'Free will and mental disorder: Exploring the relationship'. *Theoretical Medicine and Bioethics*, December, 31(6): 429–43.

Proctor, R. (1988). *Racial Hygiene: Medicine under the Nazis*. Cambridge, MA: Harvard University Press.

Raine, A., Buchsbaum, M. and LaCasse, L. (1997). 'Brain abnormalities in murderers indicated by positron emission tomography'. *Biological Psychiatry*, 42(6): 495–508.

Stern, M. (2005). *Eugenic Nation: Faults and Frontiers of Better Breeding in Modern America*. Oakland, CA: University of California Press.

Part 6

Comparative psychology

Chapter 22

Talking to the animals
Washoe and Roger Fouts

It has always been man's desire to be able to talk to animals. For years this appeared to be a forlorn hope until a group of researchers made a scientific breakthrough by teaching American Sign Language (ASL) to a chimpanzee called Washoe. Over more than 30 years Washoe appeared to show understanding, comprehension and, indeed, production of ASL, providing strong evidence that animals can learn and use language. Such research helped to develop our understanding of chimpanzee behaviour and brought to the forefront the debate about the ethical use of chimpanzees in biomedical research. One man who worked with Washoe for over 30 years as a tutor and scientist was Roger Fouts. His story is an amazing tale detailing the relationship between a chimp and a human who shared the same language and provides a remarkable insight of our own place in relation to the rest of the animal kingdom (Fouts, 1997).

Early attempts

It's not just Tarzan or Dr Dolittle who have wanted to talk to animals. Yet for the most part our attempts to converse with animals have been disappointing. One of the earliest documented scientific accounts of man's ability to talk to animals involved a horse nicknamed 'Clever Hans'. In 1891 a German called William von Osten, claimed that his horse 'Clever Hans' could answer various questions simply by tapping his hoof (Pfungst, 1911; see also Chapter 15). For mathematical questions, Hans would tap out the numbers and for answers that required letters the alphabet was encoded as 'A'= one tap; 'B'= two taps and so on. Unbelievably, it was claimed that Hans could add, subtract, multiply, divide, tell the time, work out days of the week, read, spell and understand German.

Von Osten believed that animals possessed an intelligence that is equal to that of a human. In his quest to prove this he attempted to teach animals, including a cat and a bear, how to do simple calculations; however, it was only Hans who showed any real ability. Clever Hans performed throughout Europe and became quite a sensation and crowds flocked to see his amazing performances. Hans was investigated by Professor Carl Stumpf of the Berlin School of Experimental Psychology in 1904 and his abilities were declared to be genuine. Here was an animal that did indeed seem to have some special understanding akin to some human abilities. However, in 1907 the 'Hans Commission' was set up to more rigorously test Hans's abilities. They found that Hans could only answer questions if the questioner knew the answer and the questioner was in sight of the horse. It became apparent that Hans was responding to visual cues given by the questioner. Hans noticed small involuntary movements given off by the questioner when the correct answer was reached. In response to this, Hans would stop tapping at the correct answer. The horse was not aware that the correct answer had been reached but could spot the visual cues given off by the questioner when the correct answer had been reached. Although this was a considerable trick in itself it showed that Hans did not understand German or mathematics or any other of his claimed abilities. It was shown that 'Clever Hans' was perhaps not so clever after all.

Other attempts to converse with animals have also been marked with apparent successes followed by failure. However, in the last 50 years, research has begun to demonstrate that talking to animals may not be quite the impossible goal that many people have claimed.

There is a long debate in psychology about what, if anything, sets humans apart from animals.[1] Scientists of all persuasions over the decades have attempted to analyse how similar or different humans are from the rest of the animal kingdom. Are humans qualitatively different in some important way or is there only a quantitative difference that can be measured on some sort of biological continuum?

Prior to Darwin's writing in 1859, it was generally assumed that humans were set apart from animals with the belief that we were the only beings with a soul and the capacity for speech. Many famous philosophers including Plato, Aristotle, Descartes and Huxley argued that talking with animals was an impossibility and that there was a chasm between what constitutes a human and an animal. Darwin however was unconvinced. In 1859 he postulated that humans had evolved as a result of 'descent with modification' and that humans had most likely evolved from apes living on the African Savannah. Soon evolutionary theory was used to support the idea of a continuum between humans and animals with the unfortunate result that many non-European races were treated as being lower down the continuum of civilisation and displayed as exhibits at a number of European and American Science Fairs (Savage-Rambaugh and Lewin, 1994). Indeed, there were instances (for example, St Louis World's Fair of 1904) when pygmies were housed with chimpanzees and monkeys because they were felt to be closer to such creatures than Europeans. Although his theory may have been misused in such ways, Darwin himself did not seem to recognise any obvious differences between animals and humans or indeed between different human races. In this case, could our closest living relatives manage to understand language in the same way that humans do?

Washoe: A special chimpanzee

In March 1967 a young graduate called Roger Fouts applied to the University of Nevada in Reno, USA, to study a Ph.D. in experimental psychology. Finding out that he could not afford the fees he was offered a graduate assistantship job. When he asked what the job entailed he was told very simply that it involved teaching a chimpanzee to talk. Desperate for the job and intrigued by the idea, Fouts accepted the position and so began his lifetime work with a chimp called Washoe (Fouts with Mills, 1997).

Fouts attended a job interview in August 1967 and met Allen and Beatrix Gardner, the husband and wife research team behind Project Washoe. Fouts reports that the interview showed his lack of knowledge of the topic but he got the job when he was introduced to the 2-year-old female chimpanzee, Washoe. Washoe was allowed to play at the university nursery playground on Sundays (when no children were around). After the dismal interview, Allen Gardner and Fouts walked over to the playground and Washoe spotted them from a distance. Washoe let out excited hoots and sprinted on all fours towards them. She vaulted the 4-foot high fence and jumped straight into Fouts's arms, giving him an enormous hug. Fouts believes that this incident helped him to secure the position.

One month later Fouts reported for work not at the university but at the Gardner's one-storey home with a backyard that measured 5,000 square feet plus an attached garage. Washoe lived in a trailer in the backyard of the house. This was the setting for the Gardner's chimpanzee language laboratory. On entering the house Fouts noted that everyone was whispering. The reason for

Figure 22.1 Roger Fouts and a chimpanzee
Source: Greg Williams/Rex Features

this was that the Gardners didn't want Washoe to hear any spoken language. Fouts would be conversing with Washoe exclusively using ASL and the Gardners didn't want Washoe to realise that spoken forms of communication were used by humans. Chimps cannot speak due to limitations in the physiology of their vocal tract. After struggling to get Washoe to co-operate with nappy changes in early sessions together, Fouts became preoccupied with potty training. Eventually after a series of mishaps Fouts left numerous potties around the trailer and yard and Washoe started to use them seemingly realising that it was easier to do this than using nappies. Washoe could already use some simple sign language and would often sign HURRY as she rushed across the yard to her potty and CAN'T, CAN'T in response to Fout's urgings for her to try to go to the toilet.

Chimpanzee language?

The Gardners believed that since chimpanzees were human's nearest relatives, they might have an innate capacity for language (Gardener and Gardener, 1969).

Furthermore, the results of Konrad Lorenz's cross-fostering research with ducklings and goslings, which showed that they imprinted on the first moving object they saw, suggested to the Gardners that Washoe might be able to learn many new skills given the correct environment. Earlier anecdotal cases had been reported of chimpanzees being adopted into human families and learning to do various tasks such as how to eat using knives and forks, brushing their teeth and looking through magazines, but no-one had ever successfully taught advanced sign language to a chimpanzee.[2] Indeed, the common belief in scientific circles at the time was that language was beyond the capacity of chimpanzees and apes. Fouts (and others in the field) realised that there was a fundamental problem with this argument – just because some studies had failed to teach language to apes it didn't mean that it was impossible. People might simply have been approaching the problem incorrectly. It might be a case of finding the right conditions and obtaining the right methods of teaching or training. The Gardners decided that the problem was that researchers had equated language with speech. However, speech is just one mode of language and given the physiology and behaviour of the chimpanzee it is not one that appeared promising. The Gardners decided to use ASL instead and immediately they transformed the research field. They decided to continue with the cross-fostering programme that had successfully raised chimpanzees to act very like humans but without language understanding, and to use ASL to try to add language.

The programme involved games, toys, books and magazines, all of which showed ASL being used. Researchers working with Washoe did not speak to one another but signed to one another. In short, Washoe did not hear spoken language and only experienced ASL. Washoe immediately started to sign at the same developmental rate as a human child. When she wanted a DRINK she made a fist with an outstretched thumb to her mouth; for LISTEN she would touch her ear with her index finger, and so on. After almost a year Washoe had started to combine signs such as DIRTY GOOD for her potty chair and BABY MINE to keep her doll. Washoe would also initiate language. One such example occurred on the day that Fouts was piggybacking her around and she signed YOU GO THERE. At the same time Washoe started signing FUNNY. Fouts couldn't understand why, until he felt her urine trickling down his back into his shorts!

Fouts found that the best way to get Washoe to learn was to play games. He devised numerous games of hide and seek and 'Simon says' and spent hours signing stories from books and magazines to Washoe. Later Washoe would sit at a table and draw pictures of what she had seen. Washoe would spend hours riding around on a tricycle, bouncing on mattresses or swinging around in trees.

While working with Washoe, Fouts wondered from where the chimpanzee had originated. It was believed that she had been captured by African hunters who would shoot mother chimpanzees and take the youngsters to sell in the United States. The difficult journey ensured that only 10 per cent of the captured baby chimpanzees survived the journey to the West. Nevertheless in 1966 a 10-month-old infant found herself at the medical Air Force Laboratory. The Gardners were visiting the lab in the hope of obtaining a chimp for their own research and managed to secure this infant. They brought her to their Nevada home and named her after the county in which she would live: namely Washoe. The sign they used for Washoe was a W hand sign held behind an ear meaning 'Washoe big ears'.

Washoe showed other intelligences beyond understanding of ASL. Problem solving skills were demonstrated every day – for example, when a new doormat appeared outside her trailer, Washoe initially appeared rather scared of it. She overcame her fear by placing a doll on the mat for a few minutes and checking that the doll was unharmed she accepted that she had nothing to fear from the new doormat. As any parent knows children are very good at manipulating their parents and Washoe was no exception to this. One day Fouts was tidying up after breakfast and starting to lock the food cupboards when he spotted Washoe intently looking at something she had found underneath a rock in the garden. Wondering what it might be Fouts went out to see what had interested Washoe so much. As soon as Fouts was further away from the trailer than Washoe she rushed inside opened the cupboard he had not yet locked, stole a soft drink bottle and leapt back into the safety of a tree. Fouts found nothing under the rock and realised that it had been an elaborate and deliberately planned ploy by Washoe to facilitate the stealing of the drink.

Another demonstration of Washoe's complex cognitions involved the eating of green grapes. The vines in the backyard occasionally produced rather unripe green grapes and these gave Washoe diarrhoea. Washoe realised that Fouts did not want her to eat the grapes and have to clear up afterwards so whenever she wanted something that she was not allowed she would climb up and threaten to eat grapes until Fouts gave in to her demands. If he didn't give in, she would climb to the highest branch and try to pee on him!

Fouts believed that he played the role of an older brother taking care of the youngest child. On a daily basis Fouts observed Washoe using language in her everyday life. For example, Washoe would sign QUIET to herself when she had crept into a room and wanted to remain unseen. She would play with her dolls frequently during the day and sign to them in much the same way a child would talk to her dolls. To those critics who felt Washoe was merely mimicking and copying human behaviour like a glorified circus performer, this could not have been true. She had only been surrounded by adult carers and her child-like behaviour (playing with dolls) had never been something she had observed.

Fouts used to take Washoe out in the car for trips around the city. They would visit local parks just as a parent might take out their child for a day out. These trips eventually had to be stopped because Fouts didn't want her to hear spoken language and because she caused quite a stir when people realised that a baby chimpanzee was walking around the shopping centre or park. When she had been younger Fouts could just hold her in his arms but as she grew larger this became too difficult.

Simple conditioning?

Perhaps the most popular psychological theory to explain learning was that proposed by B.F. Skinner of Harvard University (Skinner, 1950). He suggested that language learning (as with other forms of learning) could be explained by operant conditioning, namely, that behaviour is shaped by the consequences of the behaviour. Put simply, reinforcers (rewards) or punishers operate to shape and change our behaviour. If we perform an action (write an essay) and get a reward (e.g. praise) then we are likely to repeat this behaviour. If we eat a berry and we get sick we are unlikely to repeat this behaviour. We learn language the same way through reward and punishment. Parents give rewards for vocalisations (encouragement, smiles, attention) and the nearer the vocalisation to the desired word the more reward given. I know this having spent hours encouraging my own children to say 'Daddy' as their first word! The Gardners believed that this method was the way forward with Washoe and so they decided to use operant conditioning techniques. As is often the case, theory can be difficult to put into practice. They decided to use numerous rewards such as food, tickling and games. They soon realised that using such techniques was impossible. Often Washoe would move from one gesture to another occasionally making an approximation of the sign they wanted to reward. But by the time the reward (a clap, smile) was presented she had moved on to something else. After months of conditioning, Fouts reckoned that Washoe had learned one sign using these methods. Fouts believed this system would only work under extreme laboratory conditions, which may explain why Skinner made so-called 'Skinner boxes' in order to have complete control over the animal's (usually a rat's) environment.

Washoe learned signs through imitation – simply by observing them being used. She would pick up the signs without detailed instruction. For example, Fouts would point to a car and sign CAR and later Washoe would use the sign when she saw a car. Sometimes Washoe's intial signing might not be that accurate but she would perfect the sign through watching the adults around her signing. Again, this mimicked human children who may initially mispronounce words but on repeated hearings learn to say them more accurately. Fouts also helped to guide Washoe in her signing. He would point at an object and then shape her fingers into the correct sign. Washoe would learn in this way as well demonstrating a flexibility of learning in contrast to the circus performing animals she was compared with. Washoe was not being taught or conditioned in any formal way, she was learning of her own volition and in many cases she was initiating the learning through games and play. Hunger or food is supposed to be a particularly good primary reinforcer but Fouts found that Washoe's signing deteriorated if she was hungry into repetitive begging. There are studies with humans that demonstrate that positive reinforcement (e.g. money) can have negative consequences and decrease performance on creative tasks or tasks where there is a feeling that the task is worth doing for its own sake (that is, tasks with a high level of intrinsic motivation). Amabile (1985) asked 72 creative writers to write some poetry. Some were given extrinsic reasons for doing so, such as being paid, while others were given intrinsic reasons, such as enjoyment of the creative task. Their efforts were rated by 12 independent poets and the extent and quality of the intrinsic group's poetry was rated much higher than that of the extrinsic group. Other studies support these findings. Children who enjoy drawing and are offered payment for their work, draw less than those who do it just for fun and have never been offered any financial incentives. Teenagers offered money to play word games enjoy them less than those who play with no rewards (Kohn, 1999). For Washoe, learning the signs must have been rewarding in itself or allowed her to control her environment (intrinsically rewarding) so she had no need for extrinsic rewards.

With Washoe's demonstrations of blackmail and humour Fouts and the Gardners realised that chimpanzees are without doubt the closest animals to man both biologically, behaviourally and, crucially, cognitively as well. In some ways this should have come as no surprise; researchers had already shown chimps using tools to eat termites or crack open nuts, and the word 'chimpanzee' comes from a Congolese dialect meaning 'mock man'. Furthermore Sibley and Ahlquist (1984) showed that humans and chimpanzees share 98.4 per cent of their DNA. Indeed, chimpanzees are more closely related to humans than they are to gorillas or orang-utans.

Some psychologists questioned whether Washoe was using language in a similar way to humans. The Gardners and Fouts used a double blind procedure, which showed that Washoe could not have merely been responding to cues in the way that 'Clever Hans' had done years before. They arranged a cubicle in which one researcher placed objects that Washoe could see and then Washoe had to sign the object to another observer in a cubicle who could not see the original object. Washoe performed the majority of the tasks extremely well, although with replica objects like a car there were initial problems because she signed BABY to represent a miniature replica. Once this was understood by the observers her signing became much more easily understood. Eventually they found that picture slides worked just as well as real objects and the trials could proceed far more quickly. By the age of four, Washoe was getting about 80 per cent of the trials correct, however, as is often the case her mistakes revealed much about her cognitions. For example, she would sign COMB for BRUSH or COW for DOG but never got confused between categories, suggesting that she had developed a concept for categories. Her vocabulary rapidly increased and expanded to include different types of phrases such as attributive (YOUR SHOE), action (ME OPEN DOOR) and experiences (FLOWER SMELL). Fouts and the Gardners were convinced that Washoe's abilities meant that she was using language. Other psychologists accepted the evidence but still there were some who decided to redefine language in order to, as Fouts put it, keep 'all non humans out of the language club' (Fouts, 1997: 106).

Moving house

In 1970 when Washoe was about 5 years old the Gardners decided to send Washoe to the Institute of Primate Studies at Oklahoma University. There were various practical reasons for this. Washoe was outgrowing the backyard and people in the neighbourhood were starting to worry about the 'ape down the road'. After much soul searching Fouts decided that he would continue his work with Washoe and he and his family moved to Oklahoma. On 1

October 1970 Washoe was tranquillised and transported in a private lear jet to Oklahoma. Fouts was shocked to find a small concrete cage waiting for Washoe – after years of having her own trailer and sleeping in her own bed she found herself in a small cage with 20 other adult chimpanzees in nearby iron cages screaming and banging on their doors. The person in charge of this facility was Dr William Lemmon and for the next few years Fouts and Lemmon had a series of intense battles over the appropriate way to house and help Washoe. Quite unlike the techniques that Fouts had used with Washoe, Lemmon dominated the chimps at his research institute using cattle prods and pellet guns if they refused to submit to his dominance. Eventually Fouts and Lemmon came to a temporary truce whereby it was agreed that Fouts would set up his own chimpanzee colony on an island in the middle of a nearby lake. The island was man made, constructed out of concrete, amounting to dirt and scrub over about a quarter of an acre, but to Fouts it was the start of an exciting new era. Fouts realised quickly that he was an expert in chimpanzee behaviour with one chimpanzee who thought she was human but that this did not prepare him for working with other chimpanzees. Fouts was in charge of a number of chimpanzee orphans and over the coming years he worked closely with other incredible chimpanzees such as Thelma, Cindy, Booee, Bruno, Ally, Loulis, Moja, Tatu and Dar. Many of these chimpanzees had been bred and subjected to medical experimentation. Booee for example had had his corpus callosum severed (the connecting tissue between the two brain hemispheres) resulting in two independently working brains. With this new extended family all the chimps started to learn ASL from Fouts and Washoe and indeed Washoe started to learn spoken English because Fouts decided to use it with many of the other chimps who could understand it (some had been brought up in family homes). All of these other chimpanzees proved that Washoe wasn't some chimp genius but rather that all chimps are capable of learning language. All of these chimps learned at their own speed but they did all learn language.

In 1972 Fouts started to turn his academic expertise to autistic children. He started working with a 9-year-old boy called David who had shown extremely limited language abilities and who exhibited classic repetitive meaningless behaviours. Fouts decided to try to teach him ASL. Within a few sessions, David was communicating with basic ASL signs and after a few weeks he suddenly started to vocalise simple words such as 'mama' and 'drink'. Fouts moved on to other autistic children and had similar success. Fouts (and other researchers) had shown that teaching sign language opens up communication and can then lead on to speech. Later Fouts found out that the area of the brain responsible for hand movements is also implicated in speech control, suggesting that some kind of positive interaction may be occurring with ASL and speech. Fouts went on to hypothesise that early man started with non-verbal communication and this developed into basic grunts and sounds and eventually, through evolutionary pressures into an adapted anatomy (vocal tract) and spoken language. Fouts believed that language emerged culturally and he hoped that by showing captive chimpanzees signing, and teaching their young to sign, he could demonstrate this. Tool use in the wild had already been shown to be learned from parent to child in this way. After Washoe had lost her own infant, Fouts managed to persuade Washoe to adopt a 10-month-old male infant called Loulis. Fouts ensured that the researchers only ever made seven signs in the presence of Loulis. Thus any other signs that Loulis used must have been learned from other chimps. Within 8 weeks Loulis was frequently signing to humans or chimps but he never used the signs he saw the researchers using. He only seemed to learn through observation from other chimps. Fouts therefore felt he could conclude that chimps' language acquisition comes through simple learning techniques shared with humans. In numerous videotapes made over the coming years Fouts showed chimps interacting and spontaneously signing with other chimps.

There had been numerous other attempts by other researchers such as Sue Savage-Rumbaugh (with a bonobo called Kanzi) (Savage-Rumbaugh and Lewin, 1994) and Penny Patterson (with a gorilla called Koko) (Patterson, 1981) to teach language to great apes. One researcher called Herbert Terrace reported early success with his chimp called Nim Chimsky (a joke about the linguist Noam Chomsky), but later claimed that the chimp had simply been signing as a result of prompting from the researchers (in a similar way to 'Clever Hans' years before) (Terrace, 1979). Fouts successfully showed that there were important methodological problems with Terrace's approach, but it didn't stop critics of language acquisition in chimps from using it as evidence of the uniqueness of human language.

By 1974 Fouts was an internationally acclaimed academic and his family were settled in Oklahoma. However, conditions were far from ideal for Washoe and the other chimps. Fouts was also beginning to realise that although he loved Washoe as a member of his own family Washoe was still regarded as a 'scientific prisoner' by Lemmon and some of the staff. Fouts even toyed with the idea of trying to rehabilitate Washoe back into the wild in Africa but this was quickly rejected as being an impossible undertaking. Instead he set about finding a more humane sanctuary for Washoe and the other chimps. Fouts made tentative enquiries at a number of universities and eventually Central Washington University offered Fouts a tenured professorship and the opportunity to build a primate research centre. One night in August 1980 Fouts hired a trailer and drove to Ellensburg, Washington with three chimps Washoe, Loulis and Moja.

Fouts found that his research area was becoming less popular and as a result his funding was dwindling. Fouts set out to raise funds in whichever way possible – one way he found to save money was to collect out-of-date fruit and vegetables from the local markets for the chimps to eat. Fouts also became a scientific adviser for the Tarzan film *Greystoke* directed by Hugh Hudson. The money from this venture helped to develop the research facilities for the chimpanzees.

The ethics of animal research

In the late 1980s Fouts decided to turn his attention to the ethics of experimenting on the great apes. Fouts had visited enough animal laboratories to know the kind of procedures that these animals were subjected to. Often the apes are kept in isolation and yet they are social animals and Fouts's own research had shown that these were sentient beings. As well as the ethics of such experimentation, Fouts questioned the procedures, arguing that the stress experienced by the animals made them more likely to become ill and suffer from a number of psychological problems. With all such research, there is an inherent contradiction: either it is possible to extrapolate results from apes and chimps to humans because of the similarities or it isn't. If it is possible and we are arguing that they are similar enough, shouldn't they be treated in a humane way?

Fouts went on to advocate that all animal research should be abolished and that included his own. Fouts knew that it was impossible to re-integrate his chimps back into the wild so he decided to allow them to live their lives in as good an environment as possible. It took Fouts 15 years but on 7 May 1993 Fouts opened the Chimpanzee and Human Communication Institute that he had designed and helped build. The three-dimensional tropical home incorporated 5,400 square feet of ground and vegetation including indoor and outdoor exercise areas, sleeping quarters and glass-walled kitchens so that the chimps could watch their food being prepared. Fouts changed the rules about human/chimp interaction. Humans were not allowed into the chimp area except for practical reasons of cleaning or repairing the compound.

Table 22.1 Summary of reasons for using animals in psychological research

Arguments for	Arguments against
Animal research avoids testing and harming humans; thus, it is possible to use animals where it is impossible or unethical to use humans	Animals cannot report feelings/effects so we cannot be sure how much suffering they experience
Animals have fewer rights and therefore more control in the experimentation process is possible	Animals should have the same rights as humans – why should we exploit animals for our own ends?
Animals have shorter life spans and thus maturational changes can be more quickly and easily seen	One aspect of being human is that we do not exploit disadvantaged groups; this is an example of 'Speciesism'
Animal research tends to be cheaper and easier to conduct	Science should work with, not against nature
Evolutionary continuum argument: humans are animals and we learn in a similar way; thus, animal research can be generalised to humans	Animal research gives psychology and science a poor image
Animal research can enhance our theoretical knowledge	Humans are unique beings – very different from animals and thus we cannot generalise from animals to humans
Animal research can lead to direct practical uses of benefit to humans, e.g. guide dogs, the testing of drugs	Use of alternatives strategies are preferred – for example, computer simulations
Laboratory animal research can benefit the animal species represented by the research	Due to the stress suffered in the lab situation we cannot be sure that cause and effect are certain
It is man's duty and responsibility to improve human life above that of animals	If apes are so similar to humans they should be afforded similar rights as humans

Fouts opened up the compound to human visitors so that they could see the chimps and the work they had done with them. Fouts believed that this would benefit the chimpanzee cause and help educate the public about the chimpanzee research cause. Given what he has discovered about chimpanzee behaviour and culture Fouts argues that it is entirely wrong to be conducting research on them in the way that many laboratories continue to do. Fouts argues that they are our evolutionary brothers and sisters and more closely related to us than they are to monkeys or other apes. Fouts continues to promote

Figure 22.2 The Great Ape Project strives to ensure that apes are entitled to the right to life, liberty and freedom from torture

Source: © Shutterstock

The Great Ape Project, which strives to ensure that apes are entitled to the right to life, liberty and freedom from torture. Fouts argues that because we are all part of the same evolutionary chain the law should protect chimpanzees from harm in the same way that a father wouldn't be allowed to experiment on a complete stranger in order to save his daughter's life.

To this day there is a debate as to whether Washoe truly learned language (as we know it) or whether she merely learned a few words of vocabulary. As Fouts provided more evidence of Washoe's abilities, some linguists redefined what is meant by the term 'language' in order to exclude non-human language.

For 60 years man has been imprisoning chimpanzees and using them in their research programmes ostensibly for the purpose of improving the human condition often at the expense of the chimpanzee. For most of this time we did not know any better; we did not realise how closely related we are to the chimpanzee not only genetically but behaviourally and culturally– but perhaps thanks to Washoe we now do.

The end of Washoe

Washoe was the first non-human animal to acquire a human language and her adopted son Loulis was the first to acquire a human language from another chimpanzee. Washoe died after a short illness aged 42 on Tuesday 30 October 2007.

Over the years Washoe, the grand old lady of the Chimpanzee world, gave us a fascinating insight into the chimpanzee mind and as a result led us to question our own 'unique' abilities. Of course, humans are unique but perhaps Washoe has provided evidence that we're not quite as different as we like to think.

Notes

1   Psychologists often use the somewhat clumsy term 'non-human animals' to refer to 'animals' since humans are, of course, also animals. In this chapter, I will use the term 'animal' to refer to 'non-human animals'.
2   Keith and Cathy Hayes had managed to teach their chimpanzee Viki some limited sign language, see Hayes (1952).

References

Amabile, T. (1985). 'Motivation and creativity: Effects of motivational orientation on creative writers'. *Journal of Personality and Social Psychology*, 48: 393–97.

Fouts, R. with Mills, S.T. (1997). *Next of Kin*. New York: William Morrow and Company.

Gardener, R.A. and Gardener, B.T. (1969). 'Teaching sign language to a chimpanzee'. *Science*, 165(3894): 664–72.

Kohn, A. (1999). *Punished by Rewards: The Trouble with Gold Stars, Incentive Plans and Praise and Other Bribes*. Boston, MA: Houghton Mifflin.

Patterson, F.G. (1981). 'Ape language'. *Science*, 211(4477): 86–8.

Pfungst, O. (1911). Clever Hans: The Horse of Mr von Osten. New York: Henry Holt and Company.

Savage-Rumbaugh, S. and Lewin, R. (1994). *Kanzi: The Ape at the Brink of the Human Mind*. New York: John Wiley and Sons.

Sibley, C.G. and Ahlquist, J.E. (1984). 'The phylogeny of the hominoid primates, as indicated by DNA–DNA hybridization'. *Journal of Molecular Evolution*, 20: 2–15.

Skinner, B.F. (1950). 'Are theories of learning necessary?'. *Psychological Review*, 57: 193–216.

Terrace, H.S. (1979). *Nim*. New York: Knopf.

Glossary

amnesia A loss of memory due to physical or psychological trauma. There are two types:

anterograde amnesia the inability to remember new information after the amnesic episode.

retrograde amnesia the inability to recall memories from before the amnesic episode.

anal stage of development The second stage in Freud's theory of childhood psychosexual development. Here pleasure is mainly gained from the anus and its function. Toilet training is a key behaviour at this stage in a child's life, and excessive frustration or satisfaction at the anal stage can result in the child becoming fixated at this stage and develop an 'anal' character as an adult.

anxiety disorder Anxiety involves a feeling of fear and apprehension usually accompanied by increased physiological arousal. An anxiety disorder is a collection of disorders characterised by severe anxiety. Common examples of anxiety disorders include post-traumatic stress disorder (PTSD) and obsessive–compulsive disorder (OCD).

attachment A close emotional bond between two people. It usually involves mutual affection and is usually used in relation to the bond that children form with their primary caregiver, most often a parent.

aversion therapy Aversion therapy is a form of treatment (behaviour therapy) in which the patient is exposed to a stimulus that produces deviant behaviour while simultaneously being subjected to some form of punishment or discomfort. It is a form of 'positive punishment' conditioning.

behaviour therapy Any technique of behaviour change based on the laws of classical conditioning. Wolpe (1958) defined it as *'the use of experimentally established laws of learning for the purposes of changing unadaptive behaviour'.*

bulimia nervosa An eating disorder where a person eats uncontrollably (binges) and then self-induces episodes of vomiting (purging).

bystander behaviour Also called the 'bystander effect', where people who witness an emergency situation tend to do nothing to help (see Chapter 6).

case study A detailed, in-depth study of an individual or small group. Usually involves descriptions and interpretations of the case and therefore can be rather subjective. Case studies typically involve qualitative methods.

CAT scans (computerised axial tomography) A form of brain scan.

cerebellum The part of the brain near the base of the skull responsible for muscular activity, without the need of conscious awareness.

classical conditioning Also called Pavlovian conditioning (after Ivan Pavlov, who first coined the concept). Classical conditioning is learning through association, where one stimulus or event comes to predict the occurrence of another stimulus or event. A UCS is an unconditioned (unlearned) stimulus (e.g. food) and a UCR is an unconditioned (unlearned) response (e.g. salivation). After repeated pairings, a neutral stimulus (e.g. dinner bell) can become a conditioned (learned) stimulus (CS) when one salivates to the sound of the bell alone. Salivation to a dinner bell is thus an example of a conditioned (learned) response (CR).

clinical psychology The branch of psychology concerned with assessing and treating mental illness, abnormal behaviour and psychiatric problems.

cognitive psychology The branch of psychology that studies mental processes, including how people think, perceive, remember and learn.

comparative psychology The branch of psychology concerned with the study of animal behaviour and how it 'compares' to human behaviour.

corpus callosum The nerve tissue that connects both hemispheres of the brain.

defence mechanism An unconscious mechanism that protects the conscious mind from anxiety. Originally proposed by Freud, defence mechanisms help to distort reality so that people can cope better with a particular situation. The best known defence mechanism is repression.

developmental psychology The branch of psychology concerned with the study of progressive social, mental and behavioural changes in an individual from birth until death. Often the emphasis is placed on child development, although all stages can be incorporated under the 'developmental' term.

diffusion of responsibility The tendency for bystanders to be less likely to help with more people present because they believe the responsibility for helping is shared among the group and thus each individual is less likely to help.

digit span A test of short-term memory in which a participant is given a series of digits (numbers) to recall immediately. The average digit span is around seven, plus or minus two digits.

dissociation The unconscious separation of thoughts from the psyche – a detachment of the mind from emotions. Dissociation is characterised by a sense of the world as a dreamlike or unreal place and may be accompanied by poor memory of the specific events.

DSM (Diagnostic Statistical Manual) The psychiatrist's manual used in the USA. It involves a classification, definition and description of over 200 mental health disorders. The latest version is DSM IV.

electroencephalograph (EEG) A method of recording electrical activity in the brain.

epilepsy A physical condition that occurs when there is a sudden, brief change in how the brain works. When brain cells are not working properly, a person's consciousness, movement or actions may be altered for a brief time. These changes are called epileptic seizures.

episodic memory Endel Tulving (1972) first suggested that long-term memory was split into different types. Episodic memory refers to personal memories or episodes in your own life, whereas semantic memory is shared factual knowledge that we all might know.

Freud Sigmund Freud (1856–1939), the founder of psychoanalysis.

genital stage of development One of Freud's psychosexual stages. The genital stage (12 years plus) is the culmination of psychosexual development and the fixing of sexual energy in the genitals. This moves us towards sexual intercourse into adulthood.

'Genovese' syndrome The psychological phenomenon where persons are less likely to intervene in an emergency situation when others are present than when they are alone. Reasons for this include the 'diffusion of responsibility' and 'pluralistic ignorance'.

hydrocephalus This is an abnormal build-up of cerebrospinal fluid (CSF) in the ventricles of the brain. The fluid is often under increased pressure and can compress and damage the brain.

ICD (International Classification of Diseases) A classification system for physical and psychological disorders published by the World Health

Organization. The latest version is ICD-10 and covers the patterns of symptoms and course of the disorders rather than their cause or their treatment. ICD is used in the UK, whereas DSM is used in the United States.

individual differences The comparison of people's characteristics and behaviour and an acknowledgement that people differ in these respects. Individual differences are often underplayed in the scientific tradition but are acknowledged, particularly through the use of case studies.

intersex (hermaphrodites) A term used to describe people whose biological sex is ambiguous and cannot be classified as either male or female ('hermaphrodite' is the older, outdated term).

introspection The examination of one's own thoughts, impressions and feelings. This is not accepted as a scientific method in psychology.

IQ (intelligence quotient) A way of comparing the mental age of a child with their actual age. IQ is calculated by dividing mental age by actual age and multiplying by 100. The average IQ at any age is always 100.

latent stage of development Relates to Freud's psychosexual stages of development. During the latent period, the libido interests are suppressed and children concentrate more on relationships, hobbies and other interests.

lobotomy A surgical technique in which incisions are made into the frontal lobe of the brain to cut neural connections between the frontal lobe and other centres of the brain. Popularised in the 1940s, it fell into disrepute when it was found to be unsuccessful for schizophrenia and many patients were adversely affected by the procedure.

localisation of function The belief that specific areas of the cerebral cortex are responsible for specific physical or behavioural functions.

long-term memory (LTM) A memory that is said to last from 30 seconds to a lifetime.

method of loci A mnemonic device that improves memory recall. It involves learning a series of locations (for example, points on a favourite walk) and then imagining items to be recalled being placed there. To retrieve the items, you recreate the journey in your mind's eye and 'see' each item in the place you imagined it.

mnemonics Memory devices such as the method of loci (above) which help to improve memory recall.

Montessori schools These are schools run on the principles of Dr Maria Montessori. The schools emphasise a teaching method that is very 'hands-on' and one that is completely child-centred and child-directed.

MPD (multiple personality disorder) A psychiatric condition in which a patient appears to split into two or more separate personalities. Each personality may or may not be aware of the others. MPD is a relatively new disorder and extremely rare. Critics claim it is a clinical invention rather than a real disorder. The most famous case involving MPD is that of Chris Costner Sizemore.

naïve participant A participant in a research study who is not party to the aims of the study or who has been misled as to the true purpose of the study. This is in contrast to a confederate, who is 'in' on the study and knows what the research is about and the role that is expected of them.

nativist approach An approach that emphasises inborn or inherited contributions to behaviour.

nature/nurture debate A controversy in psychology about the relative importance of either inherited (e.g. genetics) or acquired (e.g. environmental influences) characteristics on behaviour.

object permanence An understanding that objects that are hidden from view continue to exist, despite there being no physical evidence for their existence. Jean Piaget claimed that children less than 8 months old were not capable of understanding object permanence.

observer bias A tendency for researchers who are aware of the hypothesis being studied to see what they *think* is happening rather than what is *actually* happening. To guard against this, it is often better to have an observer who is 'blind' to the precise aims of the study.

obsessive-compulsive disorder (OCD) A type of anxiety disorder in which a person is affected by excessive, intrusive and inappropriate obsessions and/or compulsions. The most common types are 'checkers' (persons who have to check things over and over again) and 'washers' (persons who have to wash and clean things repeatedly).

Oedipus complex In Freudian theory, the notion that young boys desire their mother sexually and thus experience rivalry with their father for their mother's affection.

operant conditioning Also called instrumental conditioning. Operant conditioning is attributed to B.F. Skinner and involves the use of consequences to shape or maintain behaviour. Operant conditioning deals with the modification of voluntary or 'operant' behaviour. An event that either increases or strengthens a response is called a reinforcer. Positive reinforcers increase the likelihood that the behaviour will increase. Punishments or negative reinforcers (the removal of an unpleasant state) make the initial behaviour less likely to occur in the future.

oral stage of development The first stage of development in Freud's theory of psychosexual development. In this stage, pleasure is mainly derived through the mouth. Excessive frustration or satisfaction may cause the person to become fixated or stuck in this stage and develop an 'oral' personality.

phallic stage The third stage in Freud's theory of psychosexual development. Occurs around the age of 3–7 years, where pleasure is mainly derived through the sexual organs. Again, excessive frustration or satisfaction may cause the person to become fixated or stuck in this stage preoccupied by sexual potency, performance or conquest.

phobias A type of anxiety disorder where there is a persistent, irrational and unreasonable fear of an object or situation.

phrenology A pseudoscience that suggested that the bumps on the surface of the skull are related to particular functions.

physiological psychology The branch of psychology that concentrates on the physiological processes that underlie behaviour.

pluralistic ignorance A situation in which everyone looks to other people in a group for guidance on how to behave. However, everyone is also looking at everyone else for guidance on how to behave and thus inaction is thought to be the norm in the situation.

primacy effect Refers to the fact that material presented first to a participant is more likely to be recalled than material that is presented later. See also recency effect.

psychoanalysis The theory devised by Freud to explain human behaviour. It is also used as the term to describe the form of treatment he devised for mental disorders.

psychodynamic approach Refers to any theory that emphasises change and development in an individual and any theory where drive is a central idea in development. The best known psychodynamic theory is Freudian psychoanalysis.

rapid eye movement (REM) Refers to those stages of sleep characterised by eye movements and dreaming. In adults, REM sleep usually occurs for about 15 minutes in every 90-minute sleep cycle.

recency effect Refers to the fact that material presented last (most recently) to a participant is more likely to be recalled than material that is presented earlier. See also primacy effect.

schizophrenia A severe mental disorder characterised by severe disruptions in psychological functioning. Main symptoms include thought, perceptual, emotional, motor and social functioning disturbances.

semantic memory A type of long-term memory associated with factual or general knowledge.

serial position effect (memory) The finding that the words at the beginning (primacy effect) and end of the list (recency effect) are recalled better than words in the middle of the list.

short-term memory (STM) Memory that lasts for less than 20 to 30 seconds.

social psychology The approach that suggests that the thoughts, feelings and behaviour of an individual are influenced by the actual, imagined or implied presence of others.

synaesthesia The experience of having a crossing over of two or more of the senses, e.g. 'seeing' spoken words in colour.

twins

    dyzygotic twins Twins that are formed from the fertilisation of two zygotes (two fertilised egg cells) and thus are non-identical twins.

    monozygotic twins Twins that are formed from the splitting of one zygote (one fertilised egg cell) and thus are genetically identical.

Wernicke's area An area of the cerebral cortex concerned with the processing of speech sounds into recognisable language. It was named after the German Carl Wernicke, who first recognised its importance.